FOR THE LOVE OF CINEMA

FOR THE LOVE OF CINEMA

Teaching Our Passion In and Outside the Classroom

Edited by Rashna Wadia Richards
and David T. Johnson

Indiana University Press

This book is a publication of

Indiana University Press
Office of Scholarly Publishing
Herman B Wells Library 350
1320 East 10th Street
Bloomington, Indiana 47405 USA

iupress.indiana.edu

The paper used in this publication meets the minimum
requirements of the American National Standard for Information
Sciences—Permanence of Paper for Printed Library Materials,
ANSI Z39.48-1992.

Manufactured in the United States of America

Cataloging information is available from the Library of Congress.

ISBN 978-0-253-02963-8 (cloth)
ISBN 978-0-253-02995-9 (paperback)
ISBN 978-0-253-03012-2 (ebook)

1 2 3 4 5   22 21 20 19 18 17

Brief excerpts of the essay "Passionate Attachments" were formerly
published in "The Company I Keep," *Film Quarterly* 68.3 (2015).
The author thanks *Film Quarterly* and the University of California
Press for permission to reprint these portions.

Contents

Acknowledgments

THIS BOOK BEGAN with a conversation at the Society for Cinema and Media Studies conference in Boston in 2012. That year we were both presenting papers on a panel on cinephilia and haunting, prompted by a line from Serge Daney, but our discussions before and after covered wider ground. As we kept talking, we realized that one of the topics animating both of us was teaching. So when we decided to take on a longer-term research project, which turned into this edited collection, we knew two things: we were keen on bringing together issues of cinephilia and pedagogy, and we wanted to retain the personal, invigorating, at times exuberant tone of our initial exchange. We are so grateful to all of our contributors for enabling us to broaden that conversation, for sharing their experiences openly, and for showing us how to talk about love in so many ways. We thank them for their stimulating scholarship and their timely attention to all of our editorial requests time and again. More than anything, we appreciate that working with them has allowed us to feel part of a vibrant community of teacher-scholars in cinema studies.

We would also like to thank Indiana University Press for enthusiastically championing this project. We're very grateful for Raina Nadine Polivka's early encouragement and for Janice Frisch's guidance throughout the process. We also want to thank Kate Schramm, Shannon Sue Brown, and Darja Malcolm-Clarke for helping us during the book's production as well as Charlie Clark at Newgen for his judicious editing. We are deeply indebted to our external readers for their detailed and thoughtful responses, which made this book much stronger. And we are grateful to friends of the project, including Christian Keathley, Girish Shambu, and many others, who buoyed us along as the manuscript came together.

We would also like to acknowledge the support we've received at our home institutions, Rhodes College and Salisbury University. Rashna completed a large portion of this book while on sabbatical, and she would like to thank Rhodes for that time away from teaching to focus on this project. Dave would like to thank the Department of English, the Fulton School, and the Salisbury University Foundation for support during the completion of this project. Most importantly, we are grateful to our students, and to our contributors' students, who motivate and inspire us everyday and make this work worthwhile.

Finally, we would like to express our deepest gratitude to our families. There have been major changes in our personal lives during the time it has taken to put this book together. Our most profound pleasures have been the birth of our children, and our challenges have included complex, lifesaving surgeries. Through it all, we're lucky to have continued working on ideas of love, which couldn't have happened without the constant nourishment provided by our little worlds. Rashna would like to thank her husband, Jason, for his steadfast love and fierce devotion, and for showing her always what is possible; her daughter, Madeleine, for teaching her about a mad love that is all out of proportion, out of control, and beyond reason; and her dog, Callie, for her high-voltage, energizing companionship. Dave would like to thank his wife, Eileen, for her love, support, affection, and, yes, patience in reminding him daily that the sky isn't falling (yet); his son, Luke, for his love and for his unbounded, unapologetic enthusiasms; and his daughter, Anne, for her love and her sweet-natured disposition. We couldn't imagine anything without them.

FOR THE LOVE OF CINEMA

Introduction

Love and Teaching, Love and Film

Rashna Wadia Richards
and David T. Johnson

"What We Have Loved"

It is hard to talk about love. It is harder still to talk about love in relation to the work we do in and outside the classroom: teaching and thinking about the movies. On more than one occasion, we've had a well-meaning acquaintance exclaim, "You must love your job!" When the subject is film, it seems to many, the work itself must be effortless and uncomplicated and pleasurable. Sadly, this kind of view is not limited to people outside the academy. In *Why Teach*, for instance, Mark Edmundson argues for rethinking the purpose of higher education, which ought to focus not on impacting careers and salaries but on changing students' minds and lives.[1] But such "a real education" cannot include film, at least not popular film, which, for Edmundson, does not lend itself to thoughtful intellectual inquiry; if you are teaching mainstream cinema, "no matter what you propose by way of analysis, things tend to bolt downhill toward an uncritical discussion of students' tastes, into what they like and don't like."[2] Even if you hope to offer "a Frankfurt School-style analysis," Edmundson suggests, "you can be pretty sure that by mid-class Adorno and Horkheimer will be consigned to the junk heap of history."[3] What you will be left with, "under the guise of serious intellectual analysis," is "what [students] most want—easy pleasure, more TV."[4] To be fair, Edmundson's critique is leveled at what he calls cultural studies, not cinema studies per se. Yet the teaching of film in general is being attacked as well, for it allows "students [to] kick loose from the critical perspective and groove to the product."[5] It would be too easy to refute this old-fashioned notion of cinema as uncritical—and it would be entirely unnecessary, especially for readers of this volume. But we would like to take on a more pernicious argument implied here: that there is a fundamental distinction between "serious intellectual analysis" and "easy pleasure." Is it possible to deconstruct this binary between evaluation and enjoyment? Can we rigorously critique that which we enjoy, even love? Given the long history of ciné-love in our field, what does it mean to teach what we love or love what we teach? These are some of the questions addressed by this collection, whose larger aim is to put cinephilia and pedagogy into a productive dialogue with each other.

Since the 1960s, love's central role in teaching has been tackled in the field of education. Influenced by Marxist theory and anticolonialist struggle, Brazilian educator Paulo Freire was among its most prominent theorists. In *Pedagogy of the Oppressed* (published in Portuguese in 1968, translated into English in 1970), Freire first argued that treating students as empty vessels to be filled with knowledge is a form of oppression; he therefore proposed rethinking the relationship between teachers and students, who would become co-creators of knowledge.[6] Love would be central to this endeavor, as "it is impossible to teach without the courage to love, . . . to speak of love without the fear of being called ridiculous, mawkish, or unscientific, if not antiscientific."[7] Love would enable teachers and students to face each other as subjective beings, become more human, and defy subjugation in all its forms. Freire's philosophy has influenced a wide range of thinkers and philosophers. Henry A. Giroux, for instance, has contended that teachers ought to be seen as "transformative intellectuals," who educate students personally and passionately rather than by simply implementing school curricula.[8] bell hooks has drawn on Freire to make a case for the liberation of the college classroom by "understanding that eros is a force that enhances our overall effort to be self-actualizing, that it can provide an epistemological grounding informing how we know what we know, enabl[ing] both professors and students to use such energy in a classroom setting in ways that invigorate discussion and excite the critical imagination."[9] In other words, for this branch of education often known as critical pedagogy, love, passion, and personal investment are not seen as antithetical to analysis, interpretation, and the creation of knowledge.

But this equation of the personal and the intellectual does not often exist in the humanities, where we see painstaking attempts at justifying our roles as professionals or experts, usually keeping our love at a distance. There are some exceptions, of course. In her inaugural address as president of the Modern Language Association in 1980, Helen Vendler drew on Wordsworth's pledge near the end of *The Prelude*, "what we have loved, / Others will love, and we will teach them how," to urge us to change the way we think about teaching, especially at the undergraduate level.[10] Instead of "scholarly or critical reflection," Vendler advocates teaching students to read in a "state of intense engagement and self-forgetfulness," such that they may also revel in "the hesitations, pleasures, and perplexities" that first inspired us to become readers and writers and college professors.[11] Although somewhat bold for encouraging students' passion rather than shying away from it, Vendler's essay simply inverts the binaristic division between love and intellectual analysis.[12] It does not help us integrate the two into our teaching. Moreover, hers is a lonely voice. For the most part, as Roger Lundin, also nodding to Wordsworth, points out, "the language of love seems so foreign to our critical enterprises and teaching concerns."[13] While the thinkers we admire and work with, from Plato to Dante to Leslie Fiedler, may have much to say about love, we hardly ever discuss love in connection with what we ourselves do. "Having been trained in the hermeneutics of suspicion," Lundin contends, "we find the disciplines of affection unnatural."[14] Is there a way around this suspicion? Is there a way to pair love and affection with skeptical reading and critical analysis?

Cinema studies may be well suited to offer a response to other disciplines that struggle with this question, since our field has long engaged with the notion of love critically. Cinephilia, broadly defined as a love of cinema, has been part of our theoretical and analytical conversations since the 1950s, and the last two decades especially have seen a resurgence of interest in this idea, which has been used for rethinking film history, theory, and analysis (as we outline in the next section). Yet the subject of teaching, while always on the periphery of cinephilia, rarely comes to bear directly on those conversations.[15] Moreover, it is unusual to see any sustained engagement with the role of love or passion in teaching scholarship more generally, even if one assumes, often quite rightly, an earnest and impassioned commitment to teaching that informs a given study. Most of the discourse on teaching, which we will discuss in greater detail later, involves texts that are either institutional histories or how-to guides. A text like William V. Costanzo's *Great Films and How to Teach Them* may claim that it "offers high school and college teachers a relevant way to engage their students through a medium that students know and love."[16] But here too love is what students naturally feel for the movies; it isn't engaged with or encouraged or scrutinized while teaching film. That is where our collection comes in. Contributors to this volume openly take on the idea of cinephilia in and outside the classroom. But instead of offering a coherent philosophy of cinephilic teaching, these essays ask how we might (and whether we should) draw on ciné-love, both ours and our students', to augment the teaching and learning of film.

We turn first to cinephilia. In the last two decades, much has been said about the revival of cinephilia in our field. But a lot of that discussion of love has come to us amid fears of death—of cinema, of cinema studies, even of cinephilia itself. In fact, cinephilia has always been tied to the idea of death, and its recent revival has clearly been affected by these melancholic declarations. We will trace each of those saturnine assertions next. Then, we turn to the scholarship of teaching. Although there is a wealth of scholarly material on teaching, that material is often seen as something apart from regular scholarship; moreover, it is often regarded suspiciously. We will delineate some reasons for such discursive doubts before thinking about the importance of writing about teaching. Finally, we will show why we regard cinephilia and teaching as allies and then turn to this collection's essays, which explore this alliance in varied ways.

Writing About Cinephilia

"Apparently, the cinema itself is full of garbage," declares Sherry (Gina Clayton), one of the two newscasters commenting on the imminent suicide of an unidentified man (David Cronenberg) in a movie theater. That is why, instead of "sitting in a comfortable chair, with that blank screen in front of [him]," she informs Rob (Jesse Collins) and the audience, he has chosen to shoot himself in the theater's restroom. A single long take of the distraught man streams live via the network's AutoBioCam, while the two faceless and ostensibly emotionless anchors simply describe what is playing out in present tense, without any sense of historical or cultural significance. After all, this isn't an ordinary suicide, but that of the last surviving Jew in the last extant picture palace, which had been long abandoned, then disguised as a garage, and will now be blown up—another event that will be covered robotically by Sherry and Rob. Just as they cannot empathize with the man who struggles mightily with pulling the trigger, they will not mourn the passing of the movies or movie theaters. They might even glibly celebrate it. That is the concern of David Cronenberg's *At the Suicide of the Last Jew in the World in the Last Cinema in the World* (2007), which laments that cinema as we know it is dead.

Despite its caustic tone, Cronenberg's four-minute film, whose title faintly echoes Rick Blaine's "of all the gin joints in all the towns in all the world" line, comes across as an elegy. It premiered on May 20, 2007, as one of thirty-four short films by renowned directors commissioned for the Cannes Film Festival's sixtieth anniversary under the banner *Chacun son cinéma: Une déclaration d'amour au grand écran*. Cronenberg's is a declaration of love that turns mournful, bemoaning the passing of the film object, the demise of the big screen that augmented its pleasures, and the rise of newer media. Interestingly, the anthology was televised on Canal+ that same night and was made available on a Region 2 DVD by Studio-Canal on the last day of the festival. Since then, it has been uploaded to YouTube. In other words, ironically, Cronenberg's dirge can now be seen almost anywhere except on the *grand écran*.

Of course, Cronenberg is not the only one fretting over the end of cinema. In that Cannes anthology, Atom Egoyan also bemoans the passing of the ritual of moviegoing. In *Artaud Double Bill* (2007), movie patrons are engaged in texting messages to friends. At one point, while watching Carl Theodor Dreyer's *The Passion of Joan of Arc* (1928), someone texts *Artaud is beautiful* rather than being absorbed in the film. For Egoyan, such technological distractions destroy the pleasures of watching movies, the engrossing social experience that for most of its history was implied by the word *cinema*, among other meanings, all of which, according to many commentators, are coming to an end. In fact, for the last two decades, filmmakers, academics, journalists, and cultural critics alike have been declaring cinema dead or dying.[17] Prompted by fin de siècle fears, and combined with reflections on cinema's centennial, these melancholic ruminations have attributed cinema's passing to the rise of digitization and computer-generated imagery, Hollywood's hyperindustrialization, declining accessibility and influence of art or experimental cinema, and especially the impact of new media. The looming demise of celluloid led *New York Press* film critic Godfrey Cheshire to speculate that "50 years from now people will regard what we call cinema as belonging to the past, i.e., to the current century."[18] Bemoaning the ineffectiveness of film preservation, Paolo Cherchi Usai seemed to anticipate Cronenberg's last moviegoer when he imagined "a final screening attended by a final audience, perhaps indeed a lonely spectator. With that, cinema will be talked about and written about as some remote hallucination, a dream that lasted a century or two."[19] Most famously, tracing cinema's first one hundred years as a life cycle, Susan Sontag argued that what was "once heralded as the art of the 20th century" is now in "ignominious, irreversible decline."[20] These pronouncements saw the economic, technological, and aesthetic transformations affecting cinema as a medium at the turn of the millennium as a calamity. Cinema, they worried, would pass away, become obsolete or altogether forgotten.

But fears of cinema's obsolescence are quite familiar and have a much longer history. They've arisen every time the medium has undergone substantial makeovers or faced significant competition from rival media: for instance, after the advent of sound in the 1920s or television in the 1950s or home video in the 1980s. "Film 'as we know it,'" as Wheeler Winston Dixon points out, "has always been dying and is always being reborn."[21] After all, the death of cinema has been anticipated almost since its invention, often with trepidation, sometimes with glee. Recall Jean-Luc Godard's tongue-in-cheek final title for *Weekend* (1967), which pronounced not only the end of that film but also *fin de cinéma*. In the wake of the collapse of the studio system, Godard was announcing hyperbolically the end of a particular kind of filmmaking, among other endings. But then Michael Witt reminds us that "commentators [were] pointing to crises in the cinema as early as the 1910s."[22] Indeed, the very moment of cinema's inception is beset with thoughts of its demise. Louis Lumière is said to have proclaimed the moving images he was screening to the first audience "an invention without a future." James Leo Cahill has done a wonderful job of demonstrating how this aphorism, much like the tale of cinema's first audience running in terror as they were assaulted with images of an oncoming train, may be apocryphal. At best, the line may be attributed to Antoine Lumière, Louis and Auguste's father, who may have been referring not to the cinematic medium but merely to the cinematograph as having no commercial future. But the attribution still persists. As Cahill rightly suggests, "it emphasizes the manner in which cinema's arrival and departure, its birth and death, have at numerous historical conjunctures been positioned as coinciding with or haunting each other."[23] Thus, we might be inclined to disregard these re-current sky-is-falling predictions and assume that every such proclamation only entails a metamorphosis rather than the end of cinema.

Still, there is something different about the most recent round of doubts about cinema's survival. For it is accompanied by thoughts of another casualty—that of the discipline itself. In pondering what will become of cinema after the disappearance of celluloid, D. N. Rodowick returns to the moment when cinema studies was established as a discipline. While the teaching of film has a long history—with film courses being offered in the United States as early as 1915, as Dana Polan has demonstrated[24]—Rodowick observes that "the emergence of professional film studies is coincident with what may now be understood as a long period of economic decline for the cinema, first in competition from broadcast television (1955–1975), and then from video and DVD (1986–present)."[25] We might see the history of film studies, he suggests provocatively, "as rising on the decline of its object."[26] Thus, each successive near-death of cinema has prompted film scholars to reassess the ontological status of the film object, thereby continually redefining and rejuvenating the field. But it appears that the most recent discourse about cinema's impending death has not been so invigorating. Instead of enthusiasm for the next phase in its evolutionary cycle, as James Naremore has recently noted, "academic specialists sometimes appear to be trying to kill off both [cinema] and themselves."[27]

Where does this suicidal impulse come from? Cinema studies has always occupied a less-than-stable terrain in the academy, with film courses and programs scattered across various departments. Add to this inherent instability the competition posed by emerging media in the last two decades, and one can see why questions about the continuance of cinema studies have arisen. Broadly speaking, there have been three different responses to the possible imminent death of the discipline: embrace, compromise, and resistance. Noël Carroll clearly appears to belong in the first camp. He was arguing back in the midnineties for renaming what we study and theorizing it as "moving images," predicting that "what we call film and, for that matter, film history will, in generations to come, be seen as part of a larger continuous history that will not be restricted to things made only in the so called medium of film but, as well, will apply to things made in the media of video, TV, computer-generated imagery, and we know not what."[28] Even those who do not advocate such a dramatic move have acknowledged, some enthusiastically and others begrudgingly, that cinema studies needs to contend with emerging media. Many of the contributors to Christine Gledhill and Linda Williams's edited collection *Reinventing Film Studies* have tried to find a middle ground, suggesting that, in an era of doubts about its future, "film studies reinvents itself by intersecting with neighboring disciplines—media studies, cultural studies, visual culture."[29] Such an intersection is clearly reflected in the 2002 addition of *Media* to the title of the Society for Cinema and Media Studies. More recently, Dudley Andrew has sounded a less conciliatory tone. In his influential essay "The Core and the Flow of Film Studies," Andrew considers film and its study as something fundamentally different from other media.[30] After offering a history of the field, he insists that film scholarship must not be subsumed under the banner of media studies. Cinema, Andrew argues, is built on the principle of *décalage*, or the "discrepancy in space and deferral or jumps in time," whereas newer media operate on immediacy.[31] Cinema studies, he suggests, has a precise object of study, and it is this "object of gaps and absences" that has led "many of the best minds in the humanities . . . to account for the most imposing medium of the twentieth century" and produce "complex, ingenious, and passionate arguments and positions."[32] It is this discourse, which is "a way of thinking" and "an instinct of looking and listening," that we are in danger of losing.[33] Cinema studies, Andrew argues, needs to be defended and sustained for the new century. Whether we sympathize more with Andrew's position, or Gledhill and Williams's, or even Carroll's, we can agree that contemporary challenges to cinema studies are real and complex. Rethinking the rationales for and the contours of cinema studies (or cinema and media studies or moving image studies) would be especially productive and revitalizing at this time.

One way many intellectuals in and outside the academy have tried to reconsider cinema studies is by drawing passionately on a discourse that led in many ways to the birth of the discipline. The story of the rise, fall, and rebirth of cinephilia has been narrated often and may be familiar to readers of this collection, so we give only a quick sketch here. Before we do, let us mention that this history is both brief and not comprehensive. Cinephilia is usually traced back to post–World War II French film culture, with the founding of film festivals (Cannes in 1946, for example), the creation of ciné clubs, and the establishment of new journals (*Cahiers du Cinéma* in 1951, *Positif* in 1952). And it is seen as lasting, in its classical phase, until around 1968. But many scholars have recently cautioned, as Adrian Martin does in his essay with Cristina Álvarez López in this volume, against a single story of cinephilia. As Fernando Ramos Arenas similarly shows, cinephilia was "not only a national but a trans-European phenomenon"; there was a vibrant exchange of film discourses among film intellectuals and enthusiasts in France, West Germany, Spain, and Italy after the war.[34] But cinephilia is even larger than a European phenomenon. And it thrived in different regions at different times. Writing about Shivendra Singh Dungarpur's *Celluloid Man* (2012), a documentary about India's premier film archivist P. K. Nair, Rowena Santos Aquino points out that cinephilia in India flourished a little later, as Nair set up the National Film Archive of India in 1964, when classical cinephilia was already beginning to wane in the West.[35] We agree that there isn't just a single kind of cinephilia. Indeed, as the varied essays in this collection demonstrate, there are different ways of talking about that passionate zeal for cinema. Still, cinephilia as a discursive concept was delineated most productively by the *Cahiers* critics from the 1950s on, and it is this cinephilia that our contributors are directly tangling with in this collection. That is why we spend some time sketching its contours here, drawing on Paul Willemen, Antoine de Baecque, and Christian Keathley, who have offered wonderful historical narratives of cinephilia.[36] They trace the concept's prehistory to the Impressionists and the Surrealists, who, in moments of *photogénie* or uncanny instants, sought to uncover and cherish peculiar moments that outdid any film's narrative and dazzled its unsuspecting spectators. Post–World War II French critics extended this notion of cinematic enchantment by constructing an argument for a way of looking at and fetishizing films' peculiar details or eccentric gestures that often existed only in the margins of the cinematic frame. Such details exceeded their narrative drives or symbolic functions; hence, they could just as easily be located in mainstream Hollywood films as in avant-garde cinema. And they sparked, as Paul Willemen contends, the desire to write, to find "formulations to convey something about the intensity of that spark."[37] The discourse that grew out of these formulations came to be known as cinephilia, a passionately subjective way of thinking and writing about cinema's inexplicable allure. It should be noted that *Cahiers* critics were writing as the slow decline of the studio system had begun. Thus, what we now call classical cinephilia developed as a response to fears about the death of a particular kind of cinema. That discourse was necessarily tinged with nostalgia for a lost object and era. Even when cinephilia morphed into *la politique des auteurs*, a theoretical method for reading films through the lens of directorial vision—a method that offered intellectual heft to what seemed suspiciously affective—it remained a melancholic discourse.

We can therefore see why cinephilia became an easy target once film scholars turned their attention to critiquing the cinematic apparatus. After the 1960s, ciné-love, for a generation trying to challenge the establishment and decry its normativity, became a bad word. As the story goes, this is the moment of the academization of cinema studies. Once semiotics ushered in a new way of analyzing moving images, cinephilia had to be left behind, rejected, even killed. As Lee Grieveson suggests in a dialogue with Laura Mulvey and Peter Wollen, the field had to transition from cinephilia to film studies because "what begins with cinephilia, with the love of Hollywood, and becomes the theoretical study of Hollywood, becomes also a sustained critique of the ideology of Hollywood."[38] Mulvey insists that the critique "was enabled by cinephilia and a deep love of Hollywood," but she concedes that it eventually led to "a rejection of your own cinephilia."[39] Thomas Elsaesser draws attention to the fact that "this 'negative' or disavowed cinephilia [was converted] into one of the founding moments of Anglo-American film studies."[40] Thus, cinephilia wasn't so much killed off as interred, waiting to be resurrected another day. This entombment lasted for about three decades, until Susan Sontag decided to dig it back up in order to fully bury it. Writing in 1995, near the beginning of the most recent round of fears about cinema's demise, Sontag argued in her now-canonical piece that ciné-love can no longer exist because films are no longer "unique, unrepeatable, magic experiences."[41] In an era that values big explosions and even bigger profits, Sontag mourned, cinema and cinephilia are both dead.

Because Sontag linked cinema's decline to the fate of cinephilia, what might've been just another dirge became a kind of rallying cry. Critics and academics alike began to revive cinephilia, refusing to let it die away along with its object of affection. Indeed, "the doom narrative," as Girish Shambu has recently pointed out, has become "an occasion and opportunity to imaginatively spell out the ways in which cinephilia lives and *might* live in its present and future mutations."[42] Thus, during the last two decades, we have seen a rigorous return to the concept of cinephilia. Some, like de Baecque and Keathley, have tried to historicize its classical incarnation, while others have tried to analyze its manifestations in contemporary film culture. There is a new ferocity in the work of these writers, who, in trying to define cinephilia for our age, almost seem to be seizing it from the jaws of death. Jonathan Rosenbaum and Adrian Martin's edited collection *Movie Mutations* begins this trend by arguing that cinema is not only not dead, but it is thriving everywhere; likewise, cinephilia is far from finished.[43] The wider availability of films on DVD and on the Internet, and the proliferation of writing about film online, has enabled new cinephilic communities to flourish on all continents. Marijke de Valck and Malte Hagener's *Cinephilia* and Scott Balcerzak and Jason Sperb's two-volume *Cinephilia in the Age of Digital Reproduction* build on that argument by offering examples of the kind of cinephilic criticism possible in the digital age.[44] Shambu's *The New Cinephilia* shows how, while similar to classical cinephilia in its drive to view and then talk or write about cinema, contemporary cinephilia is more expansive and more internationalist, "not just in terms of the films but, equally important, in terms of the cinephiles themselves."[45] Still others have tried to explore how to use cinephilia for renewing film analysis or history. In *Death 24x a Second*, Laura Mulvey suggests that watching films at home, with the ability to pause or rewind, enhances film analysis, for "today's electronic or digital spectator can find these deferred meanings that have been waiting through the decades to be seen."[46] Similarly, in *Cinematic Flashes*, Rashna Wadia Richards proposes that cinephiliac historiography can be used as a new mode of doing film history to "uncover multiple histories that might otherwise remain buried under the weight of grand narratives about classical Hollywood."[47] Together, these works show that although cinephilia is linked with death, epitaphic writing about it is clearly premature, for cinephilic discourse is alive and thriving.

This collection grows out of this contemporary revitalization of cinephilia, which also reminds us that, though broadly and simply characterized as a love of cinema, cinephilia is hard to define. It implies an obsession with cinema or its excessive details; a desire to possess cinema (whether literally, in terms of collecting, or metaphorically, in terms of fetishism); a mourning for a beloved object that the cinephile can never hold on to; a drive to talk and write about cinema in order to recapture the original moment of pleasure; a desire to write with cinema (as seen in video essays); and on and on. Recently, Jacques Rancière has suggested that "cinephilia is a relationship with cinema governed by passion rather than theory."[48] Yet we're always trying to theorize it. And that is what we find most compelling about cinephilia: no matter how we define the term, cinephilia compels us to think about both passion and theory, love and analysis, enjoyment and evaluation at once. Marijke de Valck and Malte Hagener are right when they argue that, whether classical or contemporary, cinephilia is always caught up in a kind of double bind "between the biographical and the theoretical, the singular and the general, the fragment and the whole, the incomplete and the complete, the individual and the collective."[49] It is this notion of cinephilia as simultaneously personal and intellectual that we are interested in, for it allows us to get beyond the false division between private pleasure and academic analysis. And it is this stimulating tension that links cinephilia to our teaching. For pedagogy too is both a personal experience and a theoretical concept. Rather than choosing one or the other, we find ourselves bringing both love and critical scrutiny to the movies we discuss in the classroom. Therefore, before we put these two terms in conversation with each other, we'd like to turn to the question of the scholarship of teaching.

Writing About Pedagogy

In "Teaching Programme for the Theory and Practice of Direction," Sergei Eisenstein outlines what ought to be taught to prospective film directors at a school like GIK, the state-run film institute in Moscow.[50] He lays out a four-year curriculum for the directors' program. Claiming that "none of the generally accepted academic methods of teaching is adequate for the study of the director's craft," Eisenstein champions practical or hands-on learning.[51] Thus, his essay goes on to outline methodically how the four years in this program should unfold and what should be taught each term. After beginning every module with "the most essential theoretical postulates," the teacher pitches to his students a scenario that amounts to a directorial conundrum; he then shows them "how to deduce the entirely correct and creatively compositional solution for the particular circumstances."[52] As one might expect, this pedagogical essay is systematic and highly dispassionate; each year is divided into terms, each term into divisions, and each division emphasizes specific questions to be addressed. But Eisenstein didn't just write about teaching. He himself taught at GIK throughout the 1930s. One of his students, Vladimir Nizhny, later reproduced his experience as a student in *Lessons with Eisenstein*, which demonstrates how Eisenstein put his teaching program into practice.[53] Nizhny's text reveals a different side of Eisenstein as a teacher. Instead of the detached and objective thinker we're familiar with, Eisenstein comes across as warm and spontaneous. As Ivor Montagu puts it in the book's foreword, Eisenstein's lessons "were not something to be learned by rote, or wherein laws laid down by authority of the lecturer must be accepted. They took the form of explorations, wherein lecturer and pupils together embarked on a voyage of joint discovery of truths."[54] Moreover, he invited students over to his house, lent books to and borrowed books from them, and engaged in "long intimate talks" with them.[55] Eisenstein the teacher, in other words, was less rehearsed and more personal. It is hard to write about such extemporaneous and idiosyncratic moments in teaching—hard, that is, to blend the subjective and the theoretical when writing about teaching, something we will circle back to at the end of this section.

But that isn't the only reason why writing about teaching is less commonplace. Let us turn first to more pragmatic and pressing questions that make pedagogical writing difficult. Do books about teaching count as much as books about film theories, histories, genres, or any other more conventional topic of scholarship, when it comes to hiring, tenure, and promotion decisions in an academic department? And given that such questions are often tied to the larger disciplines in which faculty work, does the field itself recognize scholars of film pedagogy with the same regard as scholars of any other specialty? How many well-known scholars of cinema studies are known primarily as scholars of pedagogy, with perhaps secondary or tertiary interests elsewhere? Although these questions may only have an immediate bearing on the careers and curriculum vitae of this volume's editors and contributors, they suggest the deeply troubled place that teaching—the activity that, for most academics, absorbs the greatest amount of energy and time when classes are under way—continues to hold in relation to the larger knowledge we generate and pursue in the form of scholarly activity.

Part of the problem may be that teaching has an undeniably performative element to it and that much of what occurs in teaching happens "live"; like scholarship on theater events, or even cinema before the advent of home-viewing technologies, the challenges of trying to capture the teaching experience and study it on the page may account in part for its uncertain place within the larger scholarly discourse of cinema studies. More deeply, one wonders if some connotation of innate ability, an idea that instructors must often challenge within the assumptions students carry about their own reading and writing potentials, still clings to the cultural image of the teacher and dissuades many academics from making it a subject of scholarly attention. This is not to say that certain dispositions are not perhaps more or less well suited for standing in front of a group of students and leading an active lecture or discussion. But as educators, disarming a given person of the belief that he or she cannot learn a skill—or, put even more simply, cannot learn—is primary to what we are charged to do. How deeply ironic it would be, then, and despite the very good work that has been done on pedagogy, both in academia generally and specifically in cinema studies, if the myth of the natural teacher were at the root of our reluctance to engage with scholarly investigations of teaching.

Some of this reluctance no doubt also relates to the place of teaching in relation to scholarship, in that the way in which one establishes a seriousness of purpose in one's professional life, as an academic, is typically through the latter and not the former. In 1990, Ernest L. Boyer famously diagnosed the problem when he coined the phrase *scholarship of teaching* to address the issue directly in *Scholarship Reconsidered.*[56] Often more commonly encountered as a reference to volumes such as this one—that is, academic research directed at pedagogical theory and practice—the scholarship of teaching, as defined by Boyer, meant something altogether different: teaching *as* scholarship, in and of itself, quite apart from any research agendas that may or may not enter the classroom in the day-to-day instruction of a given course. This was the final term in Boyer's larger expansion of the word *scholarship* into four subdivisions, moving from most to least conventional ways of understanding the term: discovery, integration, application, and teaching. That last term, especially, stood out. For while one could and still does plausibly argue that not just discovery (original research) but integration (synthesizing already existing research) as well as application (putting research into practice) comprise scholarship, could one really make the case that the day-to-day realities of the teacher—leading a discussion following a film, or writing a midterm, or grading an essay—make up scholarly activity? Boyer's radical reply to this query was a simple *yes*. For him, "teaching is . . . a dynamic endeavor involving all the analogies, metaphors, and images that build bridges between the teacher's understanding and the student's learning," an endeavor that requires a great deal of intellectual work; as Boyer argues, "those who teach must, above all, be well informed, and steeped in the knowledge of their fields. Teaching can be well regarded only as professors are widely read and intellectually engaged."[57] Although not all of Boyer's arguments may strike the contemporary reader as equally convincing, the willingness to rethink scholarship and take teaching seriously as a scholarly activity in itself remains compelling.

Of course, little of Boyer's discourse has directly inflected the way that most colleges and universities discuss professional development for the practicing academic, even if there has been robust scholarly work on the scholarship of teaching in the years since. The term itself has now been expanded to the *scholarship of teaching and learning* or SoTL, which acknowledges the growing emphasis on assessment of student learning objectives and outcomes. On many campuses, SoTL has spawned faculty development centers, which encourage the sharing of pedagogical resources and ideas, and the International Society for the Scholarship of Teaching and Learning was founded in 2004 for thinking about teaching as vital intellectual work. Nonetheless, pedagogical scholarship is typically limited to scholars of education and higher-education administrative specialties, with much less dispersal among the faculty more generally. As Beth M. Schwartz and Aeron Haynie point out, "there is still debate at many institutions as to how scholarship of teaching and learning . . . fits within instructors' professional development."[58]

Still, pedagogy as a subject of academic research does seem to have made strides for the better. In cinema studies, scholarly exchanges that foreground college-level teaching as their subject continue to appear with regularity at conferences, in journal articles, and in full-length collections. Most of these are either institutional histories or guides for teaching particular aspects of film. Dana Polan's *Scenes of Instruction*, which traces the history of film instruction before cinema studies became an academic discipline, and Lee Grieveson and Haidee Wasson's *Inventing Film Studies*, which shows how the study of film has evolved in relation to theoretical, technological, and institutional developments, are just two brilliant examples in the former category.[59] In the category of instruction manuals for teachers of film, we have Lucy Fischer and Patrice Petro's wide-ranging *Teaching Film*, edited for a Modern Language Association series on pedagogy; books in the British Film Institute's Teaching Film and Media Studies series, such as Kate Gamm's *Teaching World Cinema* and Sarah Gilligan's *Teaching Women and Film*; and books that connect cinema studies with other disciplines, such as Gregory J. Watkins's *Teaching Religion and Film* and Kathleen L. Brown's *Teaching Literary Theory Using Film Adaptations*.[60] Collectively, these books demonstrate the vibrancy and range of work being done in film pedagogy, not to mention the many outstanding journals that have devoted articles, sections, or whole issues to the subject, recently visible in the partnership between *Cinema Journal* and the online resource TeachingMedia.org, in a quarterly forum called *Cinema Journal Teaching Dossier*.

In their striking introduction for *Teaching Film*, Fischer and Petro take note of this vitality, suggesting that "the film studies field, internationally, has produced a substantial body of work on the subject."[61] Yet they qualify that remark by noting how, especially in the United States, "the writing on approaches to teaching film has been piecemeal and dispersed and, therefore, difficult for teachers to know of or track down."[62] Whatever the reasons for that dispersal, we take at least some of them to be related to the skepticism with which pedagogical scholarship is sometimes viewed, and we will use that assumption to speculate on at least two other explanations not yet explored. Near the end of their introduction, Fischer and Petro provide a brass-tacks set of questions for the novice teacher of cinema, queries intended to help someone who is brand new to the subject and/or who wishes to start a cinema course at an institution that has never had one before. The questions take little for granted, admirably giving a first-time teacher practical considerations for how to run a course on a film, from issues such as film availability to room size and projection issues. The interest here in providing specific kinds of advice is common to a great deal of pedagogical scholarship, whether making up the bulk of a given study or, as here, provided at the end (sometimes, in a book, in the appendix). This may also, however, account for one other reason why pedagogical scholarship inspires distrust: its pragmatism, or utilitarianism, gives it the rhetorical likeness of a how-to manual, which in turn makes it seem like anything but scholarship. Intellectual work often requires engaging with theories and methodologies that are by their nature removed from a sense of the everyday (or make the everyday unfamiliar), and reading something that gives instructions on how to set up a screening, or how to lead a post-screening discussion, or how to create a grading rubric, may feel less like scholarly activity because its application value is foregrounded at the level of both subject matter and tone.

In terms of the latter, to add yet another reason for the larger sense of distrust, writers must often adopt a first-person voice when recounting their experiences. Given the often contentious place of other forms of first-person writing relative to the scholarly voice—the diaristic, the journalistic, the essayistic (in the Montaignean sense)—scholarly writing about pedagogy, like writing about cinephilia itself, may again signal to the reader that *this is not scholarship*. The writer's shift into the autobiographical seems to cut against the more formal, third-person address that has traditionally conveyed dispassionate objectivity in academic research, no matter how passionate or subjective the perspectives lying behind it. And that sense of personal stake often carries with it other difficulties within the scholarship of teaching. As Randy Bass puts it, we even talk about what it is we are researching differently: in traditional scholarship, "having a 'problem' is at the heart of the investigative process," but in scholarship about teaching, "asking about a problem in one's teaching would probably seem like an accusation."[63]

Thus both cinephilia and pedagogy have garnered suspicion for offering too much subjectivity and not enough detached objectivity. Indeed, the starting point for bringing together the key terms of this volume was the overt commingling of the subjective and the objective in writing about cinephilia and about pedagogy. The two are fitting allies because they have both inspired distrust over the years, in large measure due to the blending of the personal and the intellectual, in addition to other feelings of distrust related to their discrete histories. Bringing pedagogy to bear on cinephilia, and cinephilia to bear on pedagogy, will, we hope, dispel some of that distrust and interrogate the extent to which love and passion can or should play any role in the classroom.

Writing About Cinephilia and Pedagogy

When we began working on this volume, here are some of the questions we asked ourselves and our potential contributors: Is there such a thing as a cinephilic pedagogy? Can the love of cinema inform the serious study of cinema for today's student? What does the role of a teacher as cinephile add to our understanding of ciné-love? In an era of dire pronouncements about the vitality of the humanities and the future of cinema studies, can cinephilia and pedagogy help rejuvenate each other? The original essays collected here approach these questions from multiple perspectives and locations. Initially, we assumed that some essays would tackle this relationship theoretically, while others would offer more pragmatic approaches. And while the book is divided into two sections based more or less on that logic, we ultimately found in the contributions to this volume that it is impossible to talk about cinephilia and teaching without doing both at the same time; that is, cinephilia and teaching compel us to theorize the general and demonstrate the particular simultaneously, even if we end up doing a little more of one or the other in any given moment. Therefore, all of the essays that follow weave together theory with anecdote, analysis with autobiographical moments. More than that, they mix pedagogical philosophy with case studies in ways that do not think of the two as contrary or even entirely distinct but as mutually constitutive. Unlike Helen Vendler's inversion of love and intellectual analysis, these essays demonstrate how both can happen simultaneously. Some essays draw on aspects of students' cinephilia as a technique for rethinking familiar films or generating new kinds of analyses about the medium itself. Others reflect on how their own cinephilia informs the way they teach cinema. Still others offer new ways of writing (both verbally and audiovisually) with cinephilia in the age of new media. In a wide-ranging conversation with Scott Bukatman, also noted in this volume by Tracy Cox-Stanton, Vivian Sobchack has recently suggested this about her teaching: "If I do anything for my students, I hope it's to give them a kind of confidence in those initial fascinations, not necessarily in what they 'ought' to be fascinated by."[64] In a sense, those "initial fascinations" are like cinephilic moments that all of our contributors encourage and help students build on. These essays demonstrate the various ways in which those fascinations for or love of moving images can generate stimulating and innovative cinema scholarship as well as invigorate and innovate film pedagogy.

And yet, as the reader may have already surmised, fascinations are not necessarily always cinephilic, and teaching with passion, or love, does not always mean teaching with, through, or about cinephilia. (Nor does effective teaching always demand passion—or at least, passion may manifest as something much more measured and subdued in practice, as might love.) During the editorial process for this manuscript's publication, one of our external readers wanted to know what the difference was between teaching that was informed by cinephilia specifically and teaching that, passionate though it may be, would be more about traditional film analysis and not necessarily cinephilic. It's an excellent question. When editing our writers' work, we asked them to bear this distinction in mind directly—and yet, even as we thought through the question ourselves, we understood why writers might see a productive blurring between these modes, and we hope to have given them enough latitude in this regard. The ways in which one might distinguish or not between cinephilia in the classroom and passion or love more generally are myriad, and as readers make their way through the collection, they may notice ways in which the terms are being conflated or kept distinct, as this discussion is at least provisionally attempting. Put simply, we've left these words deliberately open-ended so as to interrogate these and other ways in which cinephilia and passion and love might inform one's pedagogy (or not), and more often than not, in the spirit of much humanities research, the point here is not to arrive at a final answer but to ask better, more fully realized questions, ones we hope will stimulate other questions for our readers, whether they are progressing chronologically through the essays or tracing out some other trajectory, perhaps even just arriving at and departing from the volume via one particularly attractive piece germane to a given reader's interests. To those essays—in this case, following the former logic—this introduction now turns.

Our first section, "Theorizing Cinephilia and Pedagogy," begins with an essay by Robert B. Ray, whose work over the years has returned time and again to new writing methodologies both in his scholarship and in the classroom. In "Cinephilia as a Method," Ray revisits a figure who has become increasingly visible within cinema studies, Stanley Cavell, but also draws on an essay by a medical doctor, H. M. Evans, to consider how *wonder* might inform the classroom instructor whose perceptions of a given film have grown habitual, much like the doctor who, to be effective, must see each patient anew. As the essay unfolds, Ray also investigates the work of Eleanor Duckworth, among others, to show how wonder might inform a teaching methodology.

Following Ray, in "Passionate Attachments," Amelie Hastie explores how bodily response and the felt experience of passion inform teaching and writing. Drawing on the more well-known work of Jean Epstein, Siegfried Kracauer, and André Bazin, but juxtaposing it with writers rarely, if ever, discussed in cinema studies—the poet H.D. and the novelist Dorothy Richardson—Hastie both describes and enacts a way of responding to cinema, in a series of close readings drawn from *Whale Rider* (2002), *Ratcatcher* (1999), and *Bright Star* (2009). Explicitly foregrounding the physical dimension of cinematic response, Hastie's readings also urge us to widen the scope of cinephilia more generally, to include other voices often neglected from that pantheon.

After this essay, the volume gives voice to dissent—or at least, a cautionary word. Thomas Leitch uses his autobiographical development as a teacher and scholar to reflect on ways that he finds himself turning away from cinephilia, at least as conventionally understood, and toward cineliteracy, a more holistic set of skills that need not always be arrived at through pleasure, even if, as is apparent from reading his essay, pleasure often informs whatever his classes set out to do. In "Cinephilia and Cineliteracy in the Classroom," Leitch warns us against rushing headlong into a pedagogy informed primarily by cinephilia, since cineliteracy may serve students better over the long term. Moving through several examples, he lingers on *Out of the Past* (1947), the film that seems to offer, for him, the most possibilities for a praxis guided by cinephilia, even if ultimately one that might serve cineliteracy.

Following this essay, in a far more optimistic appraisal of cinephilia's possibilities in the classroom, Tracy Cox-Stanton dispels a common charge leveled against it: that its writings are, at best, apolitical, or at worst, reactionary. In "Nearing the Heart of a Film: Toward a Cinephilic Pedagogy," Cox-Stanton uses her own autobiographical experiences as both student and teacher to frame multiple ways of thinking about and through cinephilia, drawing upon many figures, including Christian Metz, who insists on being cognizant of one's cinematic pleasures while remaining aware of their ideological implications. As examples of her ideas in action, Cox-Stanton guides us through a key text from her own teaching, *Black Girl* (Ousmane Sembène, 1966), before turning to her latest efforts in the production of the online journal *The Cine-Files*, one with a strong connection to her pedagogy.

Next is Kalling Heck's "Movies in the Middle: Cinephilia as Lines of Becoming." For Heck, a film might offer up its own pedagogy, and pedagogical ideas more generally, via the close reading. To this extent, Heck's work responds to a recent interest in films themselves as capable of theorizing, informed here, it should come as no surprise, by Gilles Deleuze, among others. Setting out from cinema studies' own historical marginality as a discipline, Heck posits that cinephilia both demonstrates and dramatizes the continuing "emergence" of the field's own discourse and, equally, the act of learning itself, as a process always in a state of "becoming." This idea in Heck's essay also manifests as "lines of becoming" that he takes the time to trace out, through some specific examples, before turning to his own teaching, to show how a class on film comedy has benefited from a cinephilic approach.

We end the section with an essay co-authored by two well-known current practitioners and advocates of the audiovisual essay, Cristina Álvarez López and Adrian Martin. In "Audiovisual Pleasure and Narrative Cinema," Álvarez López and Martin present a two-part essay, with Martin leading off the first part with the image of teachers, via both Alain Badiou and Neil Young, as figures deeply passionate about a subject and vexed at the same time with how they might communicate that passion to students. The dynamics of cinephilia, for Martin, are "caught up in this drama," and as his section develops, he weaves his own autobiographical development as a teacher and a scholar with considerations on the audiovisual essay. Shifting into classroom praxis in the second part, Álvarez López begins by laying out many of the strategies she and Martin have used when teaching the form, and as she does so, she speculates on the ways that it might allow for other kinds of engagement outside more conventional essays assigned in college classrooms. Drawing on another proposition she formulated in 2012—"Where written texts evoke, [audiovisual] essays invoke"—Álvarez López considers how the form's "invocational character" might enable this engagement.[65]

Our second section, "Practicing Cinephilia and Pedagogy," emphasizes case studies more than theorization, though as previously noted, the interdependency of theory and praxis guides essays in this section as much as those that precede it. Embodying a robust sense of this interdependence, Kristi McKim, in "Teaching Film Nonfictionally: The Reciprocity of Pedagogy, Cinephilia, and Maternity," reflects on her teaching and her students but also often circles back to the infancy of her son Henry, both in his own sensuous experiences in those early days and in her perceptions of those experiences. Aligning her work with the feminist literary scholarship of Jane Tompkins, among others, who have brought the personal to bear on the scholarly, and vice versa, McKim moves through various moments that have informed who she is as a writer, as a teacher, as a mother, and as a person who does not cordon off these roles into separate realms but allows them to inform each other while respecting the particularities of each—and the love that each demands.

Following this piece, Steven Rybin focuses on an aspect of cinema most introductory students are likely already drawn to: the actors on-screen. In "Loving Performance: Cinephilia, Teaching, and the Stars," Rybin begins by exploring the performative dimensions of teaching itself, whether with something initially as formally resistant to interpretation as *Mothlight* (1963) or, in another example, a moment from the film *Queen Christina* (1933) and the way that Greta Garbo's own movements also resist any immediate hermeneutic device with which one might explore the text. The advantage, for Rybin, is a cinephilia-informed approach that foregrounds moments of explanatory resistance which, in turn, generate other forms of discourse, ones he explores in the latter part of his essay through specific classroom exercises that explore cinematic performance.

Such emphasis on specific exercises and films guides the next three essays as well. Allison Whitney, in "Go to the Movies! Cinephilia, Exhibition, and the

Film Studies Classroom," asks how our teaching might be informed not just by the larger preoccupations of the profession but by the specificity of place—here, Lubbock, Texas—as well as the student body that her institution, Texas Tech University, serves. In so doing, her work suggests how a regional cinephilia might guide one's pedagogy, and she explains how two assignments work within these larger aims: one, a self-ethnography of local moviegoing, with students encouraged to record all of the specific, material elements of their theatrical experience, and two, an interview project with family and friends of varying generations to ascertain constancies and changes in the exhibition experience.

Next, in "Cinephilia and Paratexts: DVD Pedagogy in the Era of Instant Streaming," Lisa Patti explores the ways students increasingly are turning away from DVD technologies and toward the cinema that can be streamed online. DVDs thus become, as Patti shows, objects of the past, ones that hold certain associations, in part imbued with nostalgia, that Patti argues might be productively used in the classroom, through cinephilia, to tease out the complicated and at times almost imperceptible shifts in the ways that instructors and their students relate to cinema. Situating Netflix as a primary platform for students' encounter with cinema, and noting her own active role in fostering that encounter by requiring students to use Netflix, Patti shows how the gaps that Netflix creates—gaps in availability of titles as well as the metaphorical gaps created in the absence of physical objects—might drive a pedagogy that looks back toward DVD technologies, through creative assignments revolving around paratexts like the DVD cover, to engage the increasingly "virtual" ways that characterize contemporary cinephilia.

Following this, Andrew Utterson focuses on a single film in "Lessons of Birth and Death: The Past, Present, and Future of Cinephilia in Martin Scorsese's *Hugo* (2011)." Here, Utterson sees a productive value in the kind of nostalgia that a film like *Hugo* trades in; given that Scorsese's fable mixes historical realities with more fantastic elements, such nostalgia is tricky to reconcile with a desire to study cinema's past in all of its richness and complexity. Yet Utterson shows that such richness and complexity need not be sacrificed in using *Hugo* as a catalyst for these conversations. On the contrary, as Utterson amply demonstrates, *Hugo* elicits queries about the past precisely because of its self-consciously illusory approach to cinema's history.

And rounding out the collection, in "Cinephilia and Philosophia: Or, Why I Don't Show *The Matrix* in Philosophy 101," Timothy Yenter begins by expressing dissatisfaction with the ways cinema has typically been used in philosophy courses—as a conduit to understanding a larger concept within philosophy, but bypassing entirely what might be useful or interesting within the cinematic experience. More specifically, Yenter feels strongly that students are being denied the ways that cinephilia opens up larger, much older questions central to philosophy:

namely, questions revolving around "the good life." While some cinema scholars may initially take issue with a phrase like *the good life*, these anxieties are likely to be put to rest as Yenter patiently leads the nonspecialist through a cogent case for why cinephilia should be more central in the philosophy classroom that chooses to engage with cinema.

This, then, is the volume you hold in your hands or, increasingly, call up onto a screen, yet another way in which the changes described in this book are represented by the ways in which you, the reader, are able to access its insights. And for those insights, we thank our contributors to this volume, for whom we have profound gratitude—for sharing their knowledge, experience, and time with us; in the writing and revision of these essays; and for what they have already taught their editors in the shaping of this volume, lessons we know will benefit our readers. Finally we must thank the students of all of our contributors and our own, for the ways that they have informed this book, directly and indirectly. We hope that all of us can continue to learn about—and yes, love—the cinema.

RASHNA WADIA RICHARDS is Associate Professor and T. K. Young Chair of English at Rhodes College. She is the author of *Cinematic Flashes: Cinephilia and Classical Hollywood* (Indiana University Press). Her essays have been published in *Criticism, Framework, Film Criticism, Quarterly Review of Film and Video*, and *Arizona Quarterly*.

DAVID T. JOHNSON is Professor of English at Salisbury University. He is the author of *Richard Linklater*, and his work has appeared in *Adaptation, The Cine-Files, Film Criticism, Film Quarterly, LOLA*, and *Reverse Shot*. From 2005 to 2016 he co-edited the journal *Literature/Film Quarterly*.

Notes

1. Mark Edmundson, *Why Teach: In Defense of a Real Education* (New York: Bloomsbury, 2013).

2. Ibid., 22.

3. Ibid.

4. Ibid.

5. Ibid.

6. Paulo Freire, *Pedagogy of the Oppressed* (Harmondsworth, UK: Penguin, 1970).

7. Paulo Freire, *Teachers as Cultural Workers: Letters to Those Who Dare to Teach* (Boulder, CO: Westview Press, 1998), 3.

8. Henry A. Giroux, *Teachers as Intellectuals: Toward a Critical Pedagogy of Learning* (Westport, CT: Bergin and Garvey, 1988), 121–128.

9. bell hooks, *Teaching to Transgress: Education as the Practice of Freedom* (New York: Routledge, 1994), 195.

10. Helen Vendler, "What We Have Loved, Others Will Love," in *Falling into Theory: Conflicting Views on Reading Literature*, ed. David H. Richter (New York: Bedford/St. Martin's, 1999).

11. Ibid., 28.

12. In that, she simply comes across as someone who condemns teachers, as Gerald Graff contends, for "becom[ing] so obsessed with sophisticated critical theories that they have lost the passion they once had for literature itself." Gerald Graff, "Disliking Books at an Early Age," in *Falling into Theory: Conflicting Views on Reading Literature*, ed. David H. Richter (New York: Bedford/St. Martin's, 1999), 39.

13. Roger Lundin, "What We Have Loved," *Pedagogy* 4 (2004): 134.

14. Ibid.

15. Tim Palmer suggests that in France cinephilia isn't just a spectatorial practice; it is very much a part of film education. Particularly at film schools like La Fémis or L'Ecole Nationale Supérieure Louis-Lumière, cinephilia is "a train of stylistic thought, a methodology instilled" in future filmmakers, who then go on to make cinephilic films. But this isn't true in classes that emphasize film analysis, which is the focus of this collection. Tim Palmer, *Brutal Intimacy: Analyzing Contemporary French Cinema* (Middletown, CT: Wesleyan University Press, 2011), 195.

16. William V. Costanzo, *Great Films and How to Teach Them* (Urbana, IL: National Council of Teachers of English, 2004).

17. There are some important countervoices, such as Jonathan Rosenbaum's; he sympathizes with Cronenberg, even thinks he himself might "qualify as Cronenberg's Last Jew," and yet remains "untroubled by the loss of the last cinema because [he] can view this particular sketch feature at home." Jonathan Rosenbaum, *Goodbye Cinema, Hello Cinephilia: Film Culture in Transition* (Chicago: University of Chicago Press, 2010), ix.

18. Godfrey Cheshire, "The Death of Film/The Decay of Cinema," *New York Press* (1999): 12.

19. Paolo Cherchi Usai, *The Death of Cinema: History, Cultural Memory and the Dark Digital Age* (London: British Film Institute, 2001), 124.

20. Susan Sontag, "The Decay of Cinema," *New York Times Magazine*, February 25, 1996, http://www.nytimes.com/1996/02/25/magazine/the-decay-of-cinema.html.

21. Wheeler Winston Dixon, "Twenty-Five Reasons Why It's All Over," in *The End of Cinema as We Know It: American Film in the Nineties*, ed. Jon Lewis (New York: New York University Press, 2001), 366.

22. Michael Witt, "The Death(s) of Cinema According to Godard," *Screen* 40 (1999): 333.

23. James Leo Cahill, ". . . and Afterwards?: Martin Arnold's Phantom Cinema," *Spectator* 27 (2007): 19.

24. Dana Polan, *Scenes of Instruction: The Beginnings of the U.S. Study of Film* (Berkeley: University of California Press, 2007).

25. D. N. Rodowick, *The Virtual Life of Film* (Cambridge, MA: Harvard University Press, 2007), 28.

26. Ibid., 29.

27. James Naremore, *An Invention Without a Future: Essays on Cinema* (Berkeley: University of California Press, 2014), 2.

28. Noël Carroll, *Theorizing the Moving Image* (Cambridge: Cambridge University Press, 1996), xiii.

29. Christine Gledhill and Linda Williams, "Introduction," in *Reinventing Film Studies*, eds. Christine Gledhill and Linda Williams (New York: Arnold, 2000), 1.

30. Dudley Andrew, "The Core and the Flow of Film Studies," *Critical Inquiry* 35 (2009): 879–915.

31. Ibid., 914.

32. Ibid., 914, 913.

33. Ibid., 913.

34. Fernando Ramos Arenas, "Writing About a Common Love for Cinema: Discourses of Modern Cinephilia as a Trans-European Phenomenon," *Trespassing Journal: An Online Journal of Trespassing Art, Science, and Philosophy* 1 (2012): 19, http://trespassingjournal.com/Is sue1/TPJ_I1_Arenas_Article.pdf.

35. Rowena Santos Aquino, "To Live (with) Cinema: Documenting Cinephilia and the Archival Impulse," *LOLA* 4 (2013), http://www.lolajournal.com/4/cinephilia.html.

36. Paul Willemen, *Looks and Frictions: Essays in Cultural Studies and Film Theory* (Bloomington: Indiana University Press, 1994); Antoine de Baecque, *La Cinéphilie: Invention d'un Regard, Histoire d'une Culture, 1944–1968* (Paris: Librarie Arthème Fayard, 2003); Christian Keathley, *Cinephilia and History, or the Wind in the Trees* (Bloomington: Indiana University Press, 2006).

37. Willemen, *Looks and Frictions*, 235.

38. Laura Mulvey and Peter Wollen, "From Cinephilia to Film Studies," in *Inventing Film Studies*, eds. Lee Grieveson and Haidee Wasson (Durham, NC: Duke University Press, 2008), 228.

39. Ibid.

40. Thomas Elsaesser, "Cinephilia or the Uses of Disenchantment," in *Cinephilia: Movies, Love and Memory*, eds. Marijke de Valck and Malte Hagener (Amsterdam: Amsterdam University Press, 2005), 32.

41. Sontag, "The Decay of Cinema."

42. Girish Shambu, *The New Cinephilia* (Montreal: Caboose, 2014), 7.

43. Jonathan Rosenbaum and Adrian Martin, eds. *Movie Mutations: The Changing Face of World Cinephilia* (London: British Film Institute, 2003).

44. Marijke de Valck and Malte Hagener, *Cinephilia: Movies, Love and Memory* (Amsterdam: Amsterdam University Press, 2005); Scott Balcerzak and Jason Sperb, *Cinephilia in the Age of Digital Reproduction: Film, Pleasure and Digital Culture*, Vol. 1 (London: Wallflower Press, 2009) and Vol. 2 (London: Wallflower Press, 2012).

45. Shambu, *The New Cinephilia*, 4.

46. Laura Mulvey, *Death 24x a Second: Stillness and the Moving Image* (London: Reaktion Books, 2006), 147.

47. Rashna Wadia Richards, *Cinematic Flashes: Cinephilia and Classical Hollywood* (Bloomington: Indiana University Press, 2013), 26.

48. Jacques Rancière, *The Intervals of Cinema*, trans. John Howe (London: Verso, 2014), 2.

49. Malte Hagener and Marijke de Valck, "Cinephilia in Transition," in *Mind the Screen: Media Concepts according to Thomas Elsaesser*, eds. Japp Kooijman, Patricia Pisters, and Wanda Strauven (Amsterdam: Amsterdam University Press, 2008), 27.

50. Sergei Eisenstein, "Teaching Programme for the Theory and Practice of Direction: How to Teach Direction," in *Sergei Eisenstein, Selected Works, Volume III, Writings 1934–47*, trans. William Powell (New York: Tauris, 2010), 74–97.

51. Ibid., 76.

52. Ibid.

53. Vladimir Nizhny, *Lessons with Eisenstein*, trans. and ed. Ivor Montagu and Jay Leyda (New York: Hill and Wang, 1962).

54. Ibid., x.

55. Ibid., xiii.

56. Ernest L. Boyer, *Scholarship Reconsidered: Priorities of the Professoriate* (New York: Carnegie Foundation for the Advancement of Teaching, 1990).

57. Ibid., 23.

58. Beth M. Schwartz and Aeron Haynie, "Faculty Development Centers and the Role of SoTL," *New Directions for Teaching and Learning* 136 (2013): 102.

59. Dana Polan, *Scenes of Instruction*; Lee Grieveson and Haidee Wasson, eds., *Inventing Film Studies* (Durham, NC: Duke University Press, 2008).

60. Lucy Fischer and Patrice Petro, eds., *Teaching Film* (New York: Modern Language Association, 2012); Kate Gamm, *Teaching World Cinema* (London: British Film Institute, 2008); Sarah Gilligan, *Teaching Women and Film* (London: British Film Institute, 2008); Gregory J. Watkins, ed., *Teaching Religion and Film* (New York: Oxford University Press, 2008); Kathleen L. Brown, *Teaching Literary Theory Using Film Adaptations* (Jefferson, NC: McFarland, 2009).

61. Fischer and Petro, *Teaching Film*, 2.

62. Ibid.

63. Randy Bass, "The Scholarship of Teaching: What's the Problem?," *Inventio: Creative Thinking about Learning and Teaching* 1 (1999).

64. Vivian Sobchack, "Vivian Sobchack in Conversation with Scott Bukatman," *Journal of E-Media Studies* 2 (2009), doi: 10.1349/PS1.1938-6060.A.338.

65. Cristina Álvarez López, "Double Lives, Second Chances," *Frames* 1 (2012), http://framescinemajournal.com/article/double-lives-second-chances/.

PART I

Theorizing Cinephilia and Pedagogy

1 Cinephilia as a Method

Robert B. Ray

Two Examples

Here is cinephilia in action: Truffaut is writing about Roger Vadim's *And God Created Woman* (1956), a surprisingly dull film, which even the usually generous Leonard Maltin can give only 2½ stars. Having acknowledged the script's banality, Truffaut nevertheless finds a moment to admire: "Brigitte Bardot lifting in her arms a little girl who wants to grab a newspaper placed out of her reach."[1] On a previous occasion, when confronted by Jean-Pierre Melville's *Bob le Flambeur* (1956), Truffaut had moved from noting the "imperfections and the amateurish side of the undertaking" to something else: "Script, mise-en-scène, intentions, all this remains vague, but what is filmed, Pigalle at daybreak, rings truer than usual, and more poetic, too."[2] Understanding cinephilia depends on recognizing what these examples have in common with Man Ray's proposition: "The worst films I've ever seen, the ones that send me to sleep, contain ten or fifteen marvelous minutes. The best films I've ever seen only contain ten or fifteen valid minutes."[3] The Truffaut examples and the Ray dictum also help make sense of Pauline Kael's initially enigmatic observation that Rossellini was "a great filmmaker who never made a great film."[4] Or, in other words, *Rome, Open City* (Roberto Rossellini, 1945) contains long stretches of melodramatic claptrap, but if you have ever seen Pina's shooting on the cobbled streets outside her apartment building, on an overcast day the color of the Germans' uniforms, you will never forget it. Speaking for cinephiles everywhere, Truffaut said that he liked films that "pulse," but they don't have to pulse all the time.[5]

The Problem

Two years ago, I found myself teaching a graduate seminar on "The Untaught Canon," well-known movies that, for one reason or another (and the reasons can prove interesting), rarely get taught: for example, *Bombshell* (Victor Fleming, 1933), *Libeled Lady* (Jack Conway, 1936), *Three Comrades* (Frank Borzage, 1938), *The Mortal Storm* (Frank Borzage, 1940), *Midnight* (Mitchell Leisen, 1939), *Remember the Night* (Mitchell Leisen, 1940), *Since You Went Away* (John Cromwell, 1944), and *The Small Back Room* (Michael Powell and Emeric Pressburger, 1949).

Each week, the students wrote two-page essays involving close stylistic analyses of particular scenes or moments. After a week devoted in part to Howard Hawks's *Air Force* (1943), one particularly conscientious student declared defeat. "I can't write about a movie like this," he complained; "the director's not doing anything." When I responded that Hawks's employers, the Hollywood moguls who both paid him well and granted him extraordinary autonomy, apparently thought that he was doing something, the student replied, "Maybe, but I can't see it. It's nothing but standard Hollywood." When he taught himself, he explained, he only used films like *L'Eclisse* (Michelangelo Antonioni, 1962) and *Last Year at Marienbad* (Alain Resnais, 1961).

This exchange is instructive. It confirms Stanley Cavell's observation that "the everyday . . . appears to us as lost to us . . . and grasping a day, accepting the everyday, the ordinary, is not a given but a task."[6] Cavell derived this insight from Wittgenstein's famous definition of that task:

> The work of the philosopher consists in assembling reminders for a particular purpose. . . . The aspects of things that are most important for us are hidden because of their simplicity and familiarity. (One is unable to notice something—because it is always before one's eyes.)[7]

We can define the work of the cinephile as calling our attention to what Cavell calls the "missable," the ordinary, uneventful moments in the movies that we commonly neglect, the kind Howard Hawks had a special talent for capturing. These events, as my student's response to them indicates, are, in Cavell's words, not only "perceptually missable" but also "intellectually dismissable." For Cavell, however, to pass over the everyday events of life "came to strike me, intermittently, not exactly as revealing my life to be unexamined, but as missed by me, lost on me."[8] His discussion of Henry James's "The Beast in the Jungle" and Max Ophuls's *Letter from an Unknown Woman* (1948) shows that, in Andrew Klevan's words, "experience lost or missed can be a matter of life and death."[9]

Sometimes, missing things can prove literally fatal. In a remarkable essay, "Wonder and the Clinical Encounter," H. M. Evans proposes that the greatest enemy of medical practice is routine, the numbing regularity of familiar illnesses and symptoms that can lull doctors into missing what lies hidden by the ordinary. "The unremarkable patient becomes routine. The routine patient becomes uninteresting. How does one respond fully and attentively to an uninteresting patient . . . ?"[10] The routine of ordinary cases, Evans explains, "impedes our full respectful attention" to the case at hand. "The challenge," Evans summarizes, lies in "maintaining respectful attentiveness." "An attitude of intense attention and an active, responsive imagination can transfigure the ordinary."[11]

Easier said than done. The graduate student struck dumb by *Air Force*'s apparently routine Hollywood style resembles the medical practitioner dulled by seeing too many cases of the flu. In both situations, experience has become a handicap, as "pattern recognition" (whether of the flu or Classic Hollywood) discourages our "remaining free to see beyond the expected classification and discern a fractionally yet crucially different 'case.'"[12] If you can only detect film style in *L'Eclisse*, you resemble a doctor who can only recognize an illness when its symptoms have reached the critical stage.

In medicine, Evans reminds us, "The stakes can be very high."[13] They can also be high elsewhere, Cavell insists. Citing Emerson and Thoreau, Cavell calls for "consulting one's experience and . . . subjecting it to examination":

> momentarily *stopping*, turning yourself away from whatever your preoccupation and turning your experience away from its expected, habitual track, to find itself, its own track: coming to attention. The moral of this practice is to educate your experience sufficiently so that it is worthy of trust . . . without this trust in one's experience, expressed as a willingness to find words for it, without thus taking an interest in it, one is without authority in one's own experience. . . . I think of this authority as the right to take an interest in your own experience. I suppose that the primary good of a teacher is to prompt his or her students to find their way to that authority; without it, rote is fate.[14]

The experience that most concerns Cavell involves the ordinary, the everyday. To that end, he regularly returns to a passage from Emerson's "The American Scholar," in which he finds an "affinity for film":

> I ask not for the great, the remote, the romantic; what is doing in Italy or Arabia; what is Greek art, or Provencal Minstrelsy; I embrace the common, I explore and sit at the feet of the familiar, the low. Give me insight into to-day, and you may have the antique and future worlds. What would we really know the meaning of? The meal in the firkin; the milk in the pan; the ballad in the street; the news of the boat; the glance of the eye; the form and the gait of the body.[15]

Like Emerson, cinephilia has often preferred "the common" to "the remote," Hawks to Antonioni, Boetticher to Bergman. It has understood that "the great, the remote" need no advocates. Instead, cinephilia has called attention to "the form and the gait of the body" of Randolph Scott, walking down a dusty street in *Decision at Sundown* (Budd Boetticher, 1957), or the food on the officers' table in *They Were Expendable* (John Ford, 1945). We don't need cinephilia to point out *Rules of the Game* (Jean Renoir, 1939); we need it for the moment in *Andy Hardy Gets Spring Fever* (W. S. Van Dyke, 1939) when a schoolteacher returns to her darkened classroom, moving in silhouette through a latticed network of shadows and light, made by the half-open venetian blinds behind her desk (Figure 1.1).

How can a doctor regularly summon Evans's "attitude of intense attention"? How do we take up Cavell's task of "accepting the everyday, the ordinary"? How

Figure 1.1. *Andy Hardy Gets Spring Fever* (W. S. Van Dyke, 1939).

does a film scholar "learn" cinephilia? These are hard questions. The answer to them lies in method.

The Methods of Wonder

Evans proposes that only by retaining a feeling for the *wonder* of medical practice, the awesome responsibility of intervening in another person's body, medically or surgically, can a physician maintain the attentiveness her work requires.

> Wonder is a very particular kind of special attentiveness (very much an attitude rather than an emotion) . . . an attitude prompted by circumstances that may be entirely ordinary yet, through our active and responsive imagination, yield an object in which the ordinary is transfigured. . . . The attitude of wonder is thus one of altered, compellingly intensified attention to something that we immediately acknowledge as somehow important . . . that we certainly do not yet understand in its fullest sense . . . something whose initial appearance to us engages our imagination before our understanding.[16]

Evans's *wonder* results in what Wittgenstein called "the dawning of an aspect," the sudden appearance of something previously missed—the duck in the gestalt image that had previously seemed to offer only a rabbit. "I should like to say," Wittgenstein commented, "that what dawns here lasts only as long as I am occupied with the object in a particular way. . . . Ask yourself 'For how long am I struck by a thing?'—'For how long do I find it *new*?'"[17]

Wittgenstein suggests that one can be prompted to notice a previously undetected aspect ("Don't you see the duck?"): "Seeing an aspect and imagining," he writes, "are subject to the will."[18] But how can we summon the attitude of wonder? For Evans, the enemies of that attitude are routine and its institutionalization, especially the protocols of insurance companies and health-care organizations.[19] Is it enough simply to call for a renewal of wonder in clinical practice?

Evans's concern, the institutionalization of routine, affects all established disciplines, especially academic ones. Since at least 1975, the escalating publishing requirements for teaching jobs have turned cinema studies into a duplicating machine reproducing nearly identical books and articles, examples of what Roland Barthes, forty-five years ago, called a new "mythological doxa . . . stock of phrases, catechistic declaration."[20] Back in 1988, Meaghan Morris had made the same scathing diagnosis:

> Sometimes, reading magazines like *New Socialist* or *Marxism Today* from the last couple of years, flipping through *Cultural Studies*, or scanning the pop-theory pile in the bookshop, I get the feeling that somewhere in some English publisher's vault there is a master-disc from which thousands of versions of the same article about pleasure, resistance, and the politics of consumption are being run off under different names with minor variations.[21]

Fast-forward to the present, and you get this actual description of a lecture in a university film series:

> In this talk, Prof. _____ will explore how Hong Kong filmmaker Stanley Kwan's *Lan Yu* ameliorates the traumatic cinematic topos of Beijing via queer "structures of feeling." The affective topography of this film is queer not so much because it features such an ordinary gay love story (as Kwan describes it). Rather, its synthesis of Beijing and Hong Kong aesthetics creates a sense of queer normativity. The traumatized national subject embraces the abject colonial subject; emotions long frozen within the palimpsest of a Beijing ethos, or commodified within the temporal spatiality of a Hong Kong topos, are expressed in real time in the presence of loving others. As a "parable of renewed Enlightenment," *Lan Yu* disrupts postcolonial narratives of neoliberalism by queering urban affectivities conditioned by the imperial and the colonized.

Traumatic cinematic topos, queer structures of feeling, affective topography, normativity, traumatized national subject, abject colonial subject, the palimpsest of a Beijing ethos, commodified, temporal spatiality, disrupts, postcolonial, neoliberalism, urban affectivities, the imperial and the colonized—the paragraph might have been written by a machine, using an algorithm derived from routine contemporary cinema studies. Instead, of course, its author is a professor, pressed for publications and in a hurry to produce them. Cavell has spotted the problem: "my impatient expressions do not allow me to know what is on my mind . . . a standard formula is ready to take over thinking for us, [so] that what is of distinct importance to us is masked by us."[22]

For twenty years, I have been looking for ways out of this cul-de-sac. In *The Avant-Garde Finds Andy Hardy*, I found inspiration in Surrealism's insistence on reopening the question of method, presumed settled by the Cartesian tradition. "We have proscribed every way of seeking the truth which does not conform to convention," André Breton announced.

> But it is important to note that there is no fixed method *a priori* for the execution of this enterprise, that until the new order it can be considered the province of poets as well as scholars, and that its success does not depend on the more or less capricious routes which will be followed.[23]

Taking up this challenge, I experimented with ways of studying ordinary movies, MGM's Andy Hardy films. These experiments involved the Surrealist devices of games, fragmentation, and collaboration. Most productive for me was an abecedarian assignment I gave to my students:

> Working with one of the course films, produce a text of 26 entries, one for each letter of the alphabet. Each entry must start with a detail from the movie you have chosen. The best entries will use details that you find especially intriguing or enigmatic to do the following:
> —first, generate knowledge about the movie at hand.
> —second, speculate about classic Hollywood filmmaking.
> —third, reflect on the cinema in general.
> Avoid initiating entires with ideas imposed on the film (e.g., "intolerance," "the male gaze"). They will inhibit your own discoveries.[24]

By prohibiting ready-made critical templates, this assignment forced students (and me) to practice what Cavell designates as "philosophical criticism," which begins with "the question . . . why one is stopped" by a detail and becomes "a matter of stopping and turning and going back over." This brand of philosophy, as Cavell defines it, turns on "responsiveness" and "not speaking first."[25] Rather than ransacking a movie for its confirmation of a pre-existing idea (postcolonialism, generic transgression, globalization, etc.), "we must let the films themselves teach us how to look at them and how to think about them."[26]

Having found a similar idea in the French Impressionists' notion of *photogénie* (which I took up in *How a Film Theory Got Lost*), I pursued this method in *The ABCs of Classic Hollywood*, again using it to study the type of movie my graduate student found unexceptional: *Grand Hotel* (Edmund Goulding, 1932), *The Philadelphia Story* (George Cukor, 1940), *The Maltese Falcon* (John Huston, 1941), and

Meet Me in St. Louis (Vincente Minnelli, 1944). And then, almost simultaneously, I read three texts that made me "stop" and "go back over" what I had been doing: (1) Wittgenstein's *Philosophical Investigations*, (2) "'What Becomes of Thinking on Film?': Stanley Cavell in Conversation with Andrew Klevan," and (3) Thoreau's *Walden*. What (besides Cavell's involvement in all three) did these things have in common? Why did they make me examine my own working methods? What do they offer as solutions to cinema studies' impasse?

We can start to answer these questions by noting that Thoreau, Wittgenstein, and Cavell all invoke some version of Evans's *wonder*. For Thoreau, the task was to awaken himself to "a miracle which is taking place every instant," the everyday details of the pond's freezing, of Concord's bells sounding in the breeze.[27] In "A Lecture on Ethics," Wittgenstein described his own intermittent sense of "absolute or ethical value" as an experience "that when I have it *I wonder at the existence of the world.*"[28] Cavell has followed a similar path, acknowledging that his first book on film, *The World Viewed*, had begun with "a certain obscurity of prompting," intuitions about the movies that, as Emerson insisted, require tuitions.[29] In "A Capra Moment," one of his best essays, Cavell devoted eight pages to a single moment from *It Happened One Night* (Frank Capra, 1934): Gable and Colbert, with their backs to the camera, walking down an empty highway, en route to the hitchhiking scene. Cavell began with only a hunch: "I knew afresh each time I viewed the film that this moment played something like an epitomizing role in the film's effect upon me, but I remained unable to find words for it sufficient to include in my critical account of the effect."[30] The essay resulted from his having found the words. "I then wrote a brief essay," Cavell told Andrew Klevan, "about simply that shot, *simply* that shot, which seemed to me to raise every issue in the whole film."[31]

Cavell describes "A Capra Moment" as "*an exercise.*"[32] Given the apparently incidental nature of Capra's scene, we might describe it as an exercise in attentiveness, a means of noticing "the missable." Film and philosophy, Cavell insists, are "both preoccupied with the everyday. . . . They are both preoccupied with ways in which we miss our lives."[33] "We must stick to the subjects of our everyday thinking," Wittgenstein counseled, "and not go astray and imagine that we have to describe extreme subtleties, which in turn we are after all quite unable to describe with the means at our disposal."[34]

Evans warns that the routine of everyday clinical practice, the loss of wonder, disables a doctor's ability to see. What's the remedy? "We must learn to reawaken and keep ourselves awake," Thoreau writes in *Walden*, "not by mechanical aids, but by an infinite expectation of the dawn."[35] That's the mission statement, but not exactly the program for achieving it. In fact, however, *Walden*, *Philosophical Investigations*, and Cavell-Klevan all suggest such a program, and it turns on *description*.

"We must do away with all *explanation*," Wittgenstein famously declared, "and description alone must take its place."[36] Thoreau had been there before him. *Walden*'s difficulty lies in the move from its first two chapters' explicit lessons to the interior chapters' factual catalogs. Thoreau's effort to keep awake involved using detailed observation to retune himself to the natural world; the goal was to love the present moment *even when nothing was happening*: "Sometimes, in a summer morning . . . I sat in my sunny doorway from sunrise till noon, rapt in a revery."[37] "These experiences," he tells us, "were very memorable and valuable to me."[38] "A Capra Moment" begins with Cavell's careful description of the scene's specifics. Because, as Cavell tells Klevan, in film "everything matters—and you do not know what everything means," because the most important thing in a movie is often "invisible. . . . It's on the surface, you can't miss it, but you inveterately miss it," we require a procedure for its retrieval.[39] That procedure begins with description.

Robert Richardson has said that "Thoreau's nearly limitless capacity for being interested is one of the most unusual and attractive things about him."[40] The seemingly endless stream of nature descriptions that fill his *Journal* and *Walden*'s inner chapters are both the reflection of and the means to that capacity. "Without interest," Cavell insists, "philosophy as I care about it most cannot proceed."[41] *Cinephilia*, of course, names a particular interest, not only in the cinema in general, but especially in what Cavell calls "the endless events . . . of film," its "fascination with, craving for, something like the accidental, the contingent."[42] Cinephilia is the movies' version of Evans's wonder, the engine of a wakeful attentiveness that notices the details hiding on the surface of the ordinary case, the routine movie—Brigitte Bardot's lifting the child to grab a newspaper from a rack just out of her reach, the bicyclist riding just outside the window of *Sunrise*'s trolley.

In a colloquium held at the University of Florida in September 2013, Andrew Klevan compared his approach to a three-legged stool, consisting of *description, interpretation, evaluation*. Anyone even slightly familiar with Truffaut's readiness to issue grades will recognize the role of evaluation in cinephilia: "A film is a born loser just because it is English." "*Giant* is everything that is contemptible in the Hollywood system." "I'll sing about . . . the virile allure of *The Narrow Margin*."[43] It's the line dividing Klevan's first two terms that's always at issue. How much description is enough? Where should description end? To what extent does any interpretation restrict, and even falsify, our experience of a movie?

These issues lie at the heart of the problem posed by *Walden*. "It cannot, I think, be denied," Cavell writes, "that *Walden* sometimes seems an enormously long and boring book." Even Emerson confided that Thoreau's writing made him "nervous and wretched."[44] Thoreau himself acknowledges that once the book leaves behind its often-excerpted first two chapters ("Economy" and "Where I

Lived, and What I Lived for") and begins what Cavell calls "its drones of fact": "An old-fashioned man would have lost his sense or died of ennui."[45] And yet Thoreau could not bring himself entirely to trust the moralizing interpretations he was tempted to impose on what he saw. Here is a characteristic passage from "Economy": Thoreau is describing how he had watched a striped snake lying "without inconvenience" on the pond's bottom for over a quarter of an hour, "perhaps because he had not yet fairly come out of his torpid state." The observation prompts a miniature sermon:

> It appeared to me that for a like reason men remain in their present low and primitive condition; but if they should feel the influence of the spring of springs arousing them, they would of necessity rise to a higher and more ethereal life.

And then, abruptly, Thoreau shifts gears:

> I had previously seen the snakes in frosty mornings in my path with portions of their bodies still numb and inflexible, waiting for the sun to thaw them. On the 1st of April it rained and melted the ice, and in the early part of the day, which was very foggy, I heard a stray goose groping about over the pond and cackling as if lost, or like the spirit of the fog.[46]

The oscillation between interpretation and description, the longing for and the resistance to easy correspondences, the commitment to saying what the woods were really like as well as what they might stand for—all lie at the heart of *Walden*. The phrase "on the 1st of April it rained and melted the ice" confirms Thoreau's proposition that "mere facts and names and dates communicate more than we suspect."[47]

Thoreau often worried about this problem—how to mix the weather report with the Lyceum sermon.[48] As early as 1841, four years before going to Walden, he had confided his impatience with a certain kind of interpretation:

> In reading a work on agriculture, I skip the author's moral reflections . . . to come at the profitable level of what he has to say. There is no science in men's religion; it does not teach me so much as the report of the committee on swine. My author shows that he has dealt in corn and turnips and can worship God with the hoe and spade, but spare me his morality.[49]

Ten years later, he had become more resolute: "I begin to see . . . objects," he wrote in his journal, "only when I leave off understanding them."[50] As Sharon Cameron observes, Thoreau's *Journal* traces "the progressive refusal to interpret the observation recorded, as if the significance of a tree were the description of that tree."[51] In this abstention, Thoreau anticipated a modernist taste: "Description is explanation," pronounced Gertrude Stein (*Lectures in America*), only to be trumped by Wallace Stevens, "Description is revelation" ("Description Without Place").

One comment on the description-interpretation divide gets at the issue. In *The Pleasure of the Text*, Roland Barthes offers this confession:

> Why do some people, including myself, enjoy in certain novels, biographies, and historical works, the representation of the "daily life" of an epoch, of a character? Why this curiosity about petty details: schedules, habits, meals, lodging, clothing, etc.? Is it the hallucinatory relish of "reality" (the very materiality of "*that once existed*")? . . .
>
> Thus, impossible to imagine a more tenuous, a more insignificant notation than that of "today's weather" (or yesterday's); and yet, the other day, reading, trying to read Amiel, irritation that the well-meaning editor (another person foreclosing pleasure) had seen fit to omit from this Journal the everyday details, what the weather was like on the shores of Lake Geneva, and retain only the insipid moral musing: yet it is this weather that has not aged, not Amiel's philosophy.[52]

Barthes's skeptical retreat from interpretation recalls Wallace Stevens's insistence that "Little of what we have believed has been true."[53] Our ideas date; the weather does not. "What the weather was like"—it's an exact description of what interested Thoreau. As he once noted, "In a journal, it is important in a few words to describe the weather, or character of the day, as it affects our feelings. That which was so important at the time cannot be unimportant to remember."[54] Meticulously described, just the details of the weather alone can achieve something: "You only need to make a faithful record of an average summer day's experience and summer mood," Thoreau writes, "and read it in the winter, and it will carry you back to more than that summer day alone could show."[55]

Description enables us to get at a film's "weather," the particularities that make it what it is. Talking to Cavell, Andrew Klevan comments on routine cinema studies: "You have a rich and detailed film and then you get an academic piece on that film that barely acknowledges any of [its] richness or detail."[56] Even someone alert to this problem can run aground. Writing about *Camille*'s fifteen-second close-up of Garbo reacting to being slapped by her lover, Klevan records his own attempt to name the reactions playing on her face (pride, defensiveness, anger, astonishment, relief, pain), only to become "conscious of the inadequacy of the specifications as each facial expression was already in the process of transforming into the next."[57] As Wittgenstein diagnosed the matter, "One thinks that one is tracing the outline of the thing's nature over and over again, and one is merely tracing round the frame through which we look at it."[58]

Cinephilia amounts to an attentive *interest* in the movies. That interest can be produced by description. Ready-made interpretations often forestall that interest. But if we want to "understand" something, will description be enough? We need another example.

Moonwatching

In *The Having of Wonderful Ideas*, Eleanor Duckworth, Jean Piaget's former student and colleague, offers a remarkable series of educational exercises (to use Cavell's term).[59] For the most part, Duckworth eschews grand statements of purpose, preferring to concentrate on the specific instructions for, and results from, her assignments. As a result, the book is at once concrete and mysterious. It resembles both *Walden* and *Philosophical Investigations*, each of which amounts to an enigmatic instruction manual for a particular activity never made fully explicit.

Perhaps Duckworth's most famous assignment began from propositions relevant to my argument:

> In my view, there are two aspects to teaching. The first is to put students into contact with phenomena related to the area to be studied—the real thing, not books or lectures about it—and to help them notice what is interesting; to engage them so they will continue to think and *wonder* [my emphasis] about it. The second is to have the students try to explain the sense they are making, and . . . to try to understand their sense.[60]

"I look for some phenomena to draw their attention," Duckworth writes, ideally "phenomena that, familiar as they are and simple as they seem, do not lend themselves to satisfactory explanations by distant theories."[61] Like the habits of the moon.

> I ask the students to keep and bring to each class a separate notebook in which they make an entry every time they see the moon—when and where they see it and what it looks like. By the first week's reporting time, at least some people have something specific they want to look for in the following week. Little by little, the assignment changes from one that is flaky, arbitrary, or easy to one that is absorbing and serious.[62]

"Having the students watch the moon," Duckworth observes, "engages [students] with phenomena. . . . I continually ask them what they notice and what they make of it, and I encourage them to do the same with each other."[63] One student records a response:

> There's so much I don't understand, and trying to understand means giving things up, at least partially trading part of a familiar way of seeing for the beginnings of another. But I also have this terrific feeling of an *opening* of things.[64]

Working from Duckworth's assignment, I asked eight graduate students enrolled in a film analysis seminar to record for ten days their observations of a

Figure 1.2. *It Happened One Night* (Frank Capra, 1934).

single scene from *It Happened One Night,* a movie as familiar as the moon, and, so it proved, equally mysterious. Here are a few responses:

> Ellie (Claudette Colbert) and Peter (Clark Gable) pretend to fool her father's detectives:
>
> - Even though the men have left, Peter buttons up Ellie's shirt for her (Figure 1.2).
> - Ellie and Peter enjoy pretending to be married more than they have enjoyed anything so far.
> - Just as junior-high children find excuses to bump up against or touch each other, Peter uses this scene as an opportunity to touch Ellie's hair, her face, her blouse, and even her legs (he parts them several times).
> - In pretending to be Ellie's husband, Peter speaks completely of domestic things: a visit to an aunt, a baby on the way, whether or not the baby will be a boy or a girl. Doing so reveals a lot about his perception of marriage.
> - Watching with the volume off, I notice that the "Wall of Jericho," which has thus far separated Peter and Ellie, now separates them from the detectives. This point in the film marks a shift; they are now "on the same side."

- During the couple's staged fight, Peter comments about a Swede "making a pass" at Ellie and portrays himself as a jealous husband. Just as Hamlet's *Mousetrap* confirms Claudius's actions, this acted scene reveals Peter's hidden desires and feelings.
  —Paulette Bane

Second motel scene, Ellie asks, "Haven't you ever been in love, Peter?":

- As Ellie asks Peter the question, she massages her arms, runs her hands down her leg, and touches her knee, before finally letting her hands fall to her sides (Figure 1.3).
- Ellie slightly bites her bottom lip before asking Peter the question. After he replies with a startled, "Me?" she again tightens her lips before speaking again.
- I'm beginning to see Ellie's arm gestures as more a squeezing movement than a massage, an indication of her discomfort and vulnerability as she puts her question to Peter.
- Ellie's body is bent forward towards the Wall of Jericho, suggesting her eagerness to hear Peter's reply. As Peter tells her that it is hard to find "someone that is real, someone that is alive," Ellie's body and eyes droop downward. Her emotion here is difficult to pinpoint. The next

Figure 1.3. *It Happened One Night* (Frank Capra, 1934).

shot is mismatched with the previous one: her head is back up, but we have not seen it lift.

- Ellie tilts her head slightly before she asks, "Have you ever thought about it at all?" When the shot switches to the center view showing both characters, we can see her shadow. In the shots of Ellie alone, we have been unable to see her shadow, an indication that the two camera set-ups have used different lighting.

- I notice that before Ellie asks Peter if she has ever been in love, her mouth is slightly open. She strokes the bed while bringing her head down, appearing unsatisfied with his reply, but uncertain how to proceed.

- The way she squeezes her arms makes her pajamas billow in the back. When she squeezes only one arm, she leans her body slightly back, an adjustment from her previous forward-leaning posture.

    —Emily Glosser

These responses show description already en route to interpretation. Pursuing this strategy can help us detect "the missable" in cinematic moments that seem ordinary. Take, for example, *It's a Wonderful Life*, a movie that almost anyone in cinema studies must feel he or she knows by heart. And yet, look what two students, Michael Vincent and Emily Glosser, prompted by the moonwatching exercise, can do with an apparently inconsequential, transitional scene (Figures 1.4–1.9).

This six-shot scene lasts exactly sixty seconds. In the newly opened Bailey Park, George's semiphilanthropic low-income-housing project, George (Jimmy Stewart) and Mary (Donna Reed) are saying goodbye to Sam Wainwright (Frank Albertson) and his wife Jane (Marian Carr), who are off to a Florida vacation. The scene, like so many in this movie, will turn on immediately noticeable contrasts and require us to reevaluate first impressions. As the two couples stand facing each other in an American shot, with a black limousine visible between them, the obvious contrast involves their clothes. George wears his typical, practical tweed suit. Mary is dressed like a bobby-soxer: skirt and sweater, scarf, and a baseball cap with the bill turned up. Sam's matching suit, obviously more elegant, is topped off by the white handkerchief in his breast pocket and the black bowler on his head. Jane's costume marks the most obvious difference between the two couples. She is thoroughly bejeweled, with her beret's elaborate pin and her brooch, necklace, earrings, and bracelet all glittering in the sunlight. She sports a white fur stole, and her black gloves and purse, complementing her perfectly tailored off-white suit, are formal: she is clearly overdressed for daytime in Bailey Park, much less for a drive to Florida. We are encouraged to dislike her.

The movie has set us up to distrust any woman who would marry Sam. Previously, the telephone-proposal scene has shown us Sam, invisible to Mary,

Figure 1.4. *It's a Wonderful Life* (Frank Capra, 1946).

Figure 1.5. *It's a Wonderful Life* (Frank Capra, 1946).

Figure 1.6. *It's a Wonderful Life* (Frank Capra, 1946).

Figure 1.7. *It's a Wonderful Life* (Frank Capra, 1946).

Figure 1.8. *It's a Wonderful Life* (Frank Capra, 1946).

Figure 1.9. *It's a Wonderful Life* (Frank Capra, 1946).

referring to her as "my girl," while another flashy, overdressed woman hangs around his neck. And yet, just as we are beginning to suspect Jane, the movie cuts to a closer shot of her asking Sam, "Why don't you have your friends join us?" Despite her appearance, she is friendly and generous. (Three shots later, her "Awfully glad to have met you, Mary" is warm and genuine.) This reversal resembles an earlier scene in the pharmacy, where after appearing to establish Mr. Gower (H. B. Warner) as a Dickensian tyrant, his temper worsened by alcohol, Capra reveals what he has withheld, the telegram notifying Mr. Gower of his son's death from influenza.[65] The movie, in other words, does to its viewer what the plot does to George: it releases new information that forces a change of heart. We learn to like Mr. Gower and Jane; George learns that he has a wonderful life.

Sam begins to reply to Jane, saying "Why, sure," as shot 3 returns to shot 1's setup, with Sam's offering the invitation Jane had suggested: "Hey, why don't you kids drive down with us, huh?" Like his chronic use of their childhood greeting, "Hee-haw!," Sam's use of "kids" suggests both his affection for the couple he has known all his life and also a blithe condescension toward them. As George pauses for a beat, our attention having been drawn to him, Emily Glosser asks us instead to notice Mary, whose face registers a series of flickering emotions: hopefulness (she looks up at George eagerly: they may get a vacation at last), deference (he will make the decision for both of them), quiet acceptance of his inevitable refusal (she looks down at the ground).

"Oh, I'm afraid I couldn't get away, Sam," George says at last, prompting shot 4 (a repeat of shot 2) and Sam's chiding answer, "Still got the nose to the old grindstone, eh?" Shot 5 resumes shot 1's setup, with Sam reminding Jane that "I offered to let George in on the ground floor of plastics, and he turned me down cold." "Plastics," of course, will become *The Graduate*'s (Mike Nichols, 1967) code term for inauthenticity, and the word reminds us of Sam's ambiguous characterization. Like Mr. Potter, he seems a somewhat unscrupulous wheeler-dealer (and perhaps a war profiteer), and also like Mr. Potter, he tempts George to give up on the Building and Loan. In fact, Sam's casual invitation here foreshadows the next scene and Mr. Potter's more dangerous offer: to come to work with him. Sam, however, is not a thorough villain. The final scene absolves him in absentia when his telegram arrives offering to advance George "up to twenty-five thousand dollars."

As the couples part, the camera now affords us a glimpse of something previously withheld: the Wainwright car has a chauffeur, a mustachioed man who seems to have escaped from a thirties gangster movie. Sam calls out his inevitable "Hee-haw!," and shot 6 shows his car driving off, the camera moving behind George and Mary, arm in arm, looking down a freshly built road in the brand-new, raw, unfinished Bailey Park. With its deep perspective following the

Wainwright car moving out of sight and George's and Mary's backs to the camera, the shot could be a film's conclusion. At the very least, it seems to mark the end of something. It does not. The scene concludes with yet another contrast: George and Mary walk back to their own much-the-worse-for-wear car, and George kicks shut its door (Figure 1.10).

But there is still something else. Cavell has urged us to consider a particularly mysterious aspect of the cinema:

> If it is part of the grain of film to magnify the feeling and meaning of a moment, it is equally part of it to counter this tendency, and instead to acknowledge the fateful fact of a human life that the significance of its moments is ordinarily not given as they are lived, so that to determine the significant crossroads of a life may be the work of a lifetime. It is as if an inherent concealment of significance, as much as its revelation, were part of the governing force of what we mean by film acting and film directing and film viewing.[66]

Learning to detect the significance of a filmed moment trains us not to miss our own lives. I seem to have offered a complete description of *It's a Wonderful Life's* brief scene, but Emily Glosser points out that I have not. After George refuses Sam's Florida vacation, Sam offers his teasing reply ("Still got the nose to the old grindstone, eh?"). Because Sam and George are doing the talking, our eyes are drawn to them and not to Mary, who as Sam says the word "plastics," gently rubs

Figure 1.10. *It's a Wonderful Life* (Frank Capra, 1946).

Figure 1.11. *It's a Wonderful Life* (Frank Capra, 1946).

her hand across her stomach (Figure 1.11). As the movie will make explicit two scenes later, she is pregnant. Her gesture is not hidden, but we (I) have been too distracted to see it.

In the retrieval of such details, in what Martin Heidegger called their "unconcealment," cinephilia justifies itself. It amounts to a specialized version of the attentiveness celebrated by Saint Augustine, who asked the earth, the living creatures, the wind and the air, the heaven, sun, moon, and stars, "What is the object of my love?"

> And I said to all these things . . . : "tell me of my God who you are not, tell me something about him." And with a great voice they cried out: "He made us." My question was the attention I gave to them, and their response was their beauty.[67]

ROBERT B. RAY is Professor of English at the University of Florida and the author of *A Certain Tendency of the Hollywood Cinema, 1930–1980*, *The Avant-Garde Finds Andy Hardy, How a Film Theory Got Lost and Other Mysteries in Cultural Studies* (Indiana University Press), *The ABCs of Classic Hollywood*, and *Walden x 40* (Indiana University Press).

Notes

1. Wheeler Winston Dixon, *The Early Film Criticism of François Truffaut* (Bloomington: Indiana University Press, 1993), 73.

2. Ibid., 154.

3. Man Ray, "Cinemage," in *The Shadow and Its Shadow: Surrealist Writings on the Cinema*, ed. Paul Hammond (London: British Film Institute, 1978), 84.

4. Quoted by Gilberto Perez, *The Material Ghost* (Baltimore, MD: Johns Hopkins University Press, 1998), 41.

5. François Truffaut, "What Do Critics Dream About?," in *The Films in My Life*, trans. Leonard Mayhew (New York: Simon and Schuster, 1975), 6.

6. Stanley Cavell, *In Quest of the Ordinary: Lines of Romanticism and Skepticism* (Chicago: University of Chicago Press, 1988), 171.

7. Ludwig Wittgenstein, *Philosophical Investigations*, trans. G.E.M. Anscombe (Oxford: Blackwell, 2001), 43 (§127 and 129).

8. Stanley Cavell, *Philosophy the Day After Tomorrow* (Cambridge, MA: Harvard University Press, 2005), 11, 12, 10.

9. Andrew Klevan, "Notes on Stanley Cavell and Philosophical Film Criticism," in *New Takes in Film-Philosophy*, eds. Havi Carel and Greg Tuck (New York: Palgrave Macmillan, 2011), 60. Cavell's discussion of the James story and the Ophuls film appears in *Cities of Words* (Cambridge, MA: Harvard University Press, 2004), 384–408.

10. H. M. Evans, "Wonder and the Clinical Encounter," *Theoretical Medicine and Bioethics* 33, no. 2 (2012): 125.

11. Ibid., 129.

12. Ibid., 131.

13. Ibid.

14. Stanley Cavell, *The Pursuits of Happiness* (Cambridge, MA: Harvard University Press, 1981), 12.

15. Ralph Waldo Emerson, *The Annotated Emerson*, ed. David Mikics (Cambridge, MA: Harvard University Press, 2012), 89–90. Cavell cites this passage in several places, including *Pursuits of Happiness*, 14.

16. Evans, "Wonder and the Clinical Encounter," 127.

17. Wittgenstein, *Philosophical Investigations*, 166, 179.

18. Ibid., 182.

19. Evans, "Wonder and the Clinical Encounter," 130.

20. "the new semiology . . . has become in some sort mythical: any student can and does denounce the bourgeois or petit-bourgeois character of such and such a form (of life, of thought, of consumption). In other words, a mythological doxa has been created: denunciation, demystification (or demythification), has itself become discourse, stock of phases, catechistic declaration." Roland Barthes, *Image-Music-Text*, trans. Stephen Heath (New York: Hill and Wang, 1977), 166.

21. Meaghan Morris, "Banality in Cultural Studies," *Discourse* 10, no. 2 (1988): 15.

22. Stanley Cavell in Conversation with Andrew Klevan, "'What Becomes of Thinking on Film?,'" in *Film as Philosophy*, eds. Rupert Read and Jerry Goodenough (New York: Palgrave Macmillan, 2005), 194.

23. André Breton, "Manifesto of Surrealism," in *Surrealism*, ed. Patrick Waldberg (New York: Oxford University Press, 1965), 66.

24. Robert B. Ray, *The ABCs of Classic Hollywood* (New York: Oxford University Press, 2008), xxiii.

25. Cavell in Conversation with Andrew Klevan, 182.

26. Cavell, *Pursuits of Happiness*, 25.

27. Henry D. Thoreau, *Walden, Civil Disobedience, and Other Writings*, ed. William Rossi (New York: Norton Critical Edition, 2008), 11.

28. Ludwig Wittgenstein, *Philosophical Occasions*, eds. James Klagge and Alfred Nordmann (Indianapolis, IN: Hackett, 1993), 41.

29. Stanley Cavell, *The World Viewed: Reflections on the Ontology of Film* (Cambridge, MA: Harvard University Press, 1979), 162.

30. Stanley Cavell, "A Capra Moment," in *Cavell on Film*, ed. William Rothman (Albany: SUNY Press, 2005), 136. For an analysis of this essay, see Robert B. Ray, "Cavell, Thoreau, and the Movies," in *Stanley Cavell, Literature, and Film: The Idea of America*, eds. Andrew Taylor and Aine Kelly (New York: Routledge, 2013), 169–184.

31. Cavell in Conversation with Andrew Klevan, 182.

32. Ibid.

33. Ibid., 206.

34. Wittgenstein, *Philosophical Investigations*, 39 (§106).

35. Thoreau, *Walden*, 64.

36. Wittgenstein, *Philosophical Investigations*, 40 (§109).

37. Ibid., 79.

38. Ibid., 120.

39. Cavell in Conversation with Andrew Klevan, 169, 189.

40. Robert Richardson, *Henry Thoreau: A Life of the Mind* (Berkeley: University of California Press, 1986), 376.

41. Cavell in Conversation with Andrew Klevan, 186.

42. Ibid., 168, 175.

43. Dixon, *The Early Film Criticism of François Truffaut*, 80, 87, 17.

44. Stanley Cavell, *The Senses of Walden* (San Francisco: North Point Press, 1981), 20, 12.

45. Ibid., 16, 90.

46. Thoreau, *Walden*, 31–32. Stephen Fender's Introduction to the Oxford World Classics edition of *Walden* alerted me to this passage's significance. Prompted by Fender, my discussion of this passage appears in my *Walden x 40: Essays on Thoreau* (Bloomington: Indiana University Press, 2012), 13–14. I have reproduced parts of it in this essay.

47. This remark appears in Thoreau's *Journal*, 27 January 1852. Rossi's Norton Critical Edition of *Walden* has it on 364.

48. The best discussion of this problem is Sharon Cameron, *Writing Nature: Henry Thoreau's Journal* (Chicago: University of Chicago Press, 1985). Cameron contrasts the *Journal*'s preference for description to *Walden*'s ambivalence about the matter.

49. Henry David Thoreau, *The Journal of Henry David Thoreau*, eds. Bradford Torrey and Francis H. Allen (New York: Dover, 1962), 1: 243.

50. Ibid., 2: 160.

51. Cameron, *Writing Nature*, 5.

52. Roland Barthes, *The Pleasure of the Text*, trans. Richard Miller (New York: Hill and Wang, 1975), 53–54.

53. Wallace Stevens, "The Noble Rider and the Sound of Words," *Stevens: Collected Poetry and Prose* (New York: Library of America, 1997), 655.

54. Thoreau, *The Journal of Henry David Thoreau*, 7: 171.

55. Ibid., 5: 454.

56. Cavell in Conversation with Andrew Klevan, 179.

57. Andrew Klevan, "Living Meaning: The Fluency of Film Performance," in *Theorizing Film Acting*, ed. Aaron Taylor (New York: Routledge, 2012), 35.

58. Wittgenstein, *Philosophical Investigations*, 41 (§114).

59. Eleanor Duckworth, *The Having of Wonderful Ideas* (New York: Teachers College Press, 2006).

60. Ibid., 173–174.

61. Ibid., 175.

62. Ibid., 176.

63. Ibid., 180.

64. Ibid., 183.

65. For a superb analysis of this scene, see George Toles, *A House Made of Light* (Detroit, MI: Wayne State University Press, 2001), 51–75.

66. Stanley Cavell, "The Thought of Movies," in *Cavell on Film*, 94.

67. Saint Augustine, *Confessions*, trans. Henry Chadwick (New York: Oxford World Classics, 2008), 183. I am grateful to Diana Senechal who, in a February 2014 talk at the University of Florida, called my attention to this passage.

2 Passionate Attachments

Amelie Hastie

> When the image is new, the world is new.
> —Gaston Bachelard

ABOUT HALFWAY THROUGH Niki Caro's 2002 *Whale Rider*, young Paikea (Keisha Castle-Hughes) seeks out her uncle Rawiri (Grant Roa) to teach her the practice of taiaha fighting, for her grandfather Koro (Rawiri Paratene) has barred her from training with his own new students because she is a girl. She comes upon Rawiri and his girlfriend, stoned and snoozing outside. When she confirms to him that Koro doesn't know that he's helping her, he utters, "Let's get it on then." In the scene that follows, using a broomstick as his taiaha, Rawiri performs directly to the camera and to us, with Paikea matching his movements behind him, while his girlfriend and buddies watch from the sidelines. Though he is a bit out of shape, his gestures are trained, both graceful and jerky, with his facial expressions punctuating his bodily movement. When he completes this performance, he stands with his body cocked to the side, loosening his mouth and nodding his head to confirm his own prowess. Classic stoner's reggae appears on the soundtrack, and his friends begin to laugh. I love this sequence. My body responds viscerally to Rawiri's movement, to his direct address, and to the music that follows. But I also love this scene because it demands that we give something over of our expectations and because it suggests that the image—an image itself of instruction—can teach us anew through seeing and feeling at once. This scene activates my imagination; as Gaston Bachelard writes, "phenomenology of the imagination cannot be content with a reduction which would make the image a subordinate means of expression; it demands, on the contrary, that images be lived directly, that they be taken as sudden events in life."[1]

One of the biggest challenges in teaching film as a medium and as a discipline to be studied is the sense of familiarity students already have with the form. One central disciplinary thrust is to defamiliarize ourselves from film in order to introduce "critical thinking." For students new to film studies this approach often means, as Christian Metz might put it, of "no longer lov[ing] the cinema."[2]

In an attempt to take their ensuing resistance into consideration, I invite students to think through their love of film as a method of creative-critical practice. Doing so still requires a kind of defamiliarization with film through our very familiarity with it, or at least an agreement to enter into an experience that may, indeed, be partially "new." To help this process along is the "fact" (albeit a phenomenological one) that films appear in a present tense, therefore allowing them "to be taken as sudden events in life," whose "images be lived directly." Allowing "images [to] be lived directly" is not to confuse the physical world and the world on-screen but to see a potential relation between them. Phenomenologically speaking, our encounter with the film—through love or hate, joy or terror, thrill or boredom—allows us to think in the presence of the medium and *with* film, not merely through or against it. In the best of cases, our love for film can then become a kind of love for the world; that love does not delimit critical practice but, in fact, enables it.

What we might thus offer our students through our co-presence with film is a shared process that enables a form of critical subjectivity to take shape. The "I" that emerges in this process is therefore not one who is merely constituted (or interpellated) by the cinema but one who speaks back to the film, who enters into conversation with the world it imagines before us. As Rawiri stares seemingly toward me, in a land outside the screen, I encounter his world and mine at once. This image also enables me to imagine the position that Paikea does not occupy herself in this scene (nor one that I occupy in my own classroom), as I face teacher and student at the same time. This spell is not broken when he breaks his stare; instead I remain heart-racingly aware of what I see before me. I share, for a moment, Rawiri's breath and his physical presence. The image teaches me to see and to feel. And this is the very sensation and process that I want to extend to my own students.

Loving Film, Historically Speaking

I tend to read Siegfried Kracauer's *Theory of Film* as an insistence not so much on a love of the world but as offering, via film, an insistence upon life itself. Certainly this approach to film, to the world, and to life is borne of his experience as a German Jew who, upon the threat of death, became an exile for the rest of his life in New York City. And like other writers who produced work contemporaneously with (and before) him, he described the film spectator. Of course, this concern is not widely known about Kracauer, nor is it widely taught, if film theory anthologies are a useful indication of an approach to his work in undergraduate classrooms; besides excerpts from *From Caligari to Hitler*, we largely know *Theory of Film* via his focus on realism and the moving image in the second and third chapters of that work, "Basic Concepts" and "The Establishment of Physical Existence." In a course I regularly teach on "Cinema and Everyday Life," I assign the majority of the book instead of excerpted chapters in order to allow students to experience the depth of Kracauer's thinking—an opportunity that I think allows us to encounter him, as Bachelard might say, "anew." Part of this opportunity is to encounter his focus on the spectator, which expands and clarifies our understanding of his phenomenological approach to film and material reality.

Of course, Kracauer himself was not a model of the embodied spectator in his own writing in the ways that writers/artists Jean Epstein or H.D. were (or as Christian Metz would become), but he does offer a vision of the viewer as one who feels *with* the images before herself or himself. For a theorist who sees film's greatest accomplishment as an art form that records the movement of life, it is significant that he sees the spectator, too, as one who moves. In part, this spectator is like a dreamer, who "drifts toward and into the objects."[3] Kracauer asks: "Does the spectator ever succeed in exhausting the objects he contemplates?" He responds: "There is no end to his wanderings."[4] And in effect the spectator embarks on a stream of consciousness whose contents, he writes, "still bear the imprint of the bodily sensations from which they issue. This stream of consciousness in a measure parallels the 'flow of life,' one of the main concerns of the medium."[5] Given this parallel, it's perhaps no surprise that, by his Epilogue, which is a return to his chapter on "The Spectator," he suggests that "in experiencing an object, we not only broaden our knowledge of its diverse qualities but in a manner of speaking incorporate it into us so that we grasp its being and its dynamics from within—a sort of blood transfusion, as it were."[6] And since we feel we may share the blood of the image, we see it as another living thing, so that "what we want is to touch reality not only with the fingertips but to seize it and shake hands with it."[7] This impulse to touch and feel the image is a lot like loving it, I think, and certainly it's an impulse shared by theorists of film over time.

Moving across historical models—as writers like Kracauer and, later, Laura Mulvey do themselves—we can see the enduring presence of affective and intellectual work that is shaped by the theorist's experience of film. But why seek this experience ingrained in their work in the first place? And why seek their experience of loving film? I would suggest that seeking and recognizing this love in theoretical writings is also a recognition of a vital epistemological structure that conjoins work across historical periods and theoretical frameworks. And it is one that often begins with the first-person pronoun, whether the collective for Kracauer or the singular for writers like Epstein and Dorothy Richardson. That pronoun marks the specificity of experience at the movies and in the world, and for these writers to whom I shall now turn, it marks also the experience of love. Undoubtedly our experience of film structures the multiple ways in which we know it: through emotion, intellect, physicality, materiality, and history itself. Grasping at the love that binds writers over time and space is a means of coming to know that critical work, like film, is a felt experience. As spectators and as writers, we can incorporate critical work "into us so that we grasp its being and its dynamics from within." We can therefore join a community of writers, one that might resemble to some small degree our own community of scholars, of teachers, of students; we can join this community as sentient beings, each of us moved by the images before us, moved to write.[8]

And so I want to focus here on sensations of experience, especially the experience of love, that wind through the pre-1968 history of film theory (in pre- and post–World War II writings), punctuated by moments in contemporary film. I turn to these texts in my classroom, as I do in my own reading and writing, in order to allow students to imagine not only film but also reading theory and writing critically anew. We see such sensations of experience in theoretical writings particularly through the figure of the "spectator," a term that for years seemed to have been invented in the late 1960s with psychoanalytic and ideological theory, honed in the 1970s by feminist theory. But of course the spectator—in her and his various guises—emerged with the medium itself. Across the history of film theory, in fact, the "spectator" is designed through an analysis and/or demonstration of experience, largely modeled through the sensations of the theorist herself or himself. I turn to this earlier body of work because the body itself is so resonant within it. In this work we witness the writer at the movies; her or his own presence, too, is predicated on the sense that film itself is based upon a kind of presence, ontological and/or phenomenological.[9] Thus is it possible for the spectator to *be with* and to *feel with* the film before her or him.[10]

And then, of course, the spectator is designed again in writing. It is through this writing that I also come to love the writers—the theorists whom I want to join as a spectator myself. That is, I seek to join the "I" not that the apparatus interpellates for us (though ideological theory would say my interpellation is complete because I here appear to deny it) but that community of spectators that the "I" in written work generates. And because these writers have taught me anew a mode of declaring my engagement with film, I seek a means in turn of conveying this process to my students through reading these theorists together.

Writing Intimately

Jean Epstein's work is being widely revived in contemporary film theory, already renewing an understanding of and a belief in the spectator (and, I'd suggest, in literary and theoretical poetics). During the same period he was writing essays and reviews and making films, the journal *Close Up* emerged across the English Channel, bringing together writers and filmmakers from England, Europe, and the United States. The Imagist poet H.D. and the novelist Dorothy Richardson, regular contributors to the journal, approached the cinema not unlike Epstein (though, with the exception of the publication of work from the journal fifteen years ago, I would not say *Close Up* is being widely revived in contemporary theory). Like Epstein (as well as his contemporaries such as Louis Delluc), H.D. often positioned herself as a spectatorial model, whose mode of writing demonstrated her experiential emphasis. Setting these writers in some conversation here, drawing out the active spectatorial experience they enact, I would argue that affect itself demonstrates the mobility of their experience, the means of a connection that produces a community of spectator-writers.

Love itself literally frames several of Epstein's essays on film. Thus his 1921 "Magnification" begins: "I will never find the way to say how much I love American close-ups. Point blank." "Langue d'Or" opens as follows: "Almost as much as they hate one another, human beings love one another."[11] "For a New Avant-Garde" begins with this claim: "I just want to say this: you have to love it and hate it at the same time—and love it as much as you hate it."[12] And "Amour de Charlot" ends thusly: "Your people, o fair king, are not made up of critics who admire you. O doleful prince of a celluloid tale, we are three hundred million who love your heart swimming in the throes of passion."[13]

In "Magnification," Epstein goes on to describe the face on the screen in such loving and intimate detail that his words, demonstrating his own affective experience, take one's breath away:

> Even more beautiful than a laugh is the face preparing for it. I must interrupt. I love the mouth which is about to speak and holds back, the gesture which hesitates between right and left, the recoil before the leap, and the moment before landing, the becoming, the hesitation, the taut spring, the prelude, and even more than all these, the piano being tuned before the overture.[14]

At this moment he appears to look in awe at the image before him, and shortly thereafter he moves closer to it:

> The close-up modifies the drama by the impact of proximity. Pain is within reach. If I stretch out my arm I touch you, and that is intimacy. I can count the eyelashes of this suffering. I would be able to taste the tears. Never before has a face turned to mine in that way. Ever closer it presses against me, and I follow it face to face. It's not even true that there is air between us; I consume it. It is in me like a sacrament. Maximum visual acuity.[15]

The act of seeing and feeling is demonstrated in his language itself: first, the breathless flux of words, and then, the staccato, its punctuation and tempo like that of a beating heart. His experience of viewing becomes our experience of reading. "Theory" in this case emerges through the form of language, itself designed after the form of film and through the language of love. While I cannot expect my students (or anyone else, for that matter) to write like Jean Epstein, I can invite them to read him—and to read his work aloud. I invite the same activity with the work of other writers, such as Bachelard. When we read together *The Poetics of Space*, I pause on Bachelard's claim about the word *vast*: "The word *vast*, then, is a vocable of breath. It is placed on our breathing, which must be slow and calm."[16] Together we say the word *vast* again and again so that they may feel it like breath itself. Doing so is a means of taking in theoretical work in a kind of parallel to how we might take in the experience of film. Moving between the two—writing and film—might allow students to come closer to Epstein's own sense of proximity: "It's not even true that there is air between us; I consume it. It is in me like a sacrament."[17] Of course doing so requires a sense of imagination, a will to believe. But then that is also the requirement of film itself.

Though three decades apart (and under very different circumstances), both Kracauer and Epstein describe the desire to reach for the image physically. We can see such desire activated in films themselves, narrating, potentially, our own experience. So, for instance, in Lynne Ramsay's *Ratcatcher* (1999), the young protagonist James (William Eadie) temporarily escapes the apartment where he lives with his family and where they are literally surrounded by garbage, for the narrative takes place during the 1973 Glasgow bin collectors' strike. He travels to the end of a bus line, crosses a field, and finds a nearly finished housing complex. He plays amid the construction, turning a metal pipe into a tool of his imagination, as he appears to become a captain of a ship surveying the world before him. Once inside the house, he treats the unfinished space as if it were complete, a house where he luxuriously lives. He lies in the tub (covered in plastic), turns the unplumbed faucet handles, pees in the unconnected toilet (then watches it seep out onto the floor). And why not dream here as if it's real—indeed, as if it's really his? For our fictional character, the unfinished house is like a materialized dream—or, from our point of view, the materialization of a film. All the pieces of the house are a part of physical reality, even if they are, for now, only representations of daily life. He both watches this other story unfold—as if the events he witnesses take place in another space and another time—and enters into it as if it were his own world. In this scene, James seizes and shakes hands with the reality before him, the space itself—and the dream it encompasses for him—becoming incorporated into him. For Kracauer or Epstein, this is our potential (and ideal) experience of film: in its revelation of actual physical existence, moving in space and evolving through time, film invites our touch, even if we almost never move our actual bodies to attempt to shake its hand.

James's dream house becomes increasingly parallel with the cinema (both the physical space and the film on the screen) as he moves through it. Thus, when he opens a door, we are situated inside as he pauses in the entrance, as if he is sneaking from behind the curtain to enter the screen. But it's also as if he is sneaking into a movie theater, and we witness him as he watches. In fact, the film cuts from his act of looking to the "screen" itself: a rectangular window frame without the pane inside, revealing an open field before it. Here the outside world is literally framed by the dream house. James climbs onto the windowsill, swings his legs over the ledge, and stares into a field of wheat before he jumps through the empty window. At the same time he enters the film screen, he also abandons it for the real world, so that in this brief moment the two become for us one and the same. Once he is outside, the frame disappears, and James runs through the field before us with the sort of abandon he almost never experiences in the rest of the film.

A contemporary of Epstein's, H.D. describes another such run of abandon in her essay "*Expiation.*" Racing to a movie theater in Lausanne, she writes:

> I was tumbled out dazed and exulted at the head of a sort of dimensional dream-tunnel. I was precipitated between so to speak, built-up and somewhat over-done little shops with windows and wares; oranges, boxes of leeks, lettuces on the pavement; bright green shutters. Dazed and re-vitalized by the run, I plunged down this little street somewhat reeling, making jig-jag to find just those shadows cut just that block (and that block) into perfect design of cobbled square and square little doorway till I found myself at the entrance of a slice of a theatre, the Palace of Lausanne.[18]

This run precedes the cinematic image she sees, but it also mirrors it, via contrast. In fact, when she watches the film (Lev Kuleshov, 1926), she sees a parallel of her sensations on-screen:

> Rain poured over a slab of earth and I felt all my preparation of the extravagantly contrasting out of doors gay little street, was almost an ironical intention, someone, something "intended" that I should grasp this, that some mind should receive this series of uncanny and almost psychic sensations in order to transmute them elsewhere; in order to translate them.[19]

Although she doesn't use the word explicitly, I find that here and elsewhere in *Close Up*, H.D. writes with love. What she often loves about the moving image is its potential challenge to us. In her second column for the journal she demands, "You and I have got to work. We have got to begin to care and to care and to care."[20] And whereas she writes that, upon seeing Carl Theodor Dreyer's *The Passion of Joan of Arc* (1928), "We are numb and beaten. We won't go a second time," she also declares that the film "is in a class by itself. And that is the trouble with it. It shouldn't be."[21] For H.D., care and work and feeling are bound together, as are the filmmaker and the spectator or the audience members as a whole. Hence she sees her run as a precipitation to her moviegoing, but of course she has written of this experience after she has seen the film. The two experiences—in the world, in the movie theater—become bound together in her state of perception and in her act of writing. The "someone, something" who "intended" that she should grasp the relation between her run and the images on the screen is transmuted into H.D. herself, she who intends for her reader to make these connections now.

I set such texts in relation together both here and in the classroom with the hope that they will come alive for my students. That is, coming into contact with the "I" of Epstein and H.D. can enable students to emerge as subjects in their own right, whose experience as active, sentient spectators informs their critical practice as thinkers and writers. In this way, too, they can begin to reoccupy the first-person pronoun that has so often been expunged (with good pedagogical reason) from their work in secondary school. From Epstein they may begin to imagine reaching out to touch the image; from H.D. they can consider what it means to "care and care and care." And from James they might take the cue to look at the screen and leap into it. In so doing, they also reenter into their own writing.

Surely, then, Epstein and H.D. both commune with the images before them. They watch in a state of heightened perception, enabled by a visceral sense of anticipation: they anticipate a kind of contact with the moving image. James, of Ramsay's *Ratcatcher*, demonstrates on-screen this experience of the viewer. Jem Cohen's 2012 *Museum Hours*, which I will draw on later, represents another facet of this exchange between viewer and screen and, in a sense, among audience members. And Jane Campion's 2009 *Bright Star* narrates an exchange between lovers Fanny Brawne (Abbie Cornish) and John Keats (Ben Whishaw) that neatly suggests our own elusive and material relationship with the moving images and the screen on which they appear, offering a further model for thinking and writing.

In Campion's film, sophisticated seamstress Brawne and poet Keats gradually fall in love, marked by a series of exchanges between them, both material and visual. Early on, as a gift to comfort him and his dying brother, Fanny makes John a basket of tuile biscuits, accented with a bronze ribbon she cuts from her sister Toots's (Edie Martin's) dress. Upon John's brother's death, Fanny embroiders a silk pillowcase for him to lay his head on. And after dispatching her younger siblings to purchase John's book, she initially asks Toots to read it aloud and then snatches the book from her, making reading itself an active material practice. Once she has read his work, Fanny asks John to instruct her in poetry. Then, about halfway through the film, we witness further tactile and visual exchanges between them when the Brawne family moves into the other half of the house that Keats and his friend Charles Brown (Paul Schneider) occupy. As Fanny and Toots unpack their room, John climbs the stairs to enter his own chamber, which shares a wall with Fanny's. He crosses the room, gently leans toward the wall, and knocks. Hearing him, Fanny crosses her own room to respond in kind. As she knocks, she, too, leans forward, so that her own shadow meets her on the wall, her forehead against an elusive image of herself. We cut to John, again in a similar position, implicitly facing her, set in the frame as if he could touch her without seeing her. His shadow, too, meets him. Their shadows double for the other, as they listen and feel for one another. This image itself, to paraphrase H.D., grasps our own affective and visceral longing, and in the profile of these hands and faces against a shared wall, this set of images represents the sense Epstein describes of the close-up: "Ever closer it presses against me, and I follow it face to face."[22]

And thus this sequence continues. After a brief moment in which Fanny, John, and Toots search for the best-smelling flower in the garden outside, we cut again to the second floor of the house. Here Fanny wraps herself in a curtain against a window; hidden to us, she reveals herself to John outside, to whom we cut, where we see him lying on the grass, looking toward her visage against the glass (a face that is still shielded from us, screened as her body is by the curtain). In the scene that follows, they converge together at a picnic, eventually seeking privacy beyond a bridge flanked by blowing reeds of grass (a moment that would delight Kracauer). John tells Fanny of a dream in which he kissed a figure he found among the branches of a tree, and soon their lips do, in fact, physically meet. After this scene, each of them daydreams independently. Fanny lies on her bed, as the curtain that shielded her from us previously now blows toward her from the open window in her room. This fabric screen glides forth to meet her as she collapses against her pillow. Outside we see John and others bird-watching; he climbs a blossoming tree and lies atop the branches, seemingly floating on a bed of flowers. These sequences both visualize and narrate a desire to see and to touch; such is the desire not just of the characters for one another but, I think, the desire of the moviegoer who sees the world anew before her, who sees the branches of a tree as a bed of flowers or a billowing curtain as a beckoning, a kiss. In their absence, then physical commingling, then absence again, Fanny and John commune with one another. In the film's ontological, visual presence (yet its world's physical absence), *we* commune with *it*.

Dorothy Richardson takes a somewhat different turn from Epstein and H.D., focusing not primarily on herself but communing with those around her in the theater. In a piece written in 1928 (the same year as H.D.'s pieces discussed earlier), she describes a woman in the theater who "in the presence of the wonders of art remains self-centred and serenely self-expressive."[23] This woman, in fact, is so annoying to those around her that Richardson composes an ironic list of do's and don'ts for behavior in the cinema. But she then argues in this spectator's favor:

> Let us attend to her, for she can lead her victim through anger to cynicism and on at last to a discovery that makes it passing strange that no male voice has been raised save in condemnation, that no man, film-lover and therefore for years past helplessly at her mercy, has risen up and cried Eureka. For she is right. For all her bad manners that will doubtless be pruned when the film becomes high art and its temple a temple of stillness save for the music that at present inspires her to do her worst, she is innocently, directly, albeit

unconsciously, upon the path that men have reached through long centuries of effort and of thought. She does not need, this type of woman clearly does not need, the illusions of art to come to the assistance of her own sense of existing. Instinctively she maintains a balance, the thing perceived and herself perceiving.[24]

Whereas H.D. frequently translated an emotional and psychic experience of film (she was, after all, an analysand of Freud's), Richardson describes the social experience of the cinema. She pictures those people around us in the theater, and as she does, she characterizes the theater itself as a physical space from which social relations emerge. Thus Richardson reveals a trust in the viewer, suggesting that in this social space we viewers have something to learn from one another, even about what it means to be a "lover" of film. What I love most about this particular passage is Richardson's insistent belief in this viewer: "She does not need, this type of woman clearly does not need."[25] My students love this piece as well (though the complex rhetorical shifts Richardson makes midway in the piece almost always throw them for a loop) because it enables them to make sense of something they see all the time at the movies but that so often escapes our focus in our insistent textual attention. In short, those bodies around us—ours included—*mean something*. We might interpret the meaning of our social experience in relation to what we see on-screen; in fact, we can interpret what we see on-screen through the actions of those around us. Richardson and this viewer together teach us both about the social codes of viewing and about the material conditions of moviegoing experiences. In effect, Richardson demands that we become active social participants as moviegoers, that we maintain a balance between "the thing perceived and herself perceiving."

Museum Hours invites such experiences of perception. It does so through its content and its form. Set in the Kunsthistorisches Museum in Vienna, the film tells the story of a museum guard, Johann (Bobby Sommer), who becomes acquainted with Anne (Mary Margaret O'Hara), a Canadian woman in town to sit vigil with a dying cousin. She frequents the museum, and the two of them also tour the city together, where he begins to see things anew. Johann's experience in the city is a model for our experience as viewers of this film; as the camera shifts from painting to painting, then around touring museum patrons, and finally into the streets outside, we also might experience a peculiar manner of seeing. Approximately halfway through the film, one such instructive sequence takes place: Johann's voice-over is describing a young guard he used to work with, who learned about the origins of the public museum. As he speaks, we linger on the faces of individual museum visitors, and then we shift to linger similarly on faces and figures within art works. From here we move to the outside, another public space engaged with looking: a kind of temporary flea market. As buyers and sellers wander around, the camera landing for a moment while a man opens up a laptop, another voice-over begins. This is not Johann, but seemingly a recorded tour guide at the museum itself, describing the Egyptian *Book of the Dead*. Surrounding the central mechanized voice is the ambient noise of a giant hall, the museum we don't see. As the guide describes the book's papyrus material and one's practice of reading it (from right to left) to the absent museumgoer, we move through the market, alighting on other forms of print material—ephemera like magazines and discarded books.

Throughout this film, we enter into a particular observational mode: humans resemble paintings in all their texture and stillness, and in the paintings we see evidence of the actions and perception of everyday life. The film demands that we make a series of connections, ones that blur distinctions between artwork and living people as well as between the interior of the museum and the exterior of the streets outside. In fact, the streets outside take on the perspective of paintings or the rooms of the museum itself; diagonal lines of roads and buildings meet as if they were parts of an interior hall (of course, the reverse is also true). These diagonals, usually in the background of the frame, enhance our sense of the depth of the space before us. In this depth is a renewed sense of dynamism, which in turn accentuates the action, however subtle, that takes place in the foreground of the moving image. The dynamism constructed in the spaces both outside and in is reflected in our fluid observational practice spurred on by the film's very structure, and by moving between the stillness of paintings and the cinematic image, each takes on the quality of the other form, decentering our own activity of looking. Thus *Museum Hours* challenges us to recognize our own acts of perception, and it particularly does so through the model of the connection forged between Johann and Anne, as they share their observations with one another and, in the case of Johann, with us. These two might harken to the social possibilities of the moviegoer as well, that which Richardson championed in her writings on film. Thus the film suggests a fluidity not just between the museum and the streets outside but also between the place in which we view the film and the world outside the space of the screen. It models for us an intimate instructional practice, a shared site of knowing.

The World in Which We Live

For me, writers like Epstein, H.D., and Richardson are easy to love. And my affection for them, in turn, makes them easy to teach. But how do I describe the feelings of intense affection I have for André Bazin, whose passion, unlike that of many of his contemporaries and protégées in *Cahiers du Cinema*, is not always on the surface of the prose itself? In part, I seek that passion out. In his most renowned essay, "The Ontology of the Photographic Image," he discusses cinema's "objectivity in time," where he states that "now, for the first time, the image of things is likewise the image of their duration, change mummified as it were."[26] And after this moment, Bazin enters into his own text. Until this point he has written only in the third person (with all the knowledge it confers), occasionally extending to the royal *we*; but here he suddenly invokes a version of himself:

> The aesthetic qualities of photography are to be sought in its power to lay bare the realities. It is not for me to separate off, in the complex fabric of the objective world, here a reflection on a damp sidewalk, there the gesture of a child. Only the impassive lens, stripping its object of all those ways of seeing it, those piled-up preconceptions, that spiritual dust and grime with which my eyes have covered it, is able to present it in all its virginal purity to my attention and consequently to my love. By the power of photography, the natural image of a world which we neither know nor can see, nature at last does more than imitate art: she imitates the artist.[27]

He, or, I should say, his "*I*," does not return for the rest of this essay (and makes nary an appearance throughout much of *What Is Cinema?*). So it seems especially significant that it—or I—appears in the declaration of love (which is also a subtle declaration against a simple understanding of film authorship). Ultimately this declaration is not surprising, given Bazin's faith, his insistence on humans' communion with the natural world, and the personalism and humanism of those philosophers and teachers who helped shape his own thinking.

Yet I must here ask myself: Am I simply a susceptible reader, as I am a susceptible viewer? Show me an image of a character sobbing—especially a character I already have feelings for—and I will likely cry with her or him. Is it just a fact that my heart swells at the mere use of the word *love* in theoretical discourse? And if so, why? Is it the kindred spirit I seek as a reader and a viewer (and a person in the world)? Is it the incongruence of finding love amid the theoretical—the speculative-scientific—that moves me? Is it that suddenly someone real, someone *imaginable*, has appeared not just in this theoretical text but in and through history? Could the theorist's writing bear the essential trace of the writer herself or himself, as Bazin suggests the film does of the object it records?

Admittedly, I can in part imagine Bazin because of Dudley Andrew's portrait of him: his descriptions of teachers who influenced him, of his love of animals (such as the crocodile he kept in his bathtub), of his home with his wife, Janine, and his son, Florent. In this way, Andrew, as a kind of interlocutor for those who knew Bazin, also becomes my teacher. In the final chapter of his biography of Bazin, Andrew writes that, in the last two years of his life,

> he appeared more emaciated than ever and friends began to observe and enjoy him with a care that betrayed their fear of soon losing him. In this last period they affectionately noted such vignettes as Bazin arguing a traffic fine with flawless syllogisms, Bazin picking up passengers at the bus stop in Nogent

because he felt it wicked to ride alone in a car with four good seats, Bazin keeping his companions laughing with droll stories as they awaited a mechanic after midnight and in the cold to fix that same car.[28]

And he goes on to discuss the dinner parties that he and Janine would throw because it was increasingly easier than going out: "No one was shocked to see him halting a discussion with a filmmaker to right a turtle or to fix Florent's train set."[29] He quotes, too, one of those filmmakers, Jean Renoir, who describes being in Bazin's house:

> In that room it seemed as though beings and things just naturally found their proper place. For me, a friend passing through, the impression was of a natural harmony, a kind of continuation or preface to the literary work of the master of the house. This surprising result can only be explained by the immense love that Bazin felt toward everything that makes up the world in which we live.[30]

And there is that word again. It is, I know, his friends' love of him and Bazin's love of the world that I now see in his writings, which themselves demonstrate his love of film as that which extends the world. As Bazin suggests, film grants us access to "a world which we neither know nor can see."[31] To Bazin, film thus demonstrates his contemporary Gaston Bachelard's claim, in a different context, that "when the image is new, the world is new."[32] Thus, what Renoir saw in his friend's house—"the immense love that Bazin felt toward everything that makes up the world in which we live"[33]—is what Bazin also saw in the essence of film. And it's what I see in passages of Bazin's (or Epstein's or Richardson's) writings. That is, these writers, like the images on-screen, like the audience members together in a movie house, and most certainly like my students in the classroom, also have existed in this world.

As Rashna Wadia Richards rightly documents in *Cinematic Flashes*, cinephilia is on the rise again; "it is commonplace," she skeptically suggests, "to observe that cinephilia has returned to film studies just when cinema appears in danger of mutating into something else."[34] But whether born out of a nostalgia for celluloid at the emergence of digital technology, or a longing for the theater coincident with an almost overwhelming increase in screenic devices of all kinds, or, as in Richards's work, an attempt to develop methodologies based on our loving experience of film, the movement to engage with the first-person subjective is returning today as well. In journals like *LOLA* or *World Picture*, in this very collection, and in communities of scholars converging in a variety of other spaces via an interest in cinephilia and in their own cinephilic impulses, a collective passion has reemerged. I also want to offer this first-person engagement to my students: to return to the "I" not as a means of producing an argument in isolation (that is, the sentence that rings as a critical death knell: "it's all subjective") but rather to emerge as a subject in relation to, or even in community with, other thinkers, writers, and moviegoers: to see that "I" as part of a resounding "we."

In 1960 Siegfried Kracauer described a shared "will to believe."[35] Some sought belief in politics, others in religion. This will emerged out of apathy, loneliness, abstractness, technological change. For Kracauer, belief seemed possible in film, in its recording and revelation of "the flow of life."[36] Here, he implied, "at least we stand a chance of finding something we did not look for, something tremendously important in its own right—the world that is ours."[37] I would hope that this contemporary movement, in a post-1968 context, might embody that work that has come since Epstein or H.D. or Bazin or Kracauer but includes them, too. Critical politics and political criticism must emerge from speaking and looking subjects—those who speak in the first person, individually and collectively. In looking at those "I"s who surround me today—writers and friends and colleagues like Kristi McKim, Rashna Richards, David Johnson, Pooja Rangan, or Girish Shambu (I could go on and on)—I think maybe we can believe in each other. That's in part the "world that is ours." And what I hope I can do as a teacher is demonstrate that will to believe—a will to believe in film but also, ultimately, in those who are learning with me, those who are writing with me, and those who might read my words.

AMELIE HASTIE is the founding Chair of the Film and Media Studies Program and Professor of English at Amherst College. She is the author of *Cupboards of Curiosity: Women, Recollection, and Film History* and *The Bigamist*. She was a member of the *Camera Obscura* editorial collective and currently writes the column "The Vulnerable Spectator" in *Film Quarterly*.

Notes

1. Gaston Bachelard, *The Poetics of Space*, trans. Maria Jolas (Boston: Beacon Press, 1994), 47.
2. Christian Metz, *The Imaginary Signifier: Psychoanalysis and Cinema* (Bloomington: Indiana University Press, 1982), 15.
3. Siegfried Kracauer, *Theory of Film: The Redemption of Physical Reality* (Oxford: Oxford University Press, 1960), 165.
4. Ibid.
5. Ibid., 166.
6. Ibid., 297.
7. Ibid.
8. Many contemporary scholars of cinephilia cite Paul Willemen's discussion of the will to articulate that love. Rashna Richards writes, "Writing or, more accurately, 'finding formulations to convey something about the intensity of that spark,' has always been, according to Willemen, a primary response to cinephilia." And in her own meditative work *Love in the Time*

of Cinema, Kristi McKim declares, "Willemen thus suggests an analytic framework governed by a temporal privileging of aesthetic immersion and revelation. We might more accurately describe Willemen's model of cinephilia as a privileging of aesthetic immersion and revelation that *becomes* an analytic framework." See Rashna Wadia Richards, *Cinematic Flashes: Cinephilia and Classical Hollywood* (Bloomington: Indiana University Press, 2013), 12, and Kristi McKim, *Love in the Time of Cinema* (London: Palgrave Macmillan, 2011), 3.

    9. In "What's the Point of an Index? Or, Faking Photographs," Tom Gunning considers André Bazin's claims about the ontological state of photographs: "For Bazin, the photograph is not a sign of something, but a presence of something, or perhaps we could say a means for putting us into the presence of something, since clearly Bazin realizes that a photograph differs from its subject." Film, too, puts us into the presence of something, and because it also "moves," its temporal state can be understood to be of the present. See Tom Gunning, "What's the Point of an Index? Or, Faking Photographs," *Nordicom Review, Special Issue: The 16th Nordic Conference on Media and Communication Research* 1–2 (2004): 46, http://www.nordicom .gu.se/sites/default/files/kapitel-pdf/157_039-050.pdf.

    10. To those who may be concerned with the ideological premises herein, consider the historical contexts of these writers, particularly the emergence of Nazism, and the traumatic effects of war, occupation, and exile. *Being with*, and *feeling with*, a film, for these writers, might mean something quite different than for the typical subject who is described in much early post-1968 critiques.

    11. Jean Epstein, "Langue d'Or," trans. Mireille Dobrzynski and Stuart Liebman, in *Jean Epstein: Critical Essays and New Translations*, eds. Sarah Keller and Jason N. Paul (Amsterdam: Amsterdam University Press, 2012), 297.

    12. Jean Epstein, "For a New Avant-Garde," trans. Stuart Liebman, in *Jean Epstein* (see note 11), 302.

    13. Jean Epstein, "Amour de Charlot," trans. Jennifer Wild, in *Jean Epstein* (see note 11), 306.

    14. Jean Epstein, "Magnification," trans. Stuart Liebman, in *French Film Theory and Criticism: A History/Anthology, 1907–1939. Vol. 1: 1907–1929*, ed. Richard Abel (Princeton, NJ: Princeton University Press, 1988), 236.

    15. Ibid., 239.

    16. Bachelard, *Poetics of Space*, 7.

    17. Epstein, "Magnification," 239.

    18. H.D. (Hilda Doolittle), *"Expiation,"* in *Close-Up 1927–1933: Cinema and Modernism*, eds. James Donald, Anne Friedberg, and Laura Marcus (Princeton, NJ: Princeton University Press, 1998), 125.

    19. Ibid.

    20. H.D., "Restraint," in *Close-Up 1927–1933: Cinema and Modernism*, eds. James Donald, Anne Friedberg, and Laura Marcus (Princeton, NJ: Princeton University Press, 1998), 112.

    21. H.D., *"Joan of Arc,"* in *Close-Up 1927–1933: Cinema and Modernism*, eds. James Donald, Anne Friedberg, and Laura Marcus (Princeton, NJ: Princeton University Press, 1998), 133.

    22. Epstein, "Magnification," 239.

    23. Dorothy Richardson, "Continuous Performance VIII [*Animal impudens . . .*]," in *Close-Up 1927–1933: Cinema and Modernism*, eds. James Donald, Anne Friedberg, and Laura Marcus (Princeton, NJ: Princeton University Press, 1998), 174.

    24. Ibid., 176.

    25. Ibid.

    26. André Bazin, "The Ontology of the Photographic Image," in *What Is Cinema? Volume 1*, trans. Hugh Gray (Berkeley: University of California Press, 2005), 14–15.

27. Ibid., 15.
28. Dudley Andrew, *André Bazin* (New York: Oxford University Press, 1978), 216.
29. Ibid., 217.
30. Ibid., 218.
31. Bazin, "The Ontology of the Photographic Image," 15.
32. Bachelard, *The Poetics of Space*, 47.
33. Andrew, *André Bazin*, 218.
34. Richards, *Cinematic Flashes*, 216.
35. Kracauer, *Theory of Film*, 291.
36. Ibid., 166.
37. Ibid., 296.

3 Cinephilia and Cineliteracy in the Classroom

Thomas Leitch

I RARELY WENT TO THE MOVIES when I was growing up. My family didn't live close to any movie theaters, my mother didn't drive, and my father rarely had either the leisure or the inclination to take in a movie. I don't recall that my parents ever went to a movie without their children, and I suspect that given an hour, I could list every single movie I saw, most of them forgettable family films at drive-in theaters, before going off to college. So from an early age my relationship with movies was very different from my relationship with books. I was an avid reader, and I loved books, but they weren't magical in the ways movies were. Reading was something I did every day; going to the movies was a special treat. Books provided me with an escape from my world, but movies promised my whole family an escape from our home—an escape into a world in which, I fervently believed, anything could happen, and I'd feel it happen kinesthetically in a way I didn't feel with books. I loved reading, but I remained hopelessly infatuated with movies.

It never occurred to me to take any film courses when I was an undergraduate at a college where Andrew Sarris taught a popular course universally known as "Wednesday Night at the Movies." Nor did my graduate program in English offer anything so frivolous as courses in the cinema. But when I had chances to teach courses that used movies, and then courses that were actually about movies, I seized them avidly. When I was offered the opportunity to cut the umbilical cord to my literary training by taking a job at which I'd be expected to teach nothing but movies, I was both daunted and delighted.

I'm not sure whether my love for movies qualifies as cinephilia—whether it's the "intense, obsessive love of cinema" David T. Johnson describes.[1] I'd be embarrassed to say how old I was when I saw my first silent film, or my first Fred Astaire film, or *The Godfather* (Francis Ford Coppola, 1972), or most of the other 1970s classics I missed when I was in school. Ever since my childhood, my moviegoing has seemed all the sweeter because I've been indulging in a long-deferred gratification and doing my best to make up for lost time. Even now, my habits as a moviegoer are dictated less by the canonical impulse that's always governed my reading, and still less by the desire to keep abreast of current developments and hold my own in Monday morning discussions of the weekend's new releases, than by a completist impulse: the need to see all of Hitchcock's films, or all of Preston Sturges's, or all of Humphrey Bogart's, no matter how terrible they are. Of course, catching up on old movies rarely sends me to movie theaters. Although I agree with Susan Sontag that "the conditions of paying attention in a domestic space are radically disrespectful of film," home is where I've watched most of the movies I've loved best.[2]

My own writing about film shows few signs of the "subjective, emotional, and equally intense response to film" that Johnson contrasts with "the more dispassionate forms of inquiry typically associated with academic research."[3] Christopher D. Morris once sympathetically referred to me as "the reader-response critic Thomas Leitch," and my inveterate habit of interrogating my highly subjective experiences of moviegoing rather than mining the emotional intensity of my responses has produced some pretty academic prose.[4] For the purposes of this essay, though, I'm going to assume that my love of movies does qualify as cinephilia, because this claim will allow me to explore a problem I can't believe is peculiar to me.

The problem is this: although my cinephilia is what originally drew me to teach movies and what makes me excited about each new course, cinephilia isn't what I teach. Nor do I have any desire to teach it. At best it's a distracting irrelevance to the activities I most value in my film classes, at worst an obstruction, an obstacle to be overcome. My lifelong love of novels has been steadily compromised over the years by twenty-five years of reviewing genre fiction, an activity that seriously diminished my appetite for browsing in bookstores long before the bookstores began to disappear. And I've certainly been able to preserve more joy in filmgoing than in reading despite my long professional association with both. But I have to admit that my love of movies, though it's been nurtured by my teaching, has been compromised by it as well. I still prefer teaching movies to teaching novels, if only because my students are much more likely to see the movies than to read the novels. I still watch movies with far more engagement and excitement if I'm considering teaching them. But once I'm committed to teaching them, I can't maintain the rapture of falling in love with them indefinitely. After all these years teaching *Casablanca* (Michael Curtiz, 1942) and *Double Indemnity* (Billy Wilder, 1944) and *Singin' in the Rain* (Gene Kelly and Stanley Donen, 1952) and *The Graduate* (Mike Nichols, 1967), I still look forward to every single time I'm going to teach them again. But I don't look forward to seeing them again. I always prefer to teach movies I love, but once I've taught them half a dozen times, I don't love them the same way anymore. Teaching the same movies over and over is a joy, but watching them over and over is a challenge.

It's particularly challenging to summon my cinephilia when I'm watching movies with my students in a classroom. Even if the room has been designed especially as a screening room, its setting on a college campus reminds me that I haven't come to have a joyous experience, even in passing; I've come as the necessary prelude to teaching the film in question. Even more than the setting, the presence of students sharpens the sense of being challenged. What if they don't like the film? What if they don't understand it? What if they're offended or traumatized? What if they laugh at all the wrong parts? No matter how often other audience members have spoiled films for me, talking during the film is the only behavior of theirs I ever worry about in advance. But I worry about students' reactions every time I show a film, especially if I've had recent problems with it. Sometimes these problems turn out to be a fluke. Next year's class doesn't titter every time Fred MacMurray calls Barbara Stanwyck "baby" in *Double Indemnity* (a total of thirty times, by the count I made one year in self-defense) or ask me what's supposed to be so funny about *Duck Soup* (Leo McCarey, 1933) or go disturbingly quiet (were those other students detached or freaked out?) as they watch *Blue Velvet* (David Lynch, 1986). And there's a special sense of triumph in overcoming students' resistance to some of my favorite films, like *Leave Her to Heaven* (John M. Stahl, 1945), by contextualizing and introducing them more carefully. But these triumphs are remote from the innocent joys of cinephilia, which involve either myself alone or myself as a single member of a large audience all reacting to a powerful moment in exactly the same way.

Don't get me wrong. It's undeniably rewarding to share movies I love with students, especially movies they've never heard of, like *The Pilgrim* (Charlie Chaplin, 1923) or *Stranger than Paradise* (Jim Jarmusch, 1984) or *Caché* (Michael Haneke, 2005). It's particularly rewarding to teach movies I like but don't yet love, since I'm convinced on the basis of long experience that teaching them will deepen the pleasure I take in them. It's been one of the great experiences of my life to watch students falling in love with particular movies or with movies in general. But these aren't the reasons why I teach movies I like or love. I'm not looking to infect students with my own cinephilia or to improve their taste by getting them to love *Vertigo* (Alfred Hitchcock, 1958) as much as I do. I choose the films I teach not because I love them but because I hope that they'll aptly illustrate topics I'd like to explore in class or serve as provocations to discussions I'd like to have. For better or worse, I've come to enjoy talking about movies more than sitting through them, and it's this love—the love of talking more critically, sensitively, and intelligently about movies—that I most hope to share with students.

In a word, then, I teach not cinephilia but cineliteracy: what James Monaco has called How to Read a Film.[5] One of the enduring joys of teaching movies is that everyone is an expert on them. When Oscar night approaches, and I ask my students who should win Best Actress or Best Supporting Actor or Best Picture, they never demur on the grounds that they aren't experts; they're perfectly confident in their expertise, and rightly so. Yet their expertise is severely limited. They're expert consumers of movies, and indeed of audiovisual entertainment across a bewildering variety of franchises, genres, and media platforms, but they're not expert analysts of them. When they begin their studies, in fact, they can barely explain why they feel as they do about the movies they love or hate, let alone what the movies are doing to encourage those feelings. My job and my joy as a teacher is to help students change from consumers to analysts of movies and along the way cast a more critical eye on their own practices as audiences and their own implication in the entertainment industry and the culture it's spawned, a womblike culture in which most of them have hitherto lived in perfect comfort without ever questioning.

When first-year students arrive in my courses announcing that they've always loved movies, I'm happy to hear about that love but no more confident that they'll do well in the courses. I certainly don't intend to turn the students who pass through my classroom into people capable of gushing about movies in the way so many of those first-years already do. And when my students leave my courses telling me that they've learned so much about movies that they'll probably never enjoy one again, I try to mitigate their sadness by reassuring them that the unquestioning, uncritical love they think has fled forever will probably return in six to eight weeks, but now, I hope, as only one of a larger repertory of possible responses to the movies.

What is the relationship between the cinephilia so many of my students claim as their birthright, a cinephilia I like to think I still share with them, and the cineliteracy I'm using my courses to promote, sometimes in the face of serious resistance? It's tempting to let this question answer itself by saying either that they're opposed impulses, like pleasure and business, or that they represent distinct developmental stages, like crawling and walking. And I think there's some truth to both of these answers. But I find the relation between the two more complicated, and the best way to explore that relation is to open both terms to closer examination.

One problem with the term *cinephilia* is that it sounds as if it's parallel to *bibliophilia*, but it isn't. Although a bibliophile is etymologically a lover of books and a cinephile a lover of movies, nobody uses either term so generally. Most of the time I've heard the word *bibliophile*, it's followed the definition in *Merriam-Webster's Collegiate Dictionary* surprisingly closely: "a lover of books, esp. for qualities of format; *also*: a book collector."[6] In common parlance, bibliophiles are not avid readers but book collectors who especially love the physical properties of books, their historical significance, and of course their monetary value. If cinephilia were really parallel to bibliophilia, then cinephiles would be film collectors who spent their time researching the provenance of their 35mm prints or comparing the resolution and sound reproduction and featurettes on different video editions. There are such people, of course, but I don't think of them as cinephiles, and I doubt they think of themselves that way either. Even in the age of home video and putatively declining interest in print culture, books continue to be collectible in ways movies are not. So right off the bat, the notion of cinephilia as collection is suspect for me, and I assume even more for my students, whose coming of age in the era of Netflix and YouTube has made them think that anyone like me who's filled his house with videos must be a bit daft.

The problems only deepen when cinephiles get down to describing their love more precisely. As the title of his essay indicates, Johnson follows Paul Willemen and Christian Keathley in emphasizing cinephilia's connection to "the encounter with a brief, incidental moment within a given film that exerts an irrational hold on the viewer."[7] He cites Keathley, who in turn briefly quotes Willemen, in describing cinephilia as "a celebration of the spectator's subjective encounter with 'fleeting, evanescent moments' in the film experience" that emphasizes "the fetishizing of fragments of a film."[8] This account of cinephilia has nothing to do with bibliophilia. If it did, bibliophiles would be defined by the furtive pleasure they take in the smallest, apparently the most inconsequential, units of their books. The only people I know like that are devotees of sexually explicit scenes who scan each new book for the good parts.

Even so, Keathley's description of cinephilia applies very illuminatingly to one dimension of my own cinephilia. But it does not begin to cover the range of my infatuation with movies. This infatuation is more precisely described by Sontag as "the desire to lose yourself in other people's lives," and "the experience of surrender to, of being transported by, what was on the screen." Like Sontag, I've always wanted "to be overwhelmed by the physical presence of the image," and incidentally by the physical power of the soundtrack—to immerse myself in an experience I think of as oceanic.[9]

As Sontag points out, this sort of cinephilia is rooted in "the experience of 'going to the movies.'"[10] Far from being restricted to microscopic, incidental moments, the pleasure I take in going to the movies operates simultaneously in many modes and on many different scales. It begins long before any given movie begins. Whether because my home life is jejune, or because I harbor sentimental memories of date nights, I still find the prospect of going to a movie theater intoxicating. The theater doesn't need to be old or storied or distinctive or even comfortable; it doesn't need to have long-standing associations with earlier pleasures—though of course these associations increase the intensity of my anticipation. The moment the lights go down can still give me the shivers. And although I have no use for the barrage of commercials and industry infomercials that increasingly precede feature films, I love watching the previews, whether because they're more condensed than the films themselves or because they constitute the last stages of foreplay before the main attraction.

If one aspect of my cinephilia focuses on the experience of going to the movies, another focuses on certain kinds of movies. Foremost among these is what Michael Wood calls "*the movies*, an independent universe, self-created, self-perpetuating, a licensed zone of unreality."[11] The movies are coextensive not with all cinema, but, at least for me, with commercial American cinema of the Hollywood studio era and films produced more or less consciously in that tradition since then. Every time I go to the cinema, I'm hoping to see another example of "the movies." This horizon of expectations, of course, is very broad, and within it I have more particular desires associated with both film genre as such and with specific genres. I go into most every film noir, every Western, and every musical expecting to be swept off my feet, whether by the liberating promise that ordinary people will sing and dance emotions I feel all the time myself or by the promise that every scene, every shot, every frame will be more powerfully evocative of the Western's libertarian promise or noir's dark worldview than anything I'm likely to see outside the movies. When Henry David Thoreau asked in *Walden*, "Why do precisely these objects which we behold make a world?," he might have been prophesying cinema's success in worldmaking, as Stanley Cavell indicated in choosing Thoreau's question as the epigraph for *The World Viewed*.[12] Not every film has this power to create a world, at least not for me, but innumerable screwball comedies and gangster films and Westerns do, and it's a special joy when nongenre films like *The Edge of Heaven* (Fatih Akin, 2007) and *The White Ribbon* (Michael Haneke, 2009) succeed in doing so, as if out of nothing, as well.

It's hard for me to recall a film noir, no matter how cheesy or formulaic, that I haven't enjoyed watching. But of course some noirs give me more pleasure than others. One of my favorites is Jacques Tourneur's *Out of the Past* (1947), which provided Robert Mitchum with his first notable starring role and Jane Greer with the juiciest role of her regrettably short career. My interest in noirs led me to the film, but in the many years since I first watched it, I've never been moved to check out most of Tourneur's other films, or Mitchum's, or even Greer's. So for me at least, the film operates within the larger signifying system of its genre, but not particularly within that of its director or stars; it's an isolated pleasure, a one-off I love partly because it's a noir, but mostly because it feels like a distillation of other noirs. Like everyone else, I love the dialogue, heavy on wisecracks like the pickup line in which Jeff Bailey, formerly Jeff Markham (Mitchum), asks Kathie Moffat (Greer) if she'll talk to him: "If I don't talk, I think. It's too late in life for me to start thinking," and his reply to the doomed accountant Leonard Eels (Ken Niles), to whom Mitchum has just been introduced as the cousin of Eels's secretary Meta Carson (Rhonda Fleming): "Your cousin is a very charming young lady." "No, he's not. His name is Norman, and he's a bookmaker in Cleveland, Ohio." The screenplay is crammed with dialogue like this, gorgeously baroque one- and two-liners that neither promote gangster realism—they're as stylized as Racine's alexandrines—nor serve a structural function apart from establishing the world of the film as its own self. And I love the film's visuals. The film establishes a systematic visual contrast between the sunlit streets of small-town Bridgeport, where Jeff has hidden from genial gangster Whit Sterling (Kirk Douglas), who's got it in for Jeff because after Whit hires him to find Kathie, the girlfriend who shoots him and runs off with forty thousand dollars, he falls for Kathie and runs off with her himself, and the noir cityscapes of San Francisco, where Jeff vainly attempts to free himself from Whit's clutches. This contrast gives a frisson to numberless individual moments, from the two shots in the opening scene when Whit's gofer Joe Stephanos (Paul Valentine), who's just accidentally come across Jeff's service station in Bridgeport, approaches Marny's Cafe across the street; to the moment in which Jeff, at the climax of a long flashback, tosses aside the towel he's been using to dry Kathie's cloudburst-drenched hair, knocking over a lamp and signaling the consummation of their romance; to the moment when Joe, sent to kill Jeff, finds him fishing in the East Walker River, and you know the spectacular natural beauty of the scene is about to serve as the backdrop to violent death.

My favorite scene in the film is pivotal to the plot. Jeff, whom Whit has sent to San Francisco ostensibly to persuade the blackmailing Eels to turn over the doctored tax returns he prepared for Whit but actually to take the fall when Joe murders Eels, has failed to prevent Eels's murder but still hopes to retrieve the tax returns, which he thinks he can use to free himself from Whit's stranglehold. Tipped off by Kathie, he goes to the Sterling Club and takes the briefcase filled with the incriminating papers from the desk of Lou Baylord (John Kellogg), the club's manager. What appeals to me about this scene, however, is not its role in the plot but its apparently casual setup and its understated exposition—the scene is played with practically no dialogue, none of it expository.

Of the nine shots in the scene, the sixth and especially the seventh stand out as particularly pleasurable. Jeff, having bypassed a pair of ineffectual security men downstairs by entering through the service door and briskly climbed a flight of stairs, enters Baylord's office as its inhabitant is trying but failing to light his cigarette with a table lighter. Baylord, seeing the stranger approach, says, "What do you want?" As the sixth shot begins, the telephone on his desk rings, and he starts to rise from his chair. Jeff, without bothering to say a word, punches him in the jaw on the cut to the seventh shot, knocking him out, and answers his phone. It's one of the guys downstairs warning him that some stranger is on his way up. Pretending to be Baylord, Jeff says, "Forget it," hangs up, and unhurriedly begins to rifle the desk drawers looking for the briefcase containing the tax returns. When he finds it behind the second drawer, he stuffs it beneath his trench coat; experimentally tries Baylord's lighter, which now works without a hitch; helps himself to one of Baylord's cigarettes; and lights up. The whole scene, especially the two-shot sequence of Jeff knocking out Baylord, answering his phone, and taking a moment to light one of his victim's cigarettes with his victim's lighter before he leaves, perfectly demonstrates his sangfroid, his unquenchable cool under intense pressure.

I've tried to indicate in this summary the ways in which many of my favorite aspects of the film, from its broadest generic context down to individual shots of dialogue, play in a larger structure that links them in wonderfully expressive ways. I'd be the last to deny that the individual moments that give me the most pleasure derive their power from these larger structures. Years ago, I heard John Fawell, speaking at the annual conference of the Literature/Film Association, give a paper, "A Smoker's Guide to Film Noir," that cataloged the many shots of smoking in *Out of the Past* and showed how they expressed the many different attitudes and relationships of the film's leading characters. But I always thought that Fawell, like me, loved these shots not because they fit into a larger pattern but because individually they were so cool, as cool as Jeff Bailey. And even if their power derived exclusively from some larger pattern that gave them meaning, I don't know why they'd be any less compelling occasions for cinephilia.

In other words, my cinephilia involves more than irrational attachments to flashing glimpses. I'm just as passionately attached to larger structures, more salient moments, more calculated effects, whole genres, even to the experience of going to the movies. My cinephilia probably involves not only the blissfully orgasmic *jouissance* of Roland Barthes's writerly discourse but the rational, planned *plaisir* of readerly discourse. I love falling into traps movies have set for me; even now my fondest memories of *The Usual Suspects* (Bryan Singer, 1995) are marked by the unalloyed delight I took in being expertly swindled.

But if I'm going to interrogate cinephilia in the light of my own experience, I ought to do the same with cineliteracy. What exactly am I trying to do when I'm teaching cineliteracy? When I don't think about it, I assume that I'm trying to teach a cinematic version of the "reading in slow motion" advocated by Reuben Brower, who recommended "slowing down the process of reading to observe what is happening, in order to attend very closely to the words, their uses, and their meanings."[13] My own version of this credo is that I'm trying to get students to shift from the *what* of a film to its *how* and *why*—from what it seems to be showing and saying to how we think about that and why, to how the film is working to make us think and feel that way, to why we have the different reactions to it that we do, and what contexts we invoke, and ought to invoke, in our attempts to make sense of the film as an object of knowledge and pleasure. The focal pedagogical activity for me is not students' individual writing, as it is for Johnson, but group discussion—or, as Johnson puts it, students' writing "less as discrete exercises in a class for a grade and more as contributions to an always already ongoing discussion."[14] In both class discussions and written assignments,

I seek to encourage not cinephilic memory or celebration but the generation and testing of new ideas.

In practice, my agenda is far more specific. When I teach *Out of the Past*, it's always as a film noir, usually because I'm teaching it in a dedicated course on noir in which I identify it as a noir romance whose hero, even as he takes the measure of the femme fatale, remains fatalistically attached to her. (When Kathie, confessing that she shot Whit, tells Jeff, "But I didn't take anything. I didn't, Jeff. Won't you believe me?" he replies, in the film's most frequently quoted line, "Baby, I don't care.") So I'm less interested in what it reveals about Tourneur's career or RKO or postwar American culture or the nature of cinematic adaptation—it's based on Daniel Mainwaring's 1946 novel *Build My Gallows High* (written under the pseudonym Geoffrey Homes), whose relatively bland dialogue it systematically pumps up to the bursting point—than in what it does with the tropes of its genre. I'm particularly interested in discussing its dialogue, its visuals, and, yes, its endlessly inventive use of cigarettes.

Whether or not they realize on their own how stylized its dialogue is, students are usually more than willing to talk about it, and I consider the discussion worthwhile if they can list their favorite (or least favorite) lines and explain why the characters in the movie don't talk like people in real life. My students are much less sensitive to the film's visuals and much less articulate when I push them to talk about individual scenes and shots. Since they don't come to the film, even in a course on film noir, expecting a barrage of night-for-night shots of rain-slicked city streets, they see nothing visually arresting about the opening sequence in Bridgeport or the careful balance of domesticated natural backdrops and faux-rustic interiors in the sequences set in Whit's house in Lake Tahoe. I consider our discussion of visuals a success if I observe that students have become more sensitive to the range of visual options available when a filmmaker is planning and shooting a given scene, and that they can talk more fully and analytically about the visual codes that help different styles of lighting, for example, express different moods, tones, relations, and impressions. Cigarettes, I'm afraid, continue to be a lost cause for me. In all the times I've taught *Out of the Past*, I've never once succeeded in getting students interested in the ways different characters in the movie use cigarettes and matches—by tossing lit matches at people who don't seem to be paying attention to them, as Joe does to The Kid (Dickie Moore), the deaf boy who helps Jeff at his garage; by taking a cigarette from a trusted friend's mouth, popping it into his own mouth, taking a single drag, and then returning it to the friend, as Jeff does with the cabdriver Petey (Wallace Scott); or simply by carrying matches to light her man's smokes without ever lighting up herself, as Ann Miller (Virginia Huston), Kathie's good-girl counterpart, does for Jeff. Even when I persuade students to take a closer look at these moments, they think

I'm overreading the film, trying to find an expressive valence in gestures that are merely designed to be realistic or fill out the frame.

Other teachers who use *Out of the Past* to foster their students' cinematic literacy might well focus on different aspects of the film. Instead of teaching it as a film noir, they could teach it as a representative RKO film, or a representative 1940s film, or a representative example of the resources of black-and-white cinematography. But whatever their focus, they'd always be using the film as an example of *something*—if not of its genre, then of its director's or stars' careers, its studio's style, its status as a literary adaptation, its frugal recycling of its theme music from earlier RKO films, its revelations about the postwar crisis in American masculinity, its critique of the American dream, its status as an industrial product designed to make money. In other words, the film would always be pressed into service as an illustration of some larger point or pattern rather than a *Ding an sich* to be appreciated or loved for itself.

In one sense, teaching the film from virtually any perspective transforms it into a documentary illustrating the nature of its genre, the individual styles of its filmmakers or stars, the operation of studio economics, the dynamics of its historical moment, or something else judged to be more important than the film itself. In another, it becomes what Lauren Berlant has called a "case" representing "a problem-event," an example specifically chosen because it "is always normative but also always a perturbation of the normative."[15] As an illustration of a given aesthetic, generic, or historical tendency, *Out of the Past* becomes "merely a case study" that "doesn't work to change the conditions of exemplarity or explanation," even as I choose and discuss it precisely in hope of changing the ways students watch and reflect on movies. In the end, the example chosen as a synecdoche becomes a challenge to the "personal or collective sensorium," which, if it ripens sufficiently, ends up challenging the verities of the profession, extending even to the choice of this example as exemplary.[16]

It's in this connection that the relation between cinephilia and cineliteracy becomes hardest to parse. I'm convinced that many teachers of cinema first sought their jobs because they loved movies so much that they wanted to immerse themselves in them in unconditional surrender. Yet the goal of teaching, or at least of my teaching, is to make this surrender a lot more conditional by scrutinizing both movies and the terms under which we immerse ourselves in them more critically than most movies want us to do. Indeed the ultimate goal of cineliteracy is not a more consuming love for movies but a more analytical disposition that can be trained on cultural phenomena whose range extends far outside the movie theater. The delight I take in drawing students into analytical discussions of movies has certainly deepened my own love of movies, but I'm not nearly so sure that it's deepened my cinephilia. Instead, it's bookended my infatuation with movies as a necessary prelude—not in my life, but in the life of my relationship with any given movie—to their ability to engender new ideas. Johnson makes something like this point when, at the end of his essay, he emphasizes the "affective dimension" of movies, "and the related sense that they are experiences as much as objects, experiences subjective in nature and yet profoundly connected to the . . . increase in an individual's ability to understand the reality of other people's lives."[17] For me at least, the experience movies offer begins with the sensational and moves toward the ideational. I want to turn each film to a use it never sought while still maintaining my love for it. Beginning by debating the problems each movie presents in the terms that movie offers, I seek in the end to encourage both my students and myself to move beyond those terms, transcending the movie's limited perspective even as I strive to remain under its spell. Any pedagogy of cinema studies that honors my own experience would have to take account of both the desire to submit to movies and the desire to put them to use—in the end, by constantly extending and reshaping the discipline that gives their analysis currency.

This observation brings me to the final problem with cinephilia and cineliteracy: the absence of any pedagogical theory that might either link them or distinguish them. For hundreds of years, university students studied the classics on the assumption that a knowledge of Greek and Roman culture was an important attainment. Homer offered a universal image of the value of adventure, Virgil the costs of war, Sophocles the fragility of human life and human identity. When education in English language and literature was added to college curriculums toward the end of the nineteenth century, the justification for studying the English classics continued to borrow its rationale from its objects of study. Horace had advised poets to make their work *dulce et utile*, and it could safely be assumed that the sweetness and usefulness of literature provided ample justification for the study of what Matthew Arnold called the best that has been thought and said in the world. When cinema followed English literature into the academy some eighty years later, its proponents assumed that the same justification applied. Under cover of cinematic classics that were plainly *dulce et utile*, genre films like *Out of the Past* eventually made themselves at home on college campuses on the grounds, as Sontag put it, that cinema was "the art of the 20th century," "an art unlike any other," "both the book of art and the book of life."[18]

What was overlooked in this rush to sanctify cinema to the study of higher education was that the case for the importance of cinema did not amount to a rationale for teaching and studying cinema. That rationale, at first artlessly borrowed from literary studies—Chaplin and Hitchcock, we were assured, were the Shakespeare and Poe of the cinema—was assumed rather than defended until the arrival of the Birmingham school of cultural studies and the grand theory of Derrida, Foucault, Althusser, and Lacan. Now it was important, indeed essential, to study movies in order to understand how we were all being manipulated or interpellated or written into a larger social discourse. These perspectives swiftly revolutionized the study of cinema. Ironically, however, they were no more cinema-specific than the old quasi-literary defenses of cinema, based as they were on models and terms set forth by theorists with no particular interest or expertise in movies themselves.

It was only at this point, as a reaction against grand theory's totalizing claims about the passive, inscribed spectator sutured into the discourse, that cinephilia could offer itself to college teachers. Speaking of the ways "cinephiliac moments" carry the potential to reveal "another history flashing through the cracks of the histories we already know," Keathley asks, "How might one 'develop' . . . one of these moments so that the resulting discourse maintains and even extends the initial experience, and at the same time constitutes part of a history in that it imparts information, knowledge, and insight?"[19] Anyone willing to open this inquiry beyond the objects of Keathley's brand of cinema will find one possibility implicit in C. S. Lewis's famous distinction between allegory and symbolism:

> [The] fundamental equivalence between the immaterial and the material may be used by the mind in two ways. . . . On the one hand you can start with an immaterial fact, such as the passions which you actually experience, and can then invent *visibilia* to express them. . . . This is allegory. . . . But there is another way of using the equivalence, which is almost the opposite of allegory, and which I would call sacramentalism or symbolism. If our passions, being immaterial, can be copied by material inventions, then it is possible that our material world in its turn is the copy of an invisible world. . . . The attempt . . . to see the archetype in the copy, is what I mean by symbolism or sacramentalism. . . . The allegorist leaves the given—his own passions—to talk of that which is confessedly less real, which is a fiction. The symbolist leaves the given to find that which is more real. To put the difference in another way, for the symbolist it is we who are the allegory.[20]

Shorn of its metaphysical overtones, this passage, a remarkably explicit prophecy of New Criticism's foundational emphasis on symbolism, asks simply which is more real, the particular material example or the idea or world it intimates and incarnates. Whether we're watching movies or teaching them, how can we trace the wider implications of each cinephiliac moment without losing the sense of its magic? Lewis doesn't answer this question, but his distinction between the manufactured *visibilia* of allegory and the intuited archetypes of symbolism offers a possible matrix for exploring this question more systematically—assuming, of course, that systematic inquiry is what we seek.

Absent this more systematic investigation, I take comfort in knowing that although I teach whole movies rather than parts of movies, even the most radiantly consonant whole plays only a small part in the matters of knowledge and inquiry

I'm most interested in. So I suspect that what Keathley is doing in the classroom is not, in the end, all that much different from what I'm doing. Even so, it's a great question he asks, even if its answer produces not so much a philosophy of teaching as a series of pedagogical tactics that may be the best we can hope for.

THOMAS LEITCH is Professor of English at the University of Delaware. His most recent books are *Wikipedia U: Knowledge, Authority, and Liberal Education in the Digital Age* and *The Oxford Handbook of Adaptation Studies*. He is currently working on *The History of American Literature on Film*.

Notes

1. David T. Johnson, "The 'Flashing Glimpse' of Cinephilia: What an Unusual Methodology Might Offer Adaptation Studies," *Adaptation* 6 (2013): 27.
2. Susan Sontag, "The Decay of Cinema," *New York Times Magazine*, February 25, 1996, http://www.nytimes.com/1996/02/25/magazine/the-decay-of-cinema.html.
3. Johnson, "The 'Flashing Glimpse' of Cinephilia," 27.
4. Christopher D. Morris, "The Direction of *North by Northwest*," *Cinema Journal* 36, no. 4 (1997): 43.
5. James Monaco, *How to Read a Film* (Oxford: Oxford University Press, 1977).
6. "Bibliophile," *Merriam-Webster's Collegiate Dictionary*, 10th ed. (Springfield, MA: Merriam-Webster, 1994), 111.
7. Johnson, "The 'Flashing Glimpse' of Cinephilia," 27.
8. Ibid.; Christian Keathley, *Cinephilia and History, or the Wind in the Trees* (Bloomington: Indiana University Press, 2006), 7; Paul Willemen "Through the Glass Darkly: Cinephilia Reconsidered," in *Looks and Frictions: Essays in Cultural Studies and Film Theory* (London: British Film Institute, 1994), 232.
9. Sontag, "The Decay of Cinema."
10. Ibid.
11. Michael Wood, *America in the Movies, or, "Santa Maria, It Had Slipped My Mind"* (New York: Basic, 1975), 8.
12. Henry David Thoreau, *A Week on the Concord and Merrimack Rivers; Walden; or, Life in the Woods; The Maine Woods; Cape Cod* (New York: Library of America, 1985), 502; Stanley Cavell, *The World Viewed: Reflections on the Ontology of Film* (Cambridge, MA: Harvard University Press, 1979).
13. Reuben A. Brower, "Reading in Slow Motion," in *In Defense of Reading*, eds. Reuben A. Brower and Richard Poirier (New York: Dutton, 1962), 4.
14. Johnson, "The 'Flashing Glimpse' of Cinephilia," 37.
15. Lauren Berlant, "On the Case," *Critical Inquiry* 33 (2007): 663, 670.
16. Ibid., 665.
17. Johnson, "The 'Flashing Glimpse' of Cinephilia," 41.
18. Sontag, "The Decay of Cinema."
19. Keathley, *Cinephilia and History*, 134.
20. C. S. Lewis, *The Allegory of Love* (Oxford: Oxford University Press, 1936), 44–45.

4 Nearing the Heart of a Film
Toward a Cinephilic Pedagogy

Tracy Cox-Stanton

Henri Langlois, the legendary director of the Cinémathèque Française, distinguished the *cinephile* from the *cinephage*. The cinephage, or film nerd, Langlois said, "sits in the front row and writes down the film credits. . . . But that's not the point of the movies. To love cinema is to love life, to really look at this window on the universe."[1] Langlois's distinction resonates for me, as it favors a definition of cinephilia that moves outward, through the eccentric desires and pleasures of the individual viewer, into the context of a surrounding world. My most rewarding moments as a film student and teacher have charted that path from individual fascination to real-life significance.

It is helpful to bisect Langlois's axiom into two complementary components: first, "really look[ing]" and second, connecting what we see and hear on the screen to the universe around us. The first component, "really looking" (and really listening), requires an appreciation of cinema's material foundation. As Rainer Werner Fassbinder has reminded us in a quote he attributes to Douglas Sirk, "You can't make films *about* things, you can only make films *with* things, with people, with light, with flowers, with mirrors, with blood, in fact with all the fantastic things which make life worth living."[2] A cinephilic approach begins with an appreciation of these *things* that make up films, deferring the meaning-making to wallow for a while in the materials of a film—noticing closely the play of light and shadow, appreciating the nuances of an actor's gesture, or recognizing the marvelous life that cinema can endow upon an otherwise banal object. Emphasizing this materiality, Nicole Brenez offers an interesting metaphor that we might borrow when we seek to clarify the project of cinephilia. She distinguishes her work from methods of film analysis that focus solely on a film's narrative or that use the film to serve a predetermined methodology, stating, "For me all these methods are interesting and valid, but in a way they are also not in the heart of what a film is. Most of them are considering films as symptoms, but they never reach the illness, if I can say that. Any kind of attempt to go to the core of the film—the visual and acoustic proposal of the film—is important and necessary."[3] I find Brenez's wonderfully perverse association of cinema with illness very provocative. We might think of cinephilia as the state of being afflicted with cinema, burdened with this exquisite illness that encourages its sufferers to indulge themselves in the effects and affects of visual and acoustic materials. Undoubtedly, cinephilia begins here, recognizing that films are made *with* things before we begin to imagine how they might also be *about* things. A great deal of inspiring and rich work has taken as its genesis (for often vastly different ends) this notion that the recent turn (or return) to cinema's materiality has reinvigorated cinema studies and offered a welcome counterbalance to the heyday of linguistic, psychoanalytic, and narratological theory. Certainly, a cinephilic method of analysis must begin with an attention to the down-and-dirty "stuff" that really makes up a film.

Fewer considerations of cinephilia, however, focus on what might be represented by the second part of Langlois's axiom, connecting the dots from the material things to the amorphous things that films might also be *about*—values, relationships, identities, pleasures, injustices—things that matter in the universe beyond the screen. These two motivations, which we might label aesthetic consciousness (really looking and listening) and social consciousness (acknowledging cinema's dialogue with real life, its intersections with ideology), should be complementary rather than antithetical. In fact, these two components are already built into the etymology of *-philia*, which refers to an unusual or excessive attraction but also to the recognition of an affinity with and connection to the other.

Thus a cinephilic pedagogy, for me, is one that encourages students to "really look at this window on the universe"—to indulge their excessive or eccentric attractions to cinema's visual and acoustic materials; but equally important is that other etymology of *-philia*, the one that emphasizes connection and camaraderie and acknowledges that cinema is not an end in itself. "To love cinema is to love life," Langlois says. For me, this dictum invokes the Bazinian emphasis on cinema's capacity to *reveal*, to interrupt our habits of seeing and lead us to unpredictable moments of insight into the universe within and beyond the screen. This is inevitably challenging—both to the student/viewer, who is typically steeped in a very specific habit of seeing, and to the professor, whose placement in the profession comes with its own unwritten rules, habits, and constraints.

The disciplinary constraints of cinema studies can be as numbing and counterproductive as the film nerd's compulsion to write down the movie credits. I sometimes think that the "default" path in academia leads one straight to filmprofessor-nerddom, where great stakes suddenly materialize around the most boring things, and all conversations lead to discussions and complaints about institutional disputes, or anxious expressions about one's place inside or outside supposedly competing schools of thought. It is easy to find oneself entrenched in a zone of "cinema studies" where our investments in actual films don't merit a mention. For me, the academic cinephage is one who grows jolly in that entrenchment and finds comfort in closing off any number of possibilities, happy to have found her niche in an institution whose boundaries she can police. The cinephile, by contrast, recognizes the necessity of remaining open to a multitude of methods, vocabularies, and interests, with the goal of interrupting rather than reinforcing her habits.[4] The cinephile promiscuously seeks methods that facilitate that impossible but divine goal: to produce something in writing that nears the heart of a film, that approaches the core of a film to both describe its manner of working and illuminate its significance to the surrounding world.[5] The return of "cinephilia" to cinema studies reinvigorates the discipline on a number of levels, reminding us of the need to deny hierarchies of professionalization and make a space for film lovers—journalists, students, scholars, fans—to engage in the questions that burn beneath our diverse devotions to the cinema.

Fascination, Double Consciousness, and Discovery

It can be useful to think of Langlois's lifework as commensurate with a cinephilic teaching pedagogy. His eccentricities and excesses were infamous, but even his worst critics agreed that Langlois created an inspiring and transformative learning environment. He juxtaposed films in thoughtful and surprising ways, encouraging viewers to see connections they wouldn't have otherwise seen, and he candidly displayed his own contagious passion for the cinema. His methods managed to tap into the longings and desires of the young generation that went on to create the French New Wave.

Even as I recognize my own nostalgia for an imagined narrative that was undoubtedly more complicated in reality, I find great inspiration in Langlois's legacy. My most ambitious goal as a teacher is to encourage my students to make connections between their own longings and the possibilities of cinema, motivating them to imagine new ways of making movies and new ways of understanding movies. At its best, syllabus construction is analogous to Langlois's programming, as we juxtapose readings and films in a manner that encourages insight. And, although it can be difficult because my own history usually differs significantly from theirs, I recognize the necessity of sharing my own cinematic passions with students. Cinema has become a meaningful part of the world I have fashioned for myself since adolescence, when I, like many of them, began to imagine a reality more in sync with my interests and ideals. So for me, there will always be a Romantic, idealist side to cinephilia—sometimes messy, self-indulgent, or nostalgic, but nonetheless passionate. I appreciate James Naremore's defense of the adolescent excesses of the French New Wave critics and filmmakers: "Before we rush to proclaim ourselves adults and scholars," he writes, "we should remember that adolescence is an important period of human development—a period of cultural resistance, when discoveries are made."[6] I think that part of my job as an educator is to encourage and validate students' individual interests and fascinations—and then, importantly, to challenge them to view those interests as the starting point of a larger discovery, a discovery that acknowledges the context of the surrounding world.

I also challenge students to view film theory as a companion in their quest, and though I don't always succeed, I work hard to convey the relevance, vigor, and geniality of film theory. In that spirit, I reject the facile opposition between cinephilia and 1970s film theory. It is easy to pull a few lines from Christian Metz's *The Imaginary Signifier* or Laura Mulvey's "Visual Pleasure" essay that seem to situate "theory" at odds with "cinephilia," but the actual relationship is much more complicated. We should remember that Metz's infamous sentence, "To be a theoretician of the cinema, one should ideally no longer love the cinema . . . ," ends with the five words "and yet still love it."[7] Metz's work describes not a dismissal of cinematic pleasure but a need to think critically about our cinematic attachments in recognition of the powerful relationship between images on the screen and lived conditions. In the excellent essay "All That Heaven Allows: What Is or Was Cinephilia?" Nico Baumbach combats the oversimplification of "*Screen* theory," reminding us that Metz proposed not a rejection of cinephilia but a "double consciousness": "For Metz, theories of cinema shouldn't be beholden to the affective attachments of cinephilia, yet at the same time, they are useless if they do not grasp the 'specific kind of love' that cinema inspired in its devotees."[8] Metz argues for a renewed, critically informed ciné-love that takes itself to task, aiming to avoid what he terms the "paralyzing bonds of a tender unconditionality."[9]

Specifically, Metz is addressing not just the love of cinema but the unconditional love of classic Hollywood cinema, a legacy of the postwar French auteurist critics that had begun to distinguish European cinema studies in the 1960s. In *Fetishism and Curiosity*, Laura Mulvey describes how she belonged to a generation of European intellectuals that "fell in love with Hollywood in its sunset years."[10] She writes, "I spent the 60s under the influence of the *Cahiers du Cinéma* and absorbed in Hollywood," until "feminism irretrievably changed the terms of the debate."[11] Although her infamous 1975 essay took a polemical tone against Hollywood's narrative and visual pleasures, her subsequent work revealed a more complicated and nuanced redefinition of her own cinephilia that abated the disempowered pleasure of submitting to the image. Rather, she recounts how her feminist consciousness enabled a new relationship to Hollywood cinema, "released from subordination to the image, . . . [and] moving out of entranced fascination with the Hollywood screen . . . to discover a distance from it that then brought its own rewards of intellectual curiosity and pleasure."[12] Mulvey describes here a pleasure that is surely familiar to most contemporary students and professors of cinema studies—the pleasure of contemplation and analysis, the conscious appreciation of images and sounds, the joy of supplementing the viewing experience with an interrogation.

My own cinephilic history differs significantly from Mulvey's. As Jonathan Rosenbaum, Adrian Martin, Nicole Brenez, and others aptly illuminate in *Movie Mutations*, despite alarmist proclamations to the contrary, cinephilia did not die after technological and cultural mutations of the 1970s and 1980s significantly altered moviegoing.[13] Rather, cinephilia itself mutated. The first movies I loved were not 35mm prints of classic Hollywood but VHS tapes of European art cinema. The late 1980s and early 1990s offered an interesting historical moment for budding cinephiles. I remember being told that "film is dead" just as it was beginning to live for me, on glitched-up, decaying-before-your-eyes videotapes. In many ways, both the medium (the clunky VHS tapes, apparatus fully on display) and the message (European art cinema) discouraged a cinephilia marked by submission, paralyzing fascination, or unconditionality. The fangirl enthrallment remained—my friends and I dressed like Anna Karina, bought Gauloises cigarettes, extoled Monica Vitti's glorious hair and tormented mien—but we simultaneously debated Godard's feminism and recognized the "separation of the elements" that make up a film. Fascination and analysis were cohorts in our ciné-love. I acknowledge now that the Mulvey/Metz generation had paved the path to the film world that we cheerfully inhabited circa 1990. By no means had we mastered all the pioneering scholarship of the 1970s, but the value of rigorous ideological analysis went unquestioned.

Further, the same awakening of ideological consciousness that marked film theory in the late 1960s informed the radical critique of authoritarian teaching methods evident in the 1968 student demonstrations and articulated so urgently in Paulo Freire's *Pedagogy of the Oppressed*.[14] The field of critical pedagogy, best represented by Freire's critique of the "banking" model of education, shared with post-1968 film theory the recognition that systems or apparatuses are implicated in power structures. Though my earliest teaching experiences fell comically short of anything espoused by Freire, this heady, antiestablishment consciousness that reverberated through the 1970s was nevertheless part and parcel of my cinephilic awakening. That ideological consciousness, I believe, is already evident in Langlois's claim that "to love cinema is to love life." That connection between cinema and the lived realities of human beings is palpable in the documentary *Phantom of the Cinémathèque* (Jacques Richard, 2004). I introduce that film to my students because it never fails to move them. They are moved by the young cinephiles' passionate defense of Henri Langlois after he was removed from his position at the Cinémathèque, and they are inspired by the urgency with which that generation linked political and artistic activity. The documentary helps students recognize a previous generation's answer to the question "What is at stake in cinema?" and invites them to contemplate that question for themselves.

I have tried here to trace the outlines of a cinephilia marked by a "double consciousness" that both indulges and interrogates our cinematic fascinations. That interrogation, for me, ultimately moves from questions about a specific film to questions about cinema in general, recognizing that ontological, aesthetic, and ideological questions underlie our entire enterprise. Being a cinephile means that I acknowledge my investment in this activity of viewing, discussing, and thinking critically about cinema, because I believe there is something at stake. Part of our interrogation, then, requires keeping key questions—What is at stake here? Why does this matter?—in close view.

For me, films matter because they allow us to see our own—and perhaps more importantly, others'—worlds anew, siphoned off from reality, placed in critical relief, ripe for insight. Thus my teaching philosophy is ultimately informed by a sense of "cinema as discovery" that probably has its roots in Bazinian humanism. I see more continuity than rupture in the movement from Bazin's "classical" theory to post-1968 "contemporary" theory. Bazin pointed to the urgency of cinema's relationship to the real world, and contemporary theory, in many ways, took him to task.

To initiate a classroom conversation about the relationship between cinema and the real world, I have sometimes assigned Mark Edmundson's book *Why Read?*, using it as a springboard to contemplate "why watch?" Edmundson argues for a humanistic literary education that echoes Langlois's distinction between the film nerd and the true cinephile: "My job as a Romanticist," Edmundson writes, "is not primarily to say unprecedented things about the Romantics. . . . My job is to continue the lives of the poets on in the present, to make them available to those living now who might need them."[15] I identify with Edmundson's sense of humility—"self-annulment"[16] he calls it—in the face of great films, artists, and thinkers, and I regularly rely on those "greats"—the ones who have moved me, the ones I have studied closely—to lift my classes when my own energy and intellect inevitably sag.

De Sica's Little Sister and the "Believing Game"

The sense of self-annulment valued by Edmundson echoes Bazin's ideas about one of his own "greats," Vittorio De Sica. In Bazin's essay on De Sica, he writes that the true merit of *Bicycle Thieves* (1948) lies in "not betraying the essence of things, in allowing them first of all to exist for their own sakes, freely; it is in loving them in their singular individuality. 'My little sister reality,' says De Sica, and she circles about him like the birds around Saint Francis. Others put her in a cage or teach her to talk, but De Sica talks with her and it is the true language of reality that we hear, the words that cannot be denied, that only love can utter."[17] It has always seemed to me that this idea of "little sister reality" perfectly encapsulates what is at stake in cinema as a window on the universe, and ultimately, what is at stake in education in general. Movies invite us to inhabit other realities, offering the potential to transform ourselves, if we are willing to reimagine our relationship to the world around us.

I enjoy teaching the film *Black Girl* (Ousmane Sembène, 1966) because it conveys colonialism's horrific reverberations in a brilliantly terse and cinematic way, and it encourages a conversation about "little sister reality." With subtlety and restraint, the film invites the viewer to inhabit its protagonist Diouana's (Mbissine Thérèse Diop's) reality. But because Diouana's truth—she is a young Senegalese woman who moves to France to serve as nanny, maid, and cook for a white French family—differs so significantly from that of most young Americans, students can have a difficult time making the transition. If the viewer doesn't submit to Diouana's point of view, the film's tragic denouement can be surprising and vexing. Almost always, one or more students will express their consternation with Diouana's seeming surrender—"That ending came out of nowhere. Why did she do that? I wanted her to fight!" a student will inevitably complain, wanting to blame Diouana herself for the nightmare of colonialism conveyed by the film.

The film's failure, for this student, can be illuminating. A viewer who has found *Black Girl*'s ending perplexing is a viewer who has failed to follow the film's acoustic and visual proposal, perhaps because the leap from his or her own reality to "Diouana's reality" is too great. But in class, we can walk back through the film, trying again to *really examine* the way the film constructs events from Diouana's point of view, focalizing the narrative not only via sound (we hear Diouana's inner monologue through voice-over) but more subtly through its mise-en-scène. As scholars of film performance have reminded us, in the cinema, a character is inextricable from a performer. We might explore the trajectories of gesture, costume, deportment, and mobility that Diouana displays across the expanse of the narrative and notice more closely her interaction with objects. The film's most significant object, of course, is its final signifier, the mask. The mask brings together all the film's themes about the ambiguity of meaning and the immense consequences of that ambiguity. The mask is an object onto which both colonized and colonizer look, and yet they see entirely different things. Even as we acknowledge that fact, and even as the film's final image moves us deeply, it also forces us to reconcile with our own ignorance of the mask's many possible signifieds. The final, haunting image of *Black Girl* depicts a little boy in close-up, holding the mask to his face, looking directly into the camera. *Cahiers* critic Serge Daney once discussed his preference for "films that looked back at you . . . from their otherness,"[18] a description that always comes to my mind when I teach *Black Girl*. For not only does the image literally turn the gaze onto the spectator, but it makes us humbly aware of our inadequacy, and it stirs us to remedy our ignorance.

This expansion of the spectator's point of view is accomplished not just through narrative characterization but through film language—thus "little sister reality" isn't necessarily achieved in every story about a little girl. It is easy enough to imagine a multitude of filmic approaches that would happily "put her in a cage or teach her to talk." The films I most enjoy teaching, the ones I am most beholden to in my own education, are those that require us to slow down and really see, hear, and feel a new reality. I encourage students to think about what the film is asking of them as a spectator, to recognize that films speak in a variety of languages, and that they don't always deliver themselves neatly in a wrapped box for our easy consumption. In a sense, what I am arguing for in "little sister reality" is submission, precisely the mechanism that Metz's sense of "double consciousness" warns us against. However, I want to suggest that submission can be a tool in the service of double consciousness—especially when it requires submission to an unfamiliar, even uncomfortable, point of view or way of seeing.

In Bazin's praise of De Sica, for example, the critical theorist in me zeros in on his phrase "the essence of things," mentally highlighting it and scribbling question marks in the margins; but at the same time, I have learned that there is much to be gained from inhabiting his idea, temporarily submitting to that which immediately raises my ire. I have learned this mostly through teaching literary and film theory and struggling with students' often quick and decisive dismissal of ideas they are only beginning to understand. Students are sometimes unwilling to "try on"—even momentarily—ideas that are foreign, unfashionable, or potentially unsettling. Television "news" shows and social media disputes have taught them, I fear, to confront new problems by developing a quick and thundering opinion. To counteract that, in film theory courses, I sometimes say to students, "We are all going to be phenomenologists today," or "This week, we all believe that psychoanalysis can illuminate a great deal about the cinema." Whether encountering a new theory or a foreign film, there is much to be gained by temporarily quieting one's inner critic, suspending the Socratic dialogue, and inhabiting the new perspective.

As long ago as 1973, the pedagogical theorist Peter Elbow introduced the compelling concept of "the believing game," designed to counterbalance the more familiar "doubting game" that we have traditionally rewarded in the classroom.[19] Elbow writes, "We haven't learned to use belief as a *tool*—as we use doubt as a tool."[20] In many ways, Elbow's notion of a "believing game" articulates the pedagogical ramifications of De Sica's "little sister reality" and helps me appreciate the ways that self-annulment or submission can lead to knowledge. Elbow writes, "Our best hope for finding invisible flaws in what we can't see in our own thinking is to enter into *different* ways of thinking or . . . points of view that carry different assumptions. Only from a new vantage point can we see our normal point of view from the outside and thereby notice assumptions that our customary point of view keeps hidden."[21] Cinema, in its constant offering of a new vantage point, in its easy estrangement of the everyday, seems uniquely suited to accomplish this task.

Movies, Moments, and Paralysis

One of the things that makes teaching film so challenging is that the audience is undeniably a moving target. When I began teaching as a graduate assistant in the early 1990s, I was nearly the same age as my students; we shared cultural references and certain ways of being in the world. I find that today's students deeply challenge my assumptions about the connection between cinephilia and adolescent rebellion and discovery. Although diverse in many ways, most of today's students grew up with a significant library of DVDs available from birth, aligning their ciné-love more often with childhood than adolescence. This distinguishes them from previous generations whose investment in the movies coincided with a more rebellious, self-aware, and exploratory stage of life. My students watched movies throughout their childhood and youth in the manner that my own generation watched television. Movies, for them, were always plentiful, taken for granted, regularly present as "background noise," and thus not particularly "curated" with much intention. They sometimes associate cinema with the routine and comfortable, posing a challenge to the revelatory perspective that I hope to facilitate.

I find Robin Wood's 1986 study of Reagan-era blockbusters alarmingly prescient of today's situation. Wood identifies a trend that emerged in the late 1980s: "the curious and disturbing phenomenon of children's films conceived and marketed largely for adults."[22] He enumerates the key characteristics of these films: their regression of the viewer to childhood, their use of dazzling special effects, their pretense of originality and innovation, their appeal to an audience's sense of helplessness in the face of immense world problems, their anxiety about American capitalism's totalitarianism, and their ultimate restoration of patriarchal authority. The blockbusters he critiques invoke regressive fantasies of childhood, sheltering the viewer from the responsibilities and uncomfortable realities of the world outside, bringing great comfort and effectively shutting the curtain to Langlois's "window on the universe." "Reassurance is the keynote," he writes.[23] In effect, he is describing the pleasurable paralysis and regressive submission that Metz and Mulvey aimed to undo.

The blockbuster mentality that Wood illuminates has nearly consumed the mainstream film industry that provides today's students with a steady diet of entertainment from childhood on. My own teaching experiences confirm Barbara

Klinger's findings in *Beyond the Multiplex* that students' relationships to cinema and cinephilia have been radically altered by the plentitude of movies they grew up with in their homes, enabling repeat viewings of childhood favorites.[24] I have been surprised to hear bright college students—*graduate* students—recount the great pleasure of a *Goonies* marathon weekend, for example. Cinephilia, for today's students, is complicated by their nostalgia for a childhood that so cogently linked comfort and pleasure with repeat viewings of blockbuster movies. The situation Wood begins to illuminate in the 1980s has come to full fruition—it is not uncommon that my college students and my elementary-aged sons eagerly anticipate the same movies these days.

As a teacher I am challenged to expand my students' sense of cinema's possibilities and yet remain flexible in my own cinematic judgments. My knee-jerk judgments of their generation can reflect my own paralysis, my own refusal to inhabit "millennial student reality," as much as theirs. I ask them to investigate their fascination, to see what's useful in it, to write about it, identifying potential "fires" of interest that underlie their seeming couch-potato submission. I have sometimes taught essays from *The Movie That Changed My Life,* in which well-known writers reflect on their favorite films, analyzing their fascinations and tracing the convoluted ways that a particular movie helped them chart their path in life.[25] The essays are useful because they allow the films to exist in their complexity, helping students recognize the ultimate ambiguity of our attractions and reminding me that precious few movies are either wholly inane or wholly progressive.

My goal is to introduce students to the pleasures of intellectual curiosity and double consciousness, retaining yet remotivating their cinematic attractions. I encourage them to indulge their research skills as they reconsider particular movies that have been important to them, exploring how historic context and scholarly ideas can deepen their understanding of the film and help them grasp their own relationship to it. Alongside Robin Wood's work, they might consider how *The Goonies* (Richard Donner, 1985) legitimates a particular type of wish fulfillment in watching a gang of adventurous, unruly children change their world. That discussion might lead to a viewing of *Zero for Conduct* (Jean Vigo, 1933) and invite students to contemplate how films from other national and historic contexts offer different appeals to the same base longings. A little bit of research might uncover Roger Ebert's 1985 review of *The Goonies* that eerily confirms Wood's claims: "More things happen in this movie than in six ordinary action films," Ebert writes. "There's not just a thrill a minute; there's a thrill, a laugh, a shock, and a special effect." In fact, Ebert's main critique of the film is that it fails to live up to *E.T.* (Steven Spielberg, 1982), which, in his words, invites the audience "to wonder, and to dream."[26] This investigation could lead to a stimulating and fruitful discussion of wonder and curiosity, from Descartes to Mulvey: What does it mean to wonder? Why does Wood critique wonder and Ebert embrace it? How has wonder changed through history? How would we characterize the Spielbergian sense of wonder? How do we discern for ourselves the difference between mind-numbing wonder and liberating wonder?

Other possibilities for mobilizing cinephilia in the classroom look less to the "movie that changed my life" and more to "the moment that sparked my fire." In different ways, Paul Willemen, Robert B. Ray, Christian Keathley, George Toles, and Rashna Wadia Richards have focused on the cinephilic tendency to fetishize individual, fleeting, and eccentric moments within a film, suggesting that an attention to those moments might not promote paralyzing unconditionality but instead facilitate knowledge.[27] Ray's *The Avant-Garde Finds Andy Hardy* and *How a Film Theory Got Lost and Other Mysteries in Cultural Studies* outline provocative methods for mobilizing our attraction to cinema's enigmatic details, modeled after surrealist games. Ray proposes a set of instructions to students: "Select a detail from a movie, one that interests you without your knowing why. Follow this detail wherever it leads and report your findings."[28] This type of assignment can provide a productive classroom exercise that simultaneously helps students understand something about a particular movie or about movies in general and at the same time legitimates and honors cinema's mysterious sensory attractions. In addition, I've found this assignment particularly helpful in combating students' paralysis or "writer's block" that sometimes occurs when they have ideas about a movie, but they don't know where to start.

Although this fetishistic, moment-based method is sometimes characterized in opposition to ideological analysis, they can, in my view, complement one another nicely. As David T. Johnson has written, a cinephile's attraction to an arresting moment need not remain personal and eccentric but can instead "face the larger critical discourse and the world itself."[29] One of my favorite essays from the British Film Institute collection *Film Moments* does just that. In "Beyond Melodrama and Realism," Laura Mulvey writes about her fascination with a scene from the Iranian film *Under the Skin of the City* (Rakhshan Bani-Etemad, 2001).[30] In the scene, almost abstract flashes of rain are followed by a woman's obsessive and overwrought gesture of washing clothes in a basin. The moment is excessive, irrational, out of keeping with the narrative requirements of the film, and yet deeply meaningful. Mulvey's analysis begins with a careful and admiring description of the moment, legitimating her sensory experience of it, and then moves outward, connecting the moment both to the possibilities of cinema and to the realities of women's lives. The film, for Mulvey, "seems to suggest that mise-en-scène must, and should, acknowledge silences rooted in oppression and repression and find some way to fill in visually for the inadequacy of language. From this perspective, the cinema's ability to move beyond language, into the cinematic, lends itself to this political form of expression and draws attention to particular conjunctures in which the political and the cinematic come together."[31] Mulvey's path of inquiry beautifully demonstrates how the "cinematic"—those sensory details that exceed language—can lead so succinctly to revelation, not only about the workings of cinema itself or about our own autobiographical investments but also about the lived realities of fellow human beings. She sees in the woman's furtive gesture an expression of unconscious, unspeakable injustice, suggesting that the scene "materialises, on film and with film, a complex interweaving of signification, reaching into the unconscious and out into the intractable reality of the everyday."[32]

Coda: Cinephiles and *The Cine-Files*

There is a reason that most essays about cinephilia these days either begin or end with a discussion of the Internet: it is undeniably altering the face of cinema studies. I confess to coming somewhat late to the game and remaining overwhelmed by the Internet's possibilities for quite some time. I remember researching the Czech film *Daisies* (Věra Chytilová, 1966) in the early 2000s and stumbling upon the most interesting and useful analysis of it, not in an established publication, but in Steven Shaviro's blog. "Does this *count?*" I wondered. The question today probably remains unanswered for many, or at least for the academic establishment that has long geared its reward system around a short list of academic presses. Distinctions that once seemed so sharp—between what "counts" and what doesn't, between academia and journalism—are blurring increasingly. I, like many others, have grown to enjoy the result.

In *The New Cinephilia*, Girish Shambu offers a lucid and enthusiastic account of how the Internet is changing cinephilia, noting especially its unprecedented enabling of conversation.[33] Websites, blogs, and social media sites have provided a uniquely fertile ground for cinephiles, as the young and old, well-known and unknown, nearby and faraway meet, united by their desire to access and share cinema's fascinations. Two sites that particularly embody this spirit of "new cinephilia" for me are Shambu's own blog "girish" and Catherine Grant's blog "Film Studies for Free."[34] These sites are motivated by an immense generosity, aiming only to share ideas and initiate discussions; the conversations they enable and the resources they provide are invaluable for the film lover and the film teacher.

In 2012, I joined the conversation myself by starting *The Cine-Files*, an online journal of cinema studies. My original impetus for the journal was pedagogical. I teach a graduate seminar on a special topic every spring. Why not, I thought, tie that topic to the production of an online journal? It seemed an excellent way to connect myself and my students to the world outside, as we appealed to academics and journalists, experts on the questions our class would ponder. *The Cine-Files* is undoubtedly a work in progress, and I see it not only as a scholarly journal but also as an experiment in twenty-first-century cinephilia. How can we use the web to bring together a diversity of individuals and perspectives united only by their devotion to questions about the cinema? The project is undeniably fueled by cinephilia because it is the quintessential labor of love; it requires an enormous amount of unpaid work—my own and others'—to keep it running. But it has brought a great sense of cinephilic camaraderie to our program and has provided some really wonderful opportunities for me and my students to connect with fellow film lovers across the world—and in the process, we produce a new and valuable resource.

The *Cine-Files*' statement of purpose ("We believe that cinema—in all its eclectic forms of the past, present, and future—is both pleasurable and substantive, and we devote these pages to its passionate analysis") reflects the sense I have argued here that cinephilia and research, pleasure and inquiry, are compatriots rather than enemies in our quest. The articles we have published offer diverse and engaging perspectives on cinema's "window on the universe," and, I hope, bear out my contention that aesthetic, historical, and philosophical inquiries sustain rather than diminish the pleasures of cinema.

A mythic feud between the sociologist Roger Caillois and the surrealist André Breton frames the dichotomy—in our case, the false dichotomy—between analysis and pleasure, demystification and submission. Their dispute was over a Mexican jumping bean: Caillois wanted to cut it open and discover the empirical mechanism behind the magic, while Breton wanted to leave the bean and its enchantment intact. Fortunately for us, the "magic" of cinema is gloriously overdetermined; there is no empirical mechanism behind its operation, ready to be unveiled and put to rest. Rather, we might think about how the sociologist and the surrealist can (and do) meet, dialogue, and debate in passionate analyses that chart their diverse paths to the heart of cinema, aiming to better understand its manner of working and to connect cinematic matter to things that matter in the world beyond the screen.

TRACY COX-STANTON is Professor of Cinema Studies at Savannah College of Art and Design. She is the founder and editor of the online journal *The Cine-Files*. She has published essays in *Camera Obscura*, *Spectator*, *Visual Arts Research*, and *Critical Essays on Mary Wollstonecraft Shelley*.

Notes

1. *The Phantom of the Cinémathèque*, dir. Jacques Richard (2004; New York: Kino Video, 2006), DVD.

2. Rainer Werner Fassbinder, "Six Films by Douglas Sirk," in *The Marriage of Maria Braun: Rainer Werner Fassbinder, Director*, ed. Joyce Rheuban (New Brunswick, NJ: Rutgers University Press, 1986), 197.

3. Nicole Brenez, "A Conversation with Nicole Brenez," *Cinética*, February 20, 2014, http://revistacinetica.com.br/english/198/.

4. An inspiring discussion between Vivian Sobchack and Scott Bukatman published in *Journal of e-Media Studies* addresses the relationship between individual cinematic fascinations and methods of writing and teaching. Sobchack describes how her own research has been motivated by unpredictable and seemingly erratic cinematic interests, and she argues for an openness and flexibility in our approach toward film analysis: "I don't have an agenda of what I'm going to be interested in. . . . Films pop up—and not always in expected places. . . . What is fascinating is trying to figure something out—and somehow, figuring it out doesn't seem to me exactly the same thing as immediately analyzing it. Certainly, I'm very aware of the methodological framework in which I'm operating. However, it's very open and responsive." "Vivian Sobchack in conversation with Scott Bukatman," *Journal of E-Media Studies* 2 (2009), doi: 10.1349/PS1.1938-6060.A.338.

5. In her essay "Writing/Images," Lesley Stern discusses the challenges of writing about the cinema. She writes, "To be in love with words and movies: this is a guarantee that you will live forever in the eighth circle of hell, where love is unrequited, over and over again. But it is also the circle that abuts both the world and paradise." *The Cine-Files* 4 (2013), http://www.thecine-files.com/current-issue-2/guest-scholars/lesley-stern/.

6. James Naremore, "Authorship and the Cultural Politics of Film Production," *Film Quarterly* 44, no. 1 (Autumn 1990): 21.

7. Christian Metz, *The Imaginary Signifier: Psychoanalysis and Cinema* (Bloomington: Indiana University Press, 1977), 15.

8. Nico Baumbach, "All That Heaven Allows: What Is or Was Cinephilia?" *Film Comment* March/April 2012: 48.

9. Metz, *The Imaginary Signifier*, 15.

10. Laura Mulvey, *Fetishism and Curiosity* (Bloomington: Indiana University Press, 1996), 19.

11. Ibid., 23.

12. Ibid., 27.

13. Jonathan Rosenbaum and Adrian Martin, eds., *Movie Mutations: The Changing Face of World Cinephilia* (London: British Film Institute, 2003).

14. Paulo Freire, *Pedagogy of the Oppressed* (Harmondsworth, UK: Penguin, 1970).

15. Mark Edmundson. *Why Read?* (New York: Bloomsbury, 2004), 90.

16. Ibid., 91.

17. André Bazin, *What Is Cinema?* Volume 2 (Berkeley: University of California Press, 1967), 69.

18. Dudley Andrew quotes Serge Daney in *What Cinema Is! Bazin's Quest and Its Charge* (Chichester, UK: Wiley-Blackwell, 2010), 45

19. Peter Elbow first introduced "the believing game" as an appendix essay in his book *Writing Without Teachers* (New York: Oxford University Press, 1973). He later developed the idea in several writings, including "The Believing Game—Methodological Believing," a paper he presented in 2008 at the Conference on College Composition and Communication. It is available in its entirety on his website, http://works.bepress.com/peter_elbow.

20. Peter Elbow, "The Believing Game—Methodological Believing" (paper presented at the annual meeting of the Conference on College Composition and Communication, New Orleans, Louisiana, April 2–5, 2008), 4, http://works.bepress.com/peter_elbow/20/.

21. Ibid., 5–6.

22. Robin Wood, "Papering the Cracks: Fantasy and Ideology in the Reagan Era," in *Movies and Mass Culture*, ed. John Belton (New Brunswick, NJ: Rutgers University Press, 1996), 205.

23. Ibid., 204.

24. Barbara Klinger, *Beyond the Multiplex: Cinema, New Technologies, and the Home* (Berkeley: University of California Press, 2006). In Chapter 4, Klinger summarizes her research about contemporary university students' home viewing practices, noting their penchant for repeat viewings.

25. David Rosenberg, ed., *The Movie That Changed My Life: Great Writers on Their Favorite Films* (New York: Penguin, 1993).

26. Roger Ebert, "The Goonies," RogerEbert.com, January 1, 1985, http://www.rogerebert .com/reviews/the-goonies-1985.

27. See, for example, Paul Willemen, *Looks and Frictions: Essays in Cultural Study and Film Theory* (Bloomington: Indiana University Press, 1994); Robert B. Ray, *The Avant-Garde Finds Andy Hardy* (Cambridge, MA: Harvard University Press, 1995); Robert B. Ray, *How a Film Theory Got Lost and Other Mysteries in Cultural Studies* (Bloomington: Indiana University Press, 2001); Christian Keathley, *Cinephilia and History, or the Wind in the Trees* (Bloomington: Indiana University Press, 2006); George Toles, "Rescuing Fragments: A New Task for Cinephilia," *Cinema Journal* 49, no. 2 (2010): 159–166; and Rashna Wadia Richards, *Cinematic Flashes: Cinephilia and Classic Hollywood* (Bloomington: Indiana University Press, 2013).

28. Ray, *How a Film Theory Got Lost*, 13.

29. David T. Johnson, "The 'Flashing Glimpse' of Cinephilia: What an Unusual Methodology Might Offer Adaptation Studies," *Adaptation* 6 (2013): 35.

30. Laura Mulvey, "Beyond Melodrama and Realism: *Under the Skin of the City* (2001)," in *Film Moments: Criticism, History, Theory*, eds. James Walters and Tom Brown (London: BFI/ Palgrave Macmillan, 2010). Mulvey's essay is also available online, reprinted with her permission in *The Cine-Files* 4 (2013), http://www.thecine-files.com/current-issue-2/guest-scholars /laura-mulvey/.

31. Mulvey, "Beyond Melodrama and Realism," 10.

32. Ibid.

33. Girish Shambu, *The New Cinephilia* (Montreal: Caboose, 2014).

34. See http://girishshambu.blogspot.com and http://filmstudiesforfree.blogspot.com.

5   Movies in the Middle

Cinephilia as Lines of Becoming

Kalling Heck

In their collection *Teaching Film*, Lucy Fischer and Patrice Petro note that film studies has been categorized by the National Research Council as "an emerging discipline" since 1995.[1] Due in part to its location in a wide range of departments, film studies or cinema studies—in all of its multifarious variants—continues to exist in a liminal space between the concrete categories of more established fields, occupying what seems to be a perpetually unsettled state. Fischer and Petro proceed by discussing some of the drawbacks of what they describe as cinema studies' "polymorphism and mobility."[2] But they also touch on the advantages of this unique position: "There is something appealing in the designation of an 'emerging discipline,' since it evokes an ideal of a discipline that is in a constant state of flux and becoming."[3] The goal of this chapter is to think through the advantages of this polymorphic state—particularly given the fact that the field has so clearly "arrived"—by exploring how cinema studies' in-between status is actually a valuable teaching tool. In order to prove the value of this proposition, the topic of cinephilia serves as a useful point of entry into the style of thought that this liminality is uniquely positioned to engender.

This chapter takes up this topic of "emergence" in the hopes of showing how the study of film, thanks in large part to its location in and among such a broad range of approaches and disciplines, is valuable for the very reason of its liminal status, its unstable position, its relationship to becoming. Cinephilia is useful here because it configures the production of knowledge in very particular ways and, in so doing, serves to provoke a productive process that allows film viewers to develop a unique relationship to the objects that they collect and collate. This is all to say that cinephilia is unique in its ability to harness the position of cinema studies, to lean upon its liminality, and to use this in-between status as a lever for producing new ideas.

Theory, broadly defined, will factor into this discussion, but rather than applying theory to the topic at hand, this chapter will endeavor to show how cinephilia constitutes the act of theorizing itself. As Fischer and Petro note, "Though essential, teaching theory is a difficult task, especially since students often expect that discussing films in class will rise only to the level of newspaper reviewing."[4] This is in my experience indeed the case, and I often find that students are blind-sided by theoretical discussion when they had expected to be "discussing movies." This chapter will demonstrate how cinephilia presents a unique solution to the problems of discussing theory at the undergraduate level by showing how the cinephilic process can itself be harnessed as a kind of *doing theory* all its own. What this means is that, like theory, cinephilia can encourage students to see the world anew and to endeavor to interpret and ultimately refigure the world(s) that they encounter, whether inside or outside the confined borders of the projected (or otherwise presented) image. Cinephilia is useful not only in its ability to help organize, connect, and interpret films, which is a significant task, but also as a system for encountering and developing new ideas, and furthermore for doing so in a way that unsettles calcified ways of seeing and knowing.

With the task of exploring the question of cinephilia's value as a uniquely productive epistemology in mind, this chapter is split into two sections. The first, titled "Producing Knowledge," deals closely with cinephilia itself and uses some of the more notable discussions of this term to explore how cinephilia can be a process that helps produce new understandings of things and signs. The second section, titled "Doing Theory," deals more closely with how this productive cinephilia is useful for teaching, and why and how it provides a unique system for helping students think differently about images and indeed about the world. Of course, the take on cinephilia presented here—that of thinking of cinephilia as a productive process akin in many ways to doing theory—is a novel one, and framing cinephilia in this way is surely an alternative vision of the subject.

Fischer and Petro build upon Christian Metz's famous statement, "Cinema is a vast subject, and there are more ways than one to enter it," by adding that it is the field's interdisciplinarity that provides these many ways to enter.[5] This chapter expands this discussion by using the topic of cinephilia not only as a new way to enter but also as a system to explore the proposition of entering into interpretation at all, and therefore as an instrument for thinking through what it means to contend with images in the first place. Ultimately, cinephilia here serves as a way to access the emergent and liminal status of the field of cinema studies and to explore the value of this unique position.

Producing Knowledge

In *Cinephilia and History, or the Wind in the Trees*, Christian Keathley notes, "By fetishizing certain shots or certain actions within shots, the cinephile reminds us of, and asks us to consider anew, the fragmented quality of all films, also reminding us of the inherent fragmentary nature of the filmmaking process."[6] This section takes up the task of addressing this fragmentary quality, and it does so in such a way as to emphasize how the cinephilic process "asks us to consider anew" these images and their statuses. That is, here I will discuss not only what cinephiles do but also what we ask when we do it. My central claim is that the questions that cinephilia asks are valuable ones and that within cinephilia is the potential for a useful style of thought that extends beyond cinema studies.

In order to explore this potential, I begin with the uses of cinephilia itself. In "Cinephilia or the Uses of Disenchantment," Thomas Elsaesser locates a kind of perpetual comparison and its subsequent disappointment at the core of the cinephile's experience. Drawing his line through Proust, Elsaesser asks:

> Savoring the sensed discrepancy between what is and what is expected, constitutes the semiotic act, so to speak, by making this difference the prerequisite for there to be any insight or feeling at all. Could it be that a similarly enacted gap is part of cinephilia's productive disenchantment?[7]

As it does for Marcel Proust in *In Search of Lost Time*, this gap, for Elsaesser, also brings about the cinephile's constant association of images. Elsaesser completes this thought by noting that "the often heard complaint that a film is 'not as good as [the director's] last one' also makes perfect sense because *disappointment redeems memory at the expense of the present*."[8] For Elsaesser, this constant comparison is the definitive task of the cinephile, and the consistent failure of a film to account for the associations with which it is connected yields a productive process that relies on a constant deferral of the current moment by putting it in the service of previous experiences.

Paul Willemen, however, argues what is essentially the opposite. For Willemen it is the "cinephiliac moment"—the "fleeting, evanescent moment" of a particular image—that gives rise to the "emotional" response that the cinephile attempts to capture.[9] This moment, which is not narrative or author dependent, is registered in excess of its meaning and dwelled upon beyond its purpose. In the case of cinephilia, for Willemen, "what is being looked for is a moment or, given that a moment is too unitary, a dimension of a moment which triggers for the viewer either the realisation or the illusion of a realisation that what is being seen is in excess of what is being shown."[10] But Willemen is careful to add that "the moment of revelation is unstable. You cannot predict with any certainty that this moment will be the cinephiliac moment."[11] For Willemen, the finding of these fleeting, revelatory moments constitutes the practice of cinephilia, moments that generate pleasure rather than disenchantment.[12]

My argument is that these divergent systems for rendering cinephilia are connected; the cinephile can simultaneously call upon previous images while experiencing an affective charge from an individuated moment. In order to break apart this binary, though, it must become clear that Elsaesser's deferral and

Willemen's moment are not necessarily mutually exclusive concepts, and that Elsaesser's association of one cinephilic moment with others may occur simultaneously with—and in some cases enact—Willemen's affective charge. Ultimately, this double movement constitutes the productive function of the cinephile's task.

For many theorists of cinephilia, however, the practices it entails—regardless of how they are constructed—are inextricably linked to a particular time and a particular space. Most famously, Susan Sontag vehemently argues that cinema, as of 1996, was suffering from severe degradation and was on the brink of demise. For Sontag, "wonder," central to her sense of what cinema had lost, came about as a result of the place of theatrical exhibition and its unique ability to "kidnap" the viewer. She writes, "to be kidnapped was to be overwhelmed by the physical presence of the image. The experience of 'going to the movies' was part of it."[13] And even more clearly, "to be kidnapped, you have to be in a movie theater, seated in the dark among anonymous strangers."[14]

In addition to spaces, for Sontag, cinephilia is linked to a particular time: the 1960s and 1970s. Sontag argues, "The 1960s and early 1970s was the feverish age of movie-going, with the full-time cinephile always hoping to find a seat as close as possible to the big screen, ideally the third row center. 'One can't live without Rossellini,' declares a character in Bertolucci's 'Before the Revolution' (1964)—and means it."[15] Keathley also locates the heyday of cinephilia in this era. For Keathley, in the 1960s and 1970s "this enthusiasm for film filtered down into general culture to the point that even 'average' moviegoers developed a respect and appreciation for the cinema as the art form for the times, and a large public happily accepted the challenges offered by ambitious, personal, unconventional films."[16]

What cinephilia implies for these authors is a process that is bound both to a particular space, the darkened theater, and a particular era, the 1960s and 1970s. But what about this period and place allows for the encapsulation and repetition that this process demands? For Sontag, "cinephilia implies that films are unique, unrepeatable, magic experiences"; they "kidnap" in the hopes of producing "wonder."[17] But what is unique and unrepeatable about the reproduced image? What is it to be kidnapped without ever leaving a space? And, finally, what begets wonderment? Cinephilia is, for Sontag, an experience that attempted to refind a particular aesthetic linked to a particular era (turn-of-the-century cinema), but this idyllic originary cinema itself relied on an unstandardized system for presentation and even projection. If something unknowable—or "magical"—is the key, then on what grounds can these fixed positions (the theater, the era) claim to be the progenitor of this unexpected, unlocatable, and uncontrollable response? The argument here is that these grounds are not as stable as they seem and that the cinephilic response can arise from a wide array of different occurrences.

Take, for instance, the flower that concludes Abbas Kiarostami's *Where Is the Friend's Home?* (1987). This flower, revealed in the last shot of the film, recalls in a single flourish the entirety of the film while simultaneously declaring its conclusion. Ahmed (Babek Ahmed Poor), whose attempts to return his friend's homework the day before led to an elderly man placing this flower in the book as a gift, has, surprisingly, completed his task. This flower indicates that he and his friend have successfully avoided punishment and that the competing rhetorics of discipline that occupy the film can in fact be navigated—a victory that is declared in such a way that exceeds this simple narrative conclusion and instead declares much more. Perhaps not qualifying for Willemen's "cinephiliac" moment by virtue of its being scripted, this ending nonetheless calls forth an affective charge that exceeds narrative closure. The origin of this charge, though, lies outside the boundaries of the film, as the moment seems to echo a previous moment that, for me, impacts this response: the conclusion of Robert Bresson's *Pickpocket* (1959), in which Michel (Martin LaSalle), the lead, famously states, "To reach you at last, what a strange path I had to take." This too is a moment that summarizes a plot while signaling a kind of triumph, one cued by the swelling of the soundtrack. These two moments coexist for me, inflecting each other with powers that neither can fully hold. And too there is the shot in Andrei Tarkovsky's *The Mirror* (1975) that similarly uses a plant, now a leaf, as a bookmark. This leaf, seen pressed in the book before it is ever seen placed in it, is likewise for me there when Ahmed turns that page.

This series of connections declares a cinephilic moment that carries its affective weight not by virtue of its being outside narrative but by its containing a kind of free-floating connection to those other texts that have moved me. To be clear, there is not disenchantment here, but there is the kind of associative process that Elsaesser considers valuable; and there is likewise no authorial or narrative remove here, but there is the kind of contingent and uncontrollable moment that Willemen finds constitutive of cinephilia. This image is, for me, an instant where the boundaries between the power of the moment and the persistence of the past collapse into a constantly expanding sphere of association and affect. But the future, too, is collapsed into this moment, for as this image reflects previous images, so too does it make space for future discoveries, a constant line of flowers found in an ever-changing book.

But what is of central importance to this interchange among images is the "me." Cinephilia helps me realize that these connections are my own and that they spiral not based on any controllable or standardizable set of principles. This is the lesson of cinephilia: that these connections are always available but also always one's own, an ever-expanding set of vital availabilities that grows not because of a preordered notion, an idea, or some sanctified ground of precise major points, but instead seemingly because of what one finds and connects on one's own. And this is key: teaching cinephilia is never exactly the teaching of film history, or culture, or some particular understanding of a film, genre, cycle, or period. The teaching of cinephilia is the teaching of one's love, for it is love that is the lesson of these connections. Love is one's own, it is to be found and celebrated, but it never quite makes sense outside of one's self. Cinephilia (and love, for that is what cinephilia is) is not about knowing the sanctioned sets of connections among things but about finding connections and knowing that connections can be found.

The cinephilic moment brings about a web of virtual connections that move among past, present, and future all at once, all the while preserving within it the possibilities of even further actualizations. What the cinephile does is collect these possibilities. Gilles Deleuze's term "recollection-image" encapsulates this process:

> Just as we perceive things in the place where they are, and have to place ourselves among these in order to perceive them, we go to look for recollection in the place where it is, we have to place ourselves within a leap into the past in general, into these purely virtual images which have been constantly preserved through time.[18]

Cinephilia can describe this process of going to look for recollection, of taking heed of Deleuze's process and constantly standing ready for just these kinds of moments, moments that themselves expand the possibilities for future recollection-images, allowing for ever deeper and wider connections. Indeed, this is what makes cinephilia unique.

But how, we must now ask, is this process valuable? How is this anything other than an obsessive ritual or an instance of an alarming degree of consumption and accumulation? To answer this question, I must turn to another example: that of a cup of water and an unbroken line. Deleuze, now writing with Felix Guattari, emphasizes the centrality of the line to the kind of movement that they describe as "becoming," the ongoing process whereby the meanings and shapes of things are deterritorialized and then reterritorialized—emptied of meaning and then re-formed in new and different ways. Deleuze and Guattari note,

> A line of becoming is not defined by points that it connects, or by points that compose it; on the contrary, it passes *between* points, it comes up through the middle, it runs perpendicular to the points first perceived, transversally to the localizable relation to distant or contiguous points. A point is always a point of origin. But a line of becoming has neither beginning nor end, departure nor arrival, origin nor destination; to speak of the absence of an origin, to make the absence of an origin the origin, is a bad play on words. A line of becoming has only a middle.[19]

What the cinephile can do is draw this line–outline, based on an ever-expanding sphere of possibilities, these disparate images in an unending system of connected cinephilic moments. This process allows the kind of becoming that Deleuze and Guattari describe, a thinking anew of the connections that are made and that can concretize into meanings, tropes, canons, whatevers. But this thinking anew, this drawing of a new line through these entrancing cinephilic moments, is not merely an action that a viewer can take upon a film. For the process here to take place, cinephilia must not be thought of as the viewer simply reconfiguring the cinematic object but as entering into relation with it—a relation that expands to impact both object and cinephile. What is *learned* here is to be found within these connections themselves; the expansion of this line through these books and flowers does not necessarily generate a tangible and functional concept, but the key is that *it might*. The possibility for new kinds of understanding is opened up again in each of these connections, and the available readings of these scenes must be revised so as to account for the possibility of new points of contact in an expanding network of associations. The lesson of cinephilia is that understandings are always available for reconfiguration and that at any moment images might arise anew to disrupt what appeared coherent and contained.

Take, for instance, the celebrated moment in *Jurassic Park* (Steven Spielberg, 1993) when the *Tyrannosaurus rex* arrives. In this exchange the *T. rex*'s approach is signaled at first through the vibrations in the otherwise insignificant cup of water on the dash of the remotely controlled SUV. This cup, clearly framed so as to reveal its stillness, ripples slightly (Figure 5.1). These ripples then repeat and increase, until finally they are accompanied by the increasing booms of the *T. rex*'s

Figure 5.1. *Jurassic Park* (Steven Spielberg, 1993).

heavy footsteps. Thus, before the animal arrives, the water seems to, and even does, speak. This cup, though, speaks not only of the coming dinosaur, not only the destruction that these booms enfold; it also signals something else. There is another kind of speaking happening here, one that is unbound to any particular origin.

Jane Bennett stresses the importance of using the term *assemblage* in her discussion of objects. Bennett defines assemblages as "ad hoc groupings of diverse elements, of vibrant materials of all sorts. Assemblages are living, throbbing confederates that are able to function despite the persistent presence of energies that confound them from within."[20] These uneven, decentered, heterogeneous collections are, for Bennett, the major way to theorize an agency of *things*. Bennett's things are always inextricably tied to the assemblage(s) that they occupy; they are impossible to pin down because they are themselves assemblages.

The cup, here, is an example par excellence of one of Bennett's "things." At first a dead object with no particular relationship to the events that this film explores, this cup of water comes alive. It awakens and begins to act. It decides, so to speak, to play a role; it stirs (and what better a thing is there for a cup of liquid to do?) and takes part in this series of events. Spielberg's singling out of this thing—an example of his celebrated attention to detail that helps this scene swell with unforeseeable thing-chatter, as his finest scenes do—likewise singles out the ability of these things to speak. What is highlighted here is the ability of this cup of water to exercise what Bennett calls "thing-power"—"the curious ability of inanimate things to animate, to act, to produce effects dramatic and subtle."[21]

The cup, this otherwise insignificant thing, has brought about surprise; it has risen up and acted in ways that could not be accounted for until after the action itself. The cup of water doesn't just imply the dinosaur's approach; it signals toward a world that lurks beneath the narrative of this film. It gestures at a world of assemblages, of irreducible complexity that exceeds context, a world that breaks forth and surprises us in new ways and with new actions. That is, this cup works to impact the drawing of the line and to direct it in new and unexpected directions.

In Jean-Luc Godard's *Two or Three Things I Know About Her* (1967) there is another cup of liquid, this time a cup of coffee (Figure 5.2). When looked into, this cup shows not just the coffee that it contains but also everything else.[22] The cup contains coffee as well as an entire universe of virtual connections that can come to impact interpretation. In Martin Scorsese's *Taxi Driver* (1976) this moment is cited, as Travis Bickle (Robert De Niro) looks into his cup, this time the water actively dissolving an effervescent antacid (Figure 5.3). As the sound of fizzing that accompanies the carbon dioxide dissolving in water overtakes the soundtrack, and the camera slowly tracks in toward the liquid, here too something is seen that is both thing and not thing at all. Within both of these cups is encapsulated the

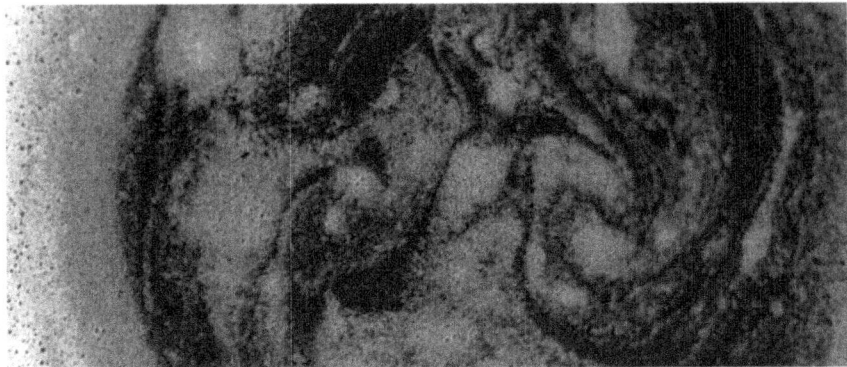

Figure 5.2. *Two or Three Things I Know About Her* (Jean-Luc Godard, 1967).

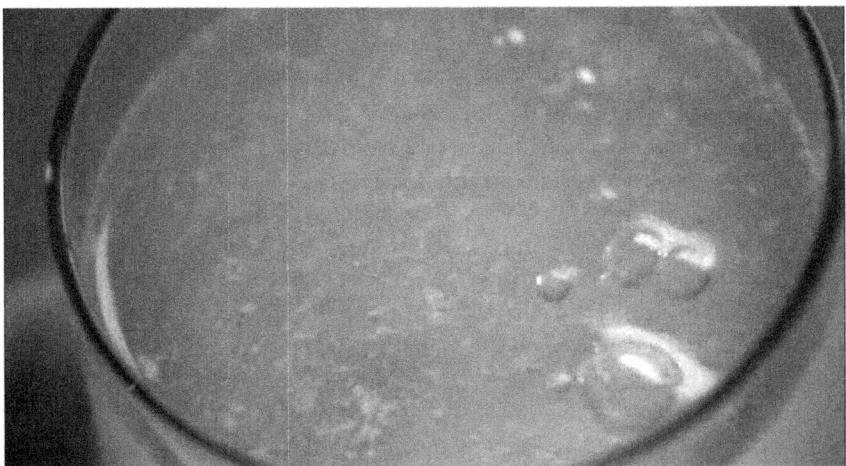

Figure 5.3. *Taxi Driver* (Martin Scorsese, 1976).

entirety of things, and too within them is each other. The reference by Scorsese—brought about by the power of Godard's moment—is a product of this earlier cup, and we can see in this fizzy liquid the assemblage that it has formed with the original cup as readily as can be seen the assemblage that is the carbon dioxide and the liquid fusing into a new mixture. But within Godard's cup there is also Scorsese's, the virtual action that was this reference, the unexpected that can arise through a series of unknowable connections that are yet to come.

Spielberg's cup also contains the universe. It points to the connection between this thing and all the other things that could be—and already are—acting with it and within it. When the characters see and are acted upon by this cup (after all, it helps in warning them in advance of the *T. rex*), it impacts the events that unfold, and therefore, narratively, this cup has played a role in determining the becoming status of those who interact with it—viewer included. Rather than recede from knowledge, this cup is listened to, and in this listening the humans who interact with it are subsequently capable of acting in new ways. The cinephile too can listen to this cup and in so doing enter into new and unknowable potentials for action.

But what it means to listen to these cups remains in this example unfinished. To listen here is to draw from these objects connections to each other but also to remain open to other potentially as yet unformed connections (other cups of water? other charging dinosaurs? other things altogether?). This is what cinephilia can do. Bennett's assemblages are not unitary, prefigured sets of things, or if they are, they are also something more. These assemblages arise unexpectedly from unforeseen and unforeseeable arrangements, and they are indeed always already breaking apart and into other arrangements as they proceed, being undone even as they are just initiated. What a cinephile does is maintain a tentative relationship to an assemblage. Or, to put it another way, what a cinephile does is allow a new assemblage, any assemblage that moves, to arise. Cinephilia institutes an awareness of assemblage as assemblage, of connection as connection, and this is why it is valuable. What it means to suggest that cinephilia holds this essential relationship to becoming is not that it alone can reveal new readings that a non-cinephile has no access to; it means that a cinephilic experience renders available new modes of connection and, even more importantly, the vantage from which to re-view these connections. For through cinephilia all connections must be seen as conditional and imbricated within a web of variation.

My connection to these cups does not in itself yield a particular or particularly compelling understanding of how these images interact, but it does constitute an available grounds for inquiry. In this regard cinephilia is significantly aligned with teaching, as the task becomes not only to find something new but also to uncover directions for these findings, to take connections like these and to begin to make them useful, universalizable, and coherent. The cinephile has discovered these connections and now may proceed to complement, contrast, and expand these discoveries. This is the path of research, but through cinephilia the beginning of research can be found, an origin that is grounded in a unique interplay between affect and association. Cinephilia privileges experience, but it does so in such a way as to always couch experience in an awareness that the connections that arise are useful but also necessarily contingent.

Deleuze and Guattari say of this process, "The line . . . does not link the wasp to the orchid, any more than it conjugates or mixes them, it passes between them, carrying them away in a shared proximity in which the discernibility of points disappears."[23] This cinephilia, what now must be described as a particular cinephilia, draws this line; it connects these disparate points not in the hopes of simply join-ing what seems incommensurate but in the hopes of dissolving the boundaries that seem to immobilize these images, that attempt to distinguish these points. The creation of a coherent whole is not the goal here; what is at stake is the con-stant reforging of connections in the hopes of finding new modes for thought. This cinephilia is helpful in that it refuses to vacate its status as middle. It refuses to figure the boundaries of the objects it can connect; it opens up new modes of action while refusing to foreclose possibilities. This cinephilia is ineffective in that it refuses figuration and therefore can never concretize the connections it brings forth, for any concretization would bring an end to its line. It is, like cinema stud-ies as a discipline, perpetually in the middle, and there it must remain, a system for rethinking things but never for allowing those things to fully take shape. This kind of cinephile functions in the dark, unceasingly forging reconnections but never bringing them into the light. Cinephilia is then truly valuable as a primer for how to break apart the boundaries that govern these objects, and it is the task of the cinephile (and the student) to deploy this project, to draw this line and make it known in the hopes of upsetting the regime of signs and showing that these things *can* be upset, a lesson that extends outward beyond merely the boundaries of the screen. What is learned thanks to this connection of cups is not a concrete idea but a way of encountering images and, subsequently, of reading them. In making a claim about, say, *Jurassic Park*, one must put these connections to work, to calcify the available understandings and bring them forth. But cinephilia is also useful in returning these calcified connections back to the realm of indetermination and, in so doing, allowing them to be revised and renewed.

Doing Theory

In a short essay on his ideas and practices for teaching film theory, Edward Bra-nigan describes film theory thusly:

> Film theory concerns the conditions and possibilities of film by addressing all films, or at least a very large number of produced films, including films not yet created. . . . What is at stake in film theory is the scale or scope of our thinking . . . Film theory does not provide a recipe or justification for the interpretation(s) of a particular film but rather examines large-scale institu-tions, conditions of or for intelligibility, and networks of changing values from which texts can and may emerge.[24]

Branigan is distinguishing film theory from criticism, and his primary tool for dividing the two is scale. Where criticism deals with particular objects and makes claims that apply primarily to an interpretation of the object under discussion, theory uses those objects to make more general claims—claims that ripple out-ward and impact things other than just our understanding of a particular film.

One set of concerns that theory helps a student understand is not only or necessarily a particular film but the circumstances that might allow for a particular interpretation—what Branigan calls the "conditions for intelligibility." Cinephilia, as described here—what with its limitless connections among and through films and constant upkeep and revision of these connections—conditions a unique process whereby the means of interpretation come into sight. For the cinephile whose cups of water carry a line among a series of films of vastly different times and spaces, and who draws these connections in an order that disrupts the coherence of direct allusion, the conditions whereby this unique kind of intelligibility is created come immediately to the fore. It is the atomization implied in this process (as represented in the previous section by the "I"s and "me"s present in the connections drawn) that comes to beg the conditions of interpretation—the idiosyncrasy of cinephilia, its forging lines that are always individuated, leads the cinephile (at least, the one discussed here) to ask *why* these lines and these connections. Of course, what always becomes clear in this process is how unstable the conditions of these understandings are, and subsequently the grounds for interpretation or the theory itself becomes the point of interest.

What cinephilia encourages is a process whereby theory, under Branigan's definition, becomes immediately available. This is not to say that the cinephilic process can account for any particular argument but that cinephilia serves as a coherent and quite useful primer, readying students to engage in theory (whether *a* theory or theory generally) as a way of looking, not dissimilar to the ones they have already developed—readying students, that is, to begin to discover the means for drawing their own lines of connection. To Branigan, "when film is considered as a discursive practice or text, it becomes a trajectory that is linked to social, historical and language issues exposed by theory."[25] Cinephilia is relevant here in that it turns each moment of a film into a trajectory, a potential movement that points to some other moment or trajectory, conditioned by an expansive web of social and historical circumstances and understandings and constituted by the contingent relationship between viewer and film.

To Branigan, the strength of theory lies in its relationship to how daily practices are encountered and navigated, making the teaching of theory an impactful and broadly valuable experience outside of simply understanding a film: "In a strict sense, films consume only a tiny sliver of one's time during a year. Nevertheless, films remain important because of profound ties to our perception of the world—to how we transform mere occasions and disconnected actions into familiar and standardized events and scenarios that demand our participation."[26] Thus, what film theory allows is a way to look at the world and see how habit has structured perception, ultimately providing a way to disrupt these perceptions and see the world anew, to reconfigure what we see and perceive and to arrange these meanings in new and valuable ways. The epistemology of the cinephile engages in just this process. The activity and interest invested in making far-reaching and highly individuated connections encourage this new way of seeing, in such a way as to embolden students, alerting them to their ability to perceive these habituated modes of vision. But it also reveals the contingency of these connections and the potential for the disruption of these narratives. The task of the cinephile is not only to "transform mere occasions and disconnected actions into familiar and standardized events and scenarios" but also to see how these actions are grounded and to find an opening that helps to see how these standardizations take shape. Ultimately, students encouraged in their cinephilia are left in a position where they are asked to build upon the cinephile's process, not only to ask what has led them to where they are but also, thanks to the context of the classroom, to have them examine these conditions, to have their interpretations verified, and, finally, to justify what has become a way of looking. Cinephilia provides a system for them to see the world too as narrativized and standardized and encourages them to discuss the conditions and, perhaps most importantly, the effects of this standardization. What is unique about cinephilia, finally, is its indecision. If interpretation concretizes, then cinephilia disrupts; it breaks things apart by pairing them with new and different things.

In the hopes of making practical what has been thus far a relatively abstract discussion, it is best now to return to one of my own classrooms as an example of the process outlined earlier. The class in question, titled "Introduction to Comedy," is a sophomore-level cinema studies course offered to help introduce students—both majors and non—to the field.[27] The sophomore-level class provides, I think, the perfect opportunity to introduce students to the idea of thinking about movies as objects worthy of thoughtful analysis and is therefore also useful in asking them to think about how they come to knowledge of a film.

This class is topical rather than a broader introduction, and it circulates around the persistence of comedy in American cinema. It is split into two halves, the first dealing with the history of American comedy—its functioning in relation to culture and the conditions of its production and development. In this first half, the students are asked to think about comedy as a mode, the boundaries that it adheres to and the standardized systems through which it meets (or fails to meet) its goals. The written texts that accompany the screenings provide interpretations or contextualizations of the films in relation to their historical moment, in terms of both industrial circumstances and American culture in general. The idea of this first portion of the class is to introduce students to a broad collection of American films from across a range of time periods (roughly one per decade until the 1980s) and to simply show films that have enticed me, for whatever reason, in my development as a cinephile.

The films shown in this first section are selected in order to forge some of the grounds for connection central to the kind of cinephilia outlined earlier. Harpo

Marx's unique mode of destruction (and disregard for narrative) in *Duck Soup* (Leo McCarey, 1933), for instance, or Jimmy Stewart's unforgettable portrayal of drunkenness in *The Philadelphia Story* (George Cukor, 1940) provide exceptional moments that, later in the class, will be mirrored in other films. But one of the things that is most striking about this first half of the class is seeing the strange and, for me, surprising moments that students single out as significant. Buster Keaton's slipping on a banana peel in *The Cameraman* (1928), for instance, took on particular value for a student, and the persistence of banana peels (and their relationship to the irony and self-awareness of the comedic mode) in our subsequent screenings ended up being a focus of many students in the class. The banana peel slip (or failure to slip, as the joke is so often subverted) is the quintessential *gag* in Donald Crafton's sense of the term: the non-narrative (or in excess of narrative) comedic element that "is marked by affective response, not set forms or clear logic."[28] The selection of this particular repeated gesture was, in light of this discussion, quite valuable, as the gag itself is structured very much like Willemen's model for cinephilia. That is, these gags operate in excess of narrative and provide some charge of pleasure. The banana peel gag in particular relies furthermore on a form of comparison, the previous presence of comedic banana peels informing this particular one and contributing to the response that it can generate. Itself mirroring the productive dynamic of past as imbricated within present that I have located in cinephilia more broadly, this banana peel recurred throughout the semester in our screenings, and its ability to simultaneously point to the present and the past provided an entry point into the readings and the class in general for a number of my students, a cinephilic beginning of sorts that pointed to new connections waiting ahead. Comedy is particularly useful in this regard, as the structure of gags so often mirrors cinephilia's own structure, particularly as it pertains to time. The readings supplied in this portion of the class provide the background necessary to locate, evaluate, and, ultimately, categorize these comedic moments in various different ways, allowing these kinds of histories to be built.

There is, however, an irreconcilable divide between the approach of this class—indeed, I would contend, the approach of any class with similar aims—and the thrust of this chapter, a divide that circulates around the process of curation. That is, the films presented in this course have been selected by me and ordered in such a way as to encourage the kinds of connections I have found essential to my own cinephilia, but this very ordering is exactly the opposite of the cinephilic process. This class, at least in its first half, is controlled, ordered, and decidedly unspontaneous. Herein lies the difficulty in teaching this kind of cinephilia: it must take place on the part of the viewer and the viewer alone, and it can never be counted or controlled, for in any ordering the spontaneity of cinephilia is already muffled. What, this discussion must now address, can be done to maintain the focus on unordered experience that, for me, is so important to cinephilia? What separates this class from one on traditional film analysis? And furthermore, how might a class encourage the kind of cinephilia described here? The advantages of this class, to extend a brief rejoinder, are hopefully addressed by the trajectory of its second half.

While the first half of the class is not necessarily easy, it is not designed to be altogether unfamiliar. The second half, however, is intended to complicate, or at least to destabilize, the first. In this second half, we study contemporary comedies—films selected in the hopes that the students are generally familiar with them. These films are paired with theories of comedy and laughter. The screenings consist generally of films that are widely available and have made some kind of impact culturally in the last few decades; they range from *Superbad* (Greg Mottola, 2007) to *Dazed and Confused* (Richard Linklater, 1993) to *Wet Hot American Summer* (David Wain, 2001). These films are then paired with readings from a wide range of theorists, including Mikhail Bakhtin, Sigmund Freud, Henri Bergson, and Simon Critchley. In this second half, the students are asked to evaluate films by putting them in relation to some of the previous films we have viewed. A common approach that I employ is to ask at the start of class which film they were reminded of in watching the contemporary one, and we proceed from that point to a discussion of particular moments that connect those two objects. One of my goals in navigating the class discussions in this latter half of the semester is to push upon the categories that cemented our earlier discussion, to ask whether *Talladega Nights: The Ballad of Ricky Bobby* (Adam McKay, 2006) shares the politics of *Duck Soup* or just its style of gag and whether these things can be easily disentangled.

In this second half, some of the advantages of cinephilia can finally be addressed. During this portion of the class, the students are asked to form connections among films that they have only recently discovered and films with which they are generally familiar. To meet this goal, I deliberately screen comedies that they have likely seen previously in the hopes of encouraging them to draw connections that are less orchestrated, less obviously predetermined. Films the students have likey seen before, particularly popular comedies with which they feel a strong connection, are in my experience those that they perceive as most calcified but that can also hold a privileged place in a student's familiarity with cinema.[29] Asking students to use these familiar texts to draw connections undermines my position as progenitor of meaning and positions students to produce their own understandings of these films that they know so well (indeed that they often know far better than I do). The readings in this second half likewise encourage students to draw wider and more daring connections. Rather than providing traditional analyses of the films we have watched (analyses that are significant in understanding the methods and reach of the cinema studies field—hence their position in the first half of the class), these readings generally predate or otherwise never directly address a film we have screened. Instead, these readings offer broader insights into humor and comedy, providing useful lenses but never proposing anything in particular about the films we have watched. Students are left to produce their own avenues for inquiry, which arise through their own means of understanding the content of the class. This approach does not provide a radical reconfiguration of the cinema studies classroom, but it does shift the emphasis from my experience of cinephilia to the students', and this is key to realizing the unique advantages of cinephilia as a model for interacting with films and texts more broadly. In this class, the students are asked to discover their own relationship to the films we have watched, and this activity is presented here as one that is continuous, taking place regardless of how many times a film has been revisited.

A primary goal of this class is to ask students to look at unfamiliar films in a familiar way and then to look at familiar films in an unfamiliar way. Furthermore, this class first asks students to think about the historical, cultural, and industrial conditions of a genre and then asks them to think about the groundings and functions of comedy in general. Its trajectory, in terms of the readings, is to request that students move from specific to broad discussions, or, per Branigan's definitions, from criticism to theory. But the ordering of the movies too asks students to draw connections between what is new and what they already know. The fact that the genre is so clearly available and familiar puts students in a position, ideally, where diverse films like *Duck Soup* and *The Philadelphia Story* require that they make very different kinds of connections to what they already think of as "American comedy." But this class also strives to group far-reaching films together into a coherent collection, despite their differences and dividing lines. The films in the second half ask students to rethink what they already know about these contemporary films by putting the students' previous knowledge in proximity to general (and quite demanding) discussions of the conditions of laughter and comedy. As an introduction to the field, then, this class not only highlights the centrality of interpretation but also asks students to draw upon their experiences of cinema (or the moving image broadly defined) in informing and pushing upon their understandings of the objects under discussion. Cinephilia conditions this system of reception, asking students to draw their own lines, always with an awareness of their being in the middle. Students are asked to embrace what they have seen and felt in watching the film and any connections they have drawn regarding it (particularly in relation to the other films they have seen). They are then presented with the task of justifying these pleasures and indeed of exploring the grounds of their responses.

These paratactic connections generate the kind of cinephilia that I have outlined in this chapter. The connections between texts and the subsequent eruption of moments that link texts together in lines of meaning that never reach a coherent conclusion are generated by linking new and old, strange and familiar, images and ideas, and then asking students to think through what they saw, thought, and felt while experiencing these films and readings. The discussion portion of this course, then, takes on a special value in that the students are free to verify and defend what they have connected. Given this approach, simply asking leading questions like "Why did you find it funny?" takes on particular significance, as they demand that students draw some connection from their experience of the film to a general understanding of humor and furthermore to another film they have watched.

Of course, the students' connections will vary greatly from one to the next, but this is the idea. The function of this class is never to come to a consensus or to arrive at a meaning but always to forge forward in the creation of new connections—an unending process that demands the constant collection and subsequent revision of ideas and ways of seeing. Ideally, this process will seep out and encourage students to gather their cinephilia and employ it as a way to see the world, a way to look at things and allow those things to interact with all the virtual connections that their past and future can allow, helping them to break apart calcified systems of knowledge and update them as well as allowing both the object of discussion and the student the space to constantly be renewed. The vision of cinephilia presented here contends that, for instance, a previous screening of *Some Like It Hot* (Billy Wilder, 1959) and discussion of Bergson's views on laughter can generate a new way of seeing *Billy Madison* (Tamra Davis, 1995)—or indeed any of these three texts. In light of this contention, the task of this class must be to avoid any particular reading of these objects and to instead encourage an understanding of the way that texts and the ideas that they contain move forward and backward through time, constantly in revision and constantly creating new lines and new directions for thought.

Speaking of what he refers to as "the ignorant schoolmaster," the pedagogical approach whereby the instructor renounces the position of authority over knowledge, Jacques Rancière presents a productive, if atomized, vision of learning that allows for the kinds of connections that are central to this discussion. According to Rancière,

> He [the ignorant schoolmaster] does not teach his pupils *his* knowledge, but orders them to venture into the forest of things and signs, to say what they have seen and what they think of what they have seen, to verify it and have it verified. What is unknown to him is the inequality of intelligence. Every distance is a factual distance and each intellectual act is a path traced between a form of ignorance and a form of knowledge, a path that constantly abolishes any fixity and hierarchy of positions with their boundaries.[30]

What Rancière here refers to as the venturing into the forest of things and signs is exactly the kind of process that cinephilia provides. Encouraged in their cinephilic wanderings, students can be confident in their ability to see a world where linkages come to disrupt meaning as readily as they clarify it, and where their knowledge of a film (or whatever else) can constantly be renewed. Cinephilia provides a way to encounter the world that unbinds concretized and paralyzed ways of seeing and to discover anew one's own relationships to these objects. That is, cinephilia helps make available a vision of the world as emergent—and indeed as liminal, unsettled, and always-in-the-middle as the field that unifies these examinations.

KALLING HECK is Lossett Visiting Assistant Professor of Media & Visual Culture at the University of the Redlands. His work addresses continental philosophy as it pertains to global art cinema, focusing on films made in the wake of transitions from authoritarianism or totalitarianism to democracy.

Notes

1. Lucy Fischer and Patrice Petro, "Introduction: Memories of Underdevelopment," in *Teaching Film*, eds. Lucy Fischer and Patrice Petro (New York: Modern Language Association, 2012), 3.

2. Ibid.

3. Ibid.

4. Lucy Fischer and Patrice Petro, "Introduction to Part 1: Theory and Representation," in *Teaching Film*, eds. Lucy Fischer and Patrice Petro (New York: Modern Language Association, 2012), 16.

5. Quoted in Lucy Fischer and Patrice Petro, "Introduction to Part 3: Interdisciplinarities," in *Teaching Film*, eds. Lucy Fischer and Patrice Petro (New York: Modern Language Association, 2012), 161.

6. Christian Keathley, *Cinephilia and History, or the Wind in the Trees* (Bloomington: Indiana University Press, 2006), 39.

7. Thomas Elsaesser, "Cinephilia or the Uses of Disenchantment," in *Cinephilia: Movies, Love and Memory*, eds. Marijke de Valck and Malte Hagener (Amsterdam: Amsterdam University Press, 2005), 33.

8. Ibid.

9. Paul Willemen, "Through the Glass Darkly: Cinephilia Reconsidered," in *Looks and Frictions: Essays in Cultural Studies and Film Theory* (Bloomington: Indiana University Press, 1994), 232–233.

10. Ibid., 247.

11. Ibid., 236.

12. Ibid., 240.

13. Susan Sontag, "The Decay of Cinema," *New York Times*, February 25, 1996, http://www .nytimes.com/1996/02/25/magazine/the-decay-of-cinema.html.

14. Ibid.

15. Ibid.

16. Keathley, *Cinephilia and History*, 2.

17. Sontag, "The Decay of Cinema."

18. Gilles Deleuze, *Cinema 2: The Time-Image*, trans. Hugh Tomlinson and Robert Galeta (New York: Continuum, 1989), 78.

19. Gilles Deleuze and Felix Guattari, *A Thousand Plateaus: Capitalism and Schizophrenia*, trans. Brian Massumi (Minneapolis: University of Minnesota Press, 1987), 293.

20. Jane Bennett, *Vibrant Matter: A Political Ecology of Things* (Durham, NC: Duke University Press, 2010), 23–24.

21. Ibid., 6.

22. Godard's cup, and its capacity to contain things other than simply coffee, is often discussed. For perhaps the best example, see John Mullarkey, *Refractions of Reality* (New York: Palgrave Macmillan, 2009), 163.

23. Deleuze and Guattari, *A Thousand Plateaus*, 294.

24. Edward Branigan, "Teaching Film Theory," in *Teaching Film*, eds. Lucy Fischer and Patrice Petro (New York: Modern Language Association, 2012), 27.

25. Ibid., 28.

26. Ibid., 29.

27. I would be remiss if I did not mention the inspiration and help of Brian Price and Ben Schneider in the creation of this class.

28. Donald Crafton, "Pie and Chase: Gag, Spectacle and Narrative in Slapstick Comedy," in *Classical Hollywood Comedy*, eds. Kristine Brunovska Karnick and Henry Jenkins (New York: Routledge, 1995), 109.

29. I have elsewhere experimented with taking into account what the students have seen in the scheduling of the class itself. This was done in the hopes of ensuring that they have seen some of the films previously outside the context of the class. It has been successful, in my experience, in terms of decentralizing the classroom, but it presents a variety of difficulties in terms of finding useful readings and ensuring the quality of the discussions.

30. Jacques Rancière, *The Emancipated Spectator*, trans. Gregory Elliot (London: Verso, 2009), 11.

6 Audiovisual Pleasure and Narrative Cinema

Cristina Álvarez López and Adrian Martin

Adrian:

Alain Badiou, at a recent American workshop, spoke wisely about the teacher/ student relationship, which he cast, in philosophical terms, as the dialogue—or nondialogue—between the *elder* and the *young*.[1] His remarks suggest to me that the teacher, naturally and necessarily, always speaks of the past, is in fact consumed and obsessed by it—for whatever degree of wisdom he or she possesses comes from having lived through a certain slice of historical/biological/cultural time, having seized it, been a part of it, and reflected on its significance. For the teacher, the past is the place where, as Neil Young once sang, "all our changes" took place; and now that it has receded a little, it is also the space that allows reflective resifting, synthesis, maybe even a little revelation. This is when teachers start citing, passionately, and with a mad, intense glimmer in their eyes, the likes of Marcel Proust, Walter Benjamin, and W. G. Sebald: all the great poets and/or prosecutors of a remembered, personal history.

The lived past carries a burning meaning, a lesson, that only the teacher can impart—and urgently so, before the flame of that message dies in the dusty oblivion of passing time, no witnesses left. "I have all I can do to keep the memory of Preston Sturges alive among readers and students who seem to be forgetting more and more of the past with each passing year of media overload," wrote Andrew Sarris in 1978.[2] The student, on the other hand, is largely unmoved by all this fussy focus on the past and its truth. He or she may see the relevance, even the importance, of History; but all he or she really cares about is the present, the *now* he or she dramatically inhabits, with all its pressing problems. Retrospection is a luxury that the young cannot afford; for the teacher, by contrast, retrospection may be the only real luxury he or she *can* afford, in his or her often materially pinched situation.

Cinephilia is caught up in this drama; it cannot help but be ensnared by it, because there is no one canon or system of "movie love" that can simply be taught or shared, at all times and all over the world. Sometimes we entertain this fantasy that there are certain films and filmmakers—*Johnny Guitar* (Nicholas Ray, 1954)? *Black Narcissus* (Michael Powell and Emeric Pressburger, 1947)? *Tokyo Story* (Yasujirō Ozu, 1953)? *Vertigo* (Alfred Hitchcock, 1958)? *Touch of Evil* (Orson Welles, 1958)? *Le Mépris* (Jean-Luc Godard, 1963)? *The Conformist* (Bernardo Bertolucci, 1970)? *Ali: Fear Eats the Soul* (Rainer Werner Fassbinder, 1974)?—that embody the eternal verities and sacred texts of the cinephile passion; sometimes we witness, powerfully in action, the charismatic transmission of shards of a certain canon from a pedagogic figurehead (on the mythic model of Henri Langlois) to a younger crowd. In this dream, cinephilia is something that *pre-exists* any one of us and into which we are veritably *initiated*: the familiar language of sects, tribes, chapels, and churches.

But cinephilia is a thousand, local, specific systems of taste, culture, and politics. It's never exactly the same thing; it changes and mutates according to where, when, and how it formulates itself. I am not saying that cinephilia is only ever local or nationalistic: quite the contrary, because it forms itself, complexly, in a series of associations, identifications, and projections, and this cross-cultural and transnational pattern or mesh differs each time. A Cuban cinephile sect in the 1970s, say, may bash its fighting culture together from bits of old *Cahiers du Cinéma* issues, film-club programming based on titles gleaned from *Film Culture* magazine or Amos Vogel's book *Film as a Subversive Art*, some Super 8 movies by local artists, a musical inspiration, favorite works of fiction, a few new and challenging premieres unveiled at a festival, and so on. Each cinephile group bears the responsibility for writing its own legend and somehow immortalizing it; if not, the rest of us are left with the same old, tired, supposedly founding tales of the Parisian Nouvelle Vague, the New German Cinema, Italian neorealism, and other lazy, curricular favorites.

You are a teacher of film, and a cinephile. The question—and the agony—you will always encounter before, during, and after any course you devise is: What is going to get across, what will communicate the cinephile passion to your young students—and hopefully ignite it within them? What is the magic madeleine to trigger their initiation into a collective past that they have not personally lived, and thus cannot remember or reremember? Will it be Howard Hawks's *Rio Bravo* (1959)? Jerry Lewis's *The Ladies Man* (1961)? Roberto Rossellini's *Viaggio in Italia* (1954)? Andrzej Wajda's *Ashes and Diamonds* (1958)? Jean-Luc Godard and Jean-Pierre Gorin's *Tout va bien* (1972)? Samuel Fuller? Glauber Rocha? Satyajit Ray? These are all examples that have failed, dismally, for me in classrooms at various times and in various places since the 1980s. Not always, but enough times that it hurts.

The disconnect between an old dream—which can sometimes mean or say little once it is unmoored from its initial cultural network—and whichever piece of the *now* that our students happen to identify with, can be extreme. And disconcerting to discover, as that abyss opens up under your teacherly feet. Hawks is "moving"? Lewis is "funny"?? Rocha is "radical"??? Many students experience the cinephile hits circa 1950–1975 as weak, incomprehensible, utterly unaffecting emanations from a distant, alien, likely dead planet—and no amount of fervent, scholarly contextualization from you, dear teacher, will alter that first impression. And yet this is a completely understandable situation, from the viewpoint of youth. Who wants to be told, ordered, commanded to love Welles, Renoir, Godard, Akerman, Mizoguchi, Costa, or anybody else?

This is a scene of crisis: a clash of incommensurable tastes belonging to teacher and student. And while, contrary to the old saying, tastes can certainly be accounted for, culturally and historically, they cannot ever be rationally wrangled, managed, or negotiated to the point of a successful victory for either party; at most, an uneasy détente ensues. Teachers are always horrified by their students' tastes—in everything. I remember, in the 1990s, thinking that my students who worshipped Hal Hartley had missed out on the "real thing," which was Mark Rappaport in the 1970s; now, when students want to write theses about the mind-numbing movies of Mumblecore, I wish they could have experienced some Hal Hartley!

Cinephilia cannot really be taught—or, if so, only as a historic object, disconnected from the present, which is a dangerous (and boring) path. More usually, it is not taught at all; few, it seems, attempt it. A long and bloody campaign was fought, decades ago, against "film appreciation" courses or "best films" curricula based solely on the professor-in-charge's subjective opinions. The result was a swing to objectivity, empiricism, and artistic non-evaluation: films can be interesting, be symptomatic, stand for something, be an intersection or conjunction of forces, but they are not for the most part masterpieces to be obediently memorized. And, no doubt, much good came from that switch-up: for starters, it separated film, TV, and media studies from the Great Books mentality that ruled university literature pedagogy well into the 1980s—and is still well and truly alive in lower levels of the educational system today.

The cinephilic spirit can be transmitted, at least to some students, in other, less direct ways—through group affects like enthusiasm, humor, excitement—but no guidebook can tell you how to institutionalize and repeat such affects successfully, from semester to semester and year to year. Cinephilia in the classroom is, therefore, hit-and-miss—and is sometimes best left at the door. Outside the classroom, other kinds of transmission/initiation can occur, and these can, alas, be rather elitist: I recall hearing an Oxbridge literary scholar boast to an audience how, while in the classroom everything was officially Classics and High Art Modernism; later, in the "tea room," especially selected students would be shown, clandestinely, some particularly artistic comic books, as jazz music played softly in the corner. Thankfully, there are more egalitarian versions of such tales that come from the merry, lusty worlds of film clubs, camps, and festivals.

Each of us finds his or her own way to cinephilia and to a community (small or large) of like-minded cinephiles—now, in the Internet age, more than ever. Speaking personally, I came, after many years, to an impasse concerning teaching and lecturing about film, since so much of it (at least in terms of screening selections) was based on my own enthusiasms. Fortunately for me, I discovered a detour that allowed a substantial rewiring of the three-way relation between film, teacher, and student: a course, mixing practice and theory, devoted to the audiovisual essay—a form I began creatively exploring in collaboration with my partner Cristina Álvarez López in 2012.

It took me a while after starting this kind of practice-based research to realize that working with the images and sounds of others breaks the type of seductive attraction that teaching—and, even more so, decades of critical writing—fosters: namely, that by speaking about, analyzing, processing, and filtering hundreds or thousands of movies, you make them, in some secret, unavowed sense, *yours,* bending them all subtly to fit and reflect the terms of your own literary or performative sensibility. And maybe that is what all the great "old school" criticism in the arts has always been about: seeing, reading, hearing, and understanding movies, for a precious moment or two, through the sensibility of that Big Other, the critic or teacher, rather than through yourself and your own ego, not to mention the prison of your own accumulated taste and culture. It's a great tradition of criticism. But the audiovisual essay, by putting us in such close contact with the filmic materials, strips out that filter and puts another kind of engagement, another kind of relation, in its place.

Cristina:

When Adrian and I began to teach our course on audiovisual essays, we were very aware of the paradox at the heart of cinephilia: a collective feeling—a shared love or appreciation of cinema—that is formed upon the individual, very personal relations, shared between the members of this community, with certain films and filmmakers. We wanted to acknowledge this paradox and take it further in order to achieve some kind of equilibrium between the different cinephilias grouped in a class—ours, and those of each particular student—and to find a way to work generatively with that multiplicity rather than enforcing one code (i.e., our code) of cinephilia.

We assigned two different exercises during the course. For the first, we chose three films that we consider rich and special, with potential to be studied audiovisually—but also three films that express something about our love and understanding of cinema. (These "canonical" films—we don't announce them as that—have included *The Night of the Hunter* [Charles Laughton, 1955], *Cat People* [Jacques Tourneur, 1942], *Alphaville* [Jean-Luc Godard, 1965], and *Point Blank*

[John Boorman, 1967].) Unsurprisingly, most students picked the most recent example we offered, which was the one they could most "relate" to on a personal level, Lynne Ramsay's *We Need to Talk About Kevin* (2011). But, even so, they were inheriting our choices, our canon, and it was revealing to see how they worked with them through their own perspective and not through ours, as we did not lecture on, screen, or even introduce these particular films to the class. Later, for the second assignment, we let them pick the films they wanted to work with, giving them the chance to connect with their own cinephilia but also challenging them to express something about it, beyond simply their liking or taste for those films.

Before this course, I had taught classes on particular filmmakers outside the academic environment, but, unlike Adrian, I had never had to assess or grade students' work. So, for me, it was difficult to tell what they were really getting from our classes; any teacher knows that students' facial expressions are not, thank God, the most reliable barometer for judging the impact of one's teaching! I have, however, read numerous academic essays by students, and I have rarely felt a strong cinephilic emotion coming from them. In the worst cases, cinema is almost completely absent, reduced to something anecdotal, barely noticed amid the stream of comments referring to the story, the plot, the characters, and so on. In the best cases (and this is also tellingly alarming), cinema is subordinated to the thought of important figures, becoming an illustration or confirmation of a theory—as proof or evidence of something supposedly higher. None of these options lets cinephilia breathe on the page.

What we propose in our course on audiovisual essays is a mixture of research, analysis, critical thinking, and artistic creation. For us, the form has to offer some insight about the films, but it also needs to work as an artistic object in itself. In academic cinema studies, the habit of quoting previous, key texts in the field is a common, even desirable practice. That's understandable: it demonstrates that students have done their homework, that they have read and familiarized themselves with prior studies. However, we have observed that this does not always help students develop their own thinking and response to films, let alone their own "voice" or sensibility as potential critics (or filmmakers). The heavy weight of quoted authority also has a dangerous edge: paralyzing the students' own creativity, their own invention, and annulling the relation between them and the films.

The audiovisual essay has been saluted as the form that finally allows us to quote, grasp, or *attain* films, with reference to Raymond Bellour's classic 1975 essay on the "unattainable text," often misread today, but it is also a highly *transformative* practice: it addresses the film through its quotable elements but, by doing so, it creates something new.[3] If there is one thing we have stressed in this course, it is that the students need to do their own thinking, to bring something of their own, to enter into a process of discovery driven by exploration, experimentation, and subjectivity. For many of them, this is liberating; for others, usually those with a more theoretical background, it is a challenge: making an audiovisual essay implies that one must rely less on what one knows beforehand and be more open to what one learns during the process.

Even the act of inserting a written quotation into a short audiovisual essay implies a series of aesthetic decisions that are not faced in written essays, where this practice is largely standardized: you need to choose a font, a color, a size; you need to decide its disposition on the screen, if the quote appears all at once or in parts; you need to calculate the time the viewer needs to read it and how this quote will interact with other materials (images and sounds) appearing previously, after, or simultaneously. So, even the simple procedure of quoting becomes a less mechanical and more creative act.

The relation between the audiovisual essay and cinephilia is a strong and productive one. It's interesting that audiovisual essays, however, invite us to rethink/replay the role of memory and impression that constitute the source of the best literature on cinephilia. Because, when we are working on an audiovisual essay, our memory of a film, the trace it has left in us, is constantly confronted with the actual material. Some years ago, I proposed this formula: "Where written texts evoke, [audiovisual] essays invoke."[4] This invocation, this bringing back of the film's pieces, makes us aware of what is actually inside that film. Even with the intention of inventively altering or modifying it later, there's always an initial moment of confrontation between your memory of the film and the film as a material object.

For some time now, I think many of us have believed, a bit naïvely, that audiovisually "quoting" a beloved moment would be enough to transmit the affects we have invested in it; however, the truth is more complex. What literature on film has done through description and evocation in order to make the reader relive a heightened moment of cinema as the writer felt it, the audiovisual essay needs to do through montage; through the interplay of sounds, text, and image; through experimenting with delay, repetition, slow motion, rhythm, progression, and so on.[5]

One thing that we always say to our students is that the process of making an audiovisual essay starts before importing the films into the editing software: it begins while watching them, it begins by noticing things—in the image and the audio—that can be selected and used. Later, the direct and strong contact with those material elements, once they have been extensively replayed and manipulated, puts students even closer to the richness and complexity of cinema. Any film is composed of multiple channels that the maker of an audiovisual essay needs to manipulate, emphasizing some and attenuating others.[6] In a written text, it is easy to ignore the channels we don't want to use or that do not fit our approach. But in an audiovisual essay, precisely because of its invocational character, those channels remain evident on the surface. Again, in an audiovisual essay, one can work toward attenuating or "erasing" them—but this implies an active and creative work, not just a passive (or even unconscious) attitude that consists in leaving them wholly aside.

This multiplicity, diversity, and richness are phenomena that can be better appreciated while working with the films. The students become aware of details they would easily overlook if writing a text; they use and experiment with these details to develop their pieces. The fact that some of them have focused on questions relating to light, color, and sound—aspects that are not only difficult to render in a written text but too often sadly ignored—is already a sign of the potential that the audiovisual essay has: to make the students connect with what cinema is on a material level. Some of their works begin from a more conventional idea but then find, in the process of development, surprising revelations. For example, one of our students who made a director study edited together several shots where the protagonists of different films performed a very similar bodily gesture. This little fragment condensed, in a powerful, intense way, something about the psychology of the characters achieved through performance and mise-en-scène; more importantly, this gesture would probably not even have been noticed if not for the process of thinking and working audiovisually. By having to make an audiovisual piece themselves, the students come to understand and grasp better how questions such as pace, rhythm, and structure are essential to the construction of any film, whether "great" or not so great.

Our title is a pun on, and also an homage to, another formative text of film theory, Laura Mulvey's "Visual Pleasure and Narrative Cinema," first published, like the English translation of "The Unattainable Text," in *Screen* in 1975.[7] All of Mulvey's work, which has included feature filmmaking and, more recently, audiovisual essays, has moved back and forth, in a sense, between the small, fleeting, detailed *pleasures* of cinema (not just visual, more truly audiovisual) that are materially etched in moments, gestures, or frames, and the ongoing, linear, more abstract movement of *narrative*, which, for her, is often aligned with a grim death drive and a moral, ideological process of fixity and closure. Like everyone, including Mulvey herself, we like a good, strong narrative, of the sort that TV series today rather than Hollywood blockbusters so expertly serve up on a regular basis; however, we have certainly become sensitive to the fact that, both for us and for our students, working on audiovisual essays seems to naturally involve a nonlinear, diachronic *decomposition* of narrative structure into its fascinating details and a turning away from those chronological "large arcs" of storytelling form that Hollywood, like all other major, commercial film/media industries around the world, enforces.

The audiovisual essay brings students closer to Shigehiko Hasumi's two major principles of film analysis, as summarized by Adrian Martin: "Firstly, one must really attend to what is there to be seen and heard on screen; and secondly, one should resist bringing to bear that which is operative 'in a domain outside the film.'"[8] While, in the written form, the temptation of reverting to what is outside the film is greater, and sometimes disguises the difficulty of concentrating on what the film itself presents, in the audiovisual essay the students are directly in touch with the film object. This, added to the process of "research done *by* the audiovisual essay, by materially working on it," is what puts the students closer to the experience of what cinephilia is and what it means—and what, most importantly, connects them to it, in the *now*, as a creative and generative force.[9]

CRISTINA ÁLVAREZ LÓPEZ is a critic and audiovisual artist. She is the co-founder of the Spanish online film journal *Transit: Cine y otros desvíos*. Her essays have appeared in *Fandor Keyframe, MUBI Notebook, LOLA, La Fuga*, and *De Filmkrant* and in books on Chantal Akerman, Bong Joon-Ho, Philippe Garrel, and Paul Schrader.

ADRIAN MARTIN is Adjunct Associate Professor of Film and Screen Studies at Monash University and a freelance writer and audiovisual artist. He is the author of seven books, the most recent being *Mise en Scène and Film Style: From Classical Hollywood to New Media Art*. He is co-editor of the online journal *LOLA* and of the book *Movie Mutations*.

Notes

1. *(notes on) Badiou on Badiou*, accessed September 12, 2014, https://badiouonbadiou.wordpress.com/.

2. Andrew Sarris, "Film Criticism in the Seventies," *Film Comment* 14, no. 1 (1978): 11.

3. This essay is reprinted as a chapter of Bellour, *The Analysis of Film* (Bloomington: Indiana University Press, 2000). We describe the piece as "misread" because it is sometimes reduced to the bald assertion that written criticism is an impossibility and that audiovisual criticism is the only possible and true, alternative path—which is nonsense in the light of Bellour's own critical practice over fifty years, which is predominantly literary, and the stated policy of the important magazine he edits, *Trafic*, which forbids illustrative imagery of any kind and enforces what Bellour (via Michel Foucault) often calls the "necessary labor of description." Bellour has himself revisited his 1975 reflection in a 2009 essay, the title of which translates as "35 Years on: Is the 'Text' Still Unattainable?," including commentary on recent audiovisual essays, which forms a chapter of his book *La querelle des dispositifs* (Paris: P.O.L., 2012).

4. Cristina Álvarez López, "Double Lives, Second Chances," *Frames* 1 (2012), http://framescinemajournal.com/article/double-lives-second-chances/.

5. See Catherine Grant and Christian Keathley, "The Use of an Illusion: Childhood Cinephilia, Object Relations, and Videographic Film Studies," *Photogénie* (2014), http://www.photogenie.be/photogenie_blog/article/use-illusion; and Adrian Martin, "The Inward/Outward

Turn," *[in]Transition* 1, no. 3 (2014), http://mediacommons.futureofthebook.org/intransi tion/2014/09/14/inwardoutward-turn.

6. See Cristina Álvarez López and Adrian Martin, "The One and the Many: Making Sense of Montage in the Audiovisual Essay," *The Audiovisual Essay* (2014), http://reframe.sussex .ac.uk/audiovisualessay/frankfurt-papers/cristina-alvarez-lopez-adrian-martin/.

7. This essay is reprinted as a chapter in Laura Mulvey, *Visual and Other Pleasures* (London: Palgrave Macmillan, 2009).

8. Adrian Martin, "Incursions," in *The Language and Style of Film Criticism*, eds. Alex Clayton and Andrew Klevan (London: Routledge, 2011), 61. The phrase from Hasumi derives from "Sunny Skies," in *Ozu's* Tokyo Story, ed. David Desser (London: Cambridge University Press, 1997), 121.

9. Cristina Álvarez López, "From Idea to Concept," *[in]Transition* 1, no. 3 (2014), http:// mediacommons.futureofthebook.org/intransition/2014/09/14/idea-concept.

PART II

Practicing Cinephilia and Pedagogy

7 Teaching Film Nonfictionally

The Reciprocity of Pedagogy, Cinephilia, and Maternity

Kristi McKim

Near the end of Ali Aydin's *Küf* (2012), Basri (Ercan Kesal) learns that his son Seyfi has been killed; framed in a sobering long take, Basri sits at his kitchen table and rocks softly as he weeps. Tears drip from his eyes; the clock ticks, and—aurally registering his slight movements—his chair gently taps against the wall, a rhythm that paces his physical expression of grief. A quiet climax of a quiet film, this scene subtly conveys Basri's interiority, all the while that our spectatorial attention sharpens within this acute perception of slightest change. Upon my screening of this film, at the 2013 New Directors/New Films Festival in New York City, I shivered and cried with astonishment at this detail. Never before had I experienced cinematic grief quite like the tapping of a chair against a wall, and the making-new that *Küf* had heretofore intimated became in this moment an extraordinary swelling up of my own emotion within this startling conveyance of despair. Furthermore, this detail exemplifies for me a profound confluence between cinephilia and teaching, a confluence that this essay proceeds to explore within both personal and academic realms.

I screened *Küf* as the first of a several-day festival experience with seven students. In fall 2012, we successfully co-wrote a proposal for funding from Hendrix College's Odyssey Program (a collegewide engaged learning program), and in March 2013 we traveled to New York for an intensive schedule of screenings and impassioned discussion. Expanded beyond classroom parameters, film pedagogy became compounded within new spatiotemporal realms of not only a festival but also a vibrant metropolis, far denser and more accelerated a city than our college town. Immediately following our screening of *Küf*, one of my students, Vincent Gammill, and I exuberantly discussed the creaking chair. As a group throughout the days that followed, we all turned to this detail as we discussed subsequent films. In the ways that this detail generated dialogue, writing, and reflection, I glimpse how perhaps cinephilia *is* pedagogy: our fascination with details incites the desire to write, share, discuss, and think about a moment in personal and worldly contexts. Moreover, the festival experience itself was laden with cinephilia, a compounding of Walter Benjamin's observations about urban experience (we discussed "love at last sight" while walking through Central Park) and Paul Willemen's conception of cinephilia as the "serialisation of moments of revelation."[1] The glee of scampering about a bustling theatrical space with students and colleagues, bursting with excitement for the excellent films we'd seen, conflated the classroom and film theater into a dreamy environment of rigorous discussion and reflection.

In the following months, students drafted and revised reviews for publication as a dossier in *Film Matters*. They workshopped their peers' reviews and refined their own. Their final version of the Introduction to their *Film Matters* dossier opens as follows:

> As the final credits of Joshua Oppenheimer's *The Act of Killing* scrolled down the screen at the New York Museum of Modern Art, we turned to one other with expressions of disbelief, anxiety, nausea, awe. For several seconds, we found ourselves unable to formulate a sentence among us—an unfamiliar state for our typically well-spoken group. The air around us seemed to vibrate. Our only response was a sort of collective paralysis; we'd been rendered immobile by the power of the moving image—itself only an illusion of movement, as we'd learned and discussed in our multiple film courses at Hendrix College. Even when our capacity for speech finally returned, we struggled to articulate just how deeply we'd been moved. This, then, comprised that tortuous moment between bodily and psychic reaction, the moment before opinion, before analysis. But our bodies had already registered *The Act of Killing*'s impact, and we could sense each other's keen distress; simultaneously, we felt some subtle connection arising from the spectatorial experience we'd shared. Our reason for being here in the first place was to work this through. Then the words erupted.[2]

That the students chose to frame their dossier with this moment attests to its significance for us all. I recall those ecstatic postscreening moments: in the shift from screening a film in the dark to applauding a filmmaker on our feet, our experience became even more physical; as we listened to Oppenheimer's gentle, eloquent, politically astute discussion of the film, I felt as if we all fell in love, together experiencing film at its most humanistic and complex.

After this question-and-answer session, I happened upon Oppenheimer in the lobby (these were the days before his meteoric ascent to Oscar-nominated stardom). In an adrenaline-surged cinephilic swoon, I gushed that the standing ovation—the physicality of the applause and the emotional and intellectual gratitude that spawned it—would undoubtedly mark one of the grandest experiences of my life; I explained how my students and I could only have dreamed of such an ethical, engaging, challenging film that showcased the virtues and limits of cinematic representation. He smiled, blushed, ducked his head in shyness, hugged me, and I can still remember the feel of his rail-thin torso, the softness of his sweater, the way he listened and spoke with gratitude and precision when I told him of my regard. The conflation of classroom and cinema, of film and filmmaker, of students and teacher, never to me felt so preciously overwhelming as in those postscreening moments. The students acknowledge this abundance and disproportion of experience to expression in their conclusion to the dossier's introduction: "as film students, film-lovers, and writers about film, we feel that through this unique opportunity, we formed cinephilic bonds and shared in our love for film."[3] The entirety of this festival experience taught me more about the kind of teacher I want to be.

During the spring 2014 semester, one year after our film festival experience, graduated seniors William Repass and Lance St. Laurent returned to Hendrix to lead discussion in my Non-Fiction Film course about *The Act of Killing*. In this vibrant conversation, those of us who participated in the festival spontaneously took turns reciting our personal encounter with the film and filmmaker; we inadvertently built upon the myth of the auteur, the genius of Oppenheimer, in ways unavoidable but nonetheless disconcerting, especially as the film challenges our praiseful adulation of film artists. We worked through the circuitous argument: *The Act of Killing* powerfully exceeds our capacity for expression because of Oppenheimer's innovation and ethics, all the while that praising Oppenheimer mildly undermines *The Act of Killing*'s critique of media. The trajectory by which our conversation about *The Act of Killing* evolved from a festival experience to an intimate writerly collaboration to a classroom discussion, from a standing ovation in New York to a Little Rock faculty dinner table to a virtual chat room to an alumni-led dialogue at Hendrix College, exemplifies the ways that studying film can transform any given space into the classroom (and can spill from the classroom into the world beyond).

Whereas this New Directors/New Films festival experience involved a variety of learning contexts, I offer another anecdote in which a traditional teaching space became strictly performative; an attempt to document my film classroom necessitated a charade of teaching, in ways that further make precious the spaces within which learning truly happens. In spring 2013, my college's publicity office asked to visit my introductory film class for their photography shoot. I conferred with my students (we had just completed a week of studying documentary, which explored how a camera alters its subject), who responded enthusiastically at the prospect of appearing in Hendrix's publicity images together as a community; thus, one morning, we posed. I self-consciously "taught" in front of the classroom, while the opening of *Bringing Up Baby* (Howard Hawks, 1938) flickered on the screen behind me. Students tried to appear involved in our "lesson," empty of content and laden with performance. This staged teaching environment—its artifice, as the photographer rearranged the students (privileging those without clashing patterned clothing, cueing their eager expressions) and asked me to "do [my] thing!"; its hilarity, as we all laughed at my inept attempts to feign natural-ness—made me yearn for the classroom sans photographer.

In addition to the artifice of the photographic scene, my then-state of early pregnancy meant I also secretly endured morning sickness; my clothes bore the haphazard unstylishness of a wardrobe almost but not quite full-on "maternity." I was and wasn't myself on that day in that hour of documentation, the photo-graphic evidence of which now appears in both Hendrix College's alumni maga-zine and its viewbook for prospective students. Though I attempted to teach as if the cameras were absent, I felt nonetheless blushingly self-conscious about "do-ing my thing" as a professor while being recorded, which further emphasizes the serendipitous combination of spontaneity, preparedness, confidence, and vulner-ability that happens within any teaching experience. Like Roland Barthes's punc-tum, the photograph records my attempt to balance my impending motherhood with my love of teaching film, this detail of my pregnancy being that upon which I fixate, the "inexhaustible element that electrifies the cinephile . . . drawn to mo-ments that rise up, like lightning flashes, ready to be activated for an alternative discourse," according to Rashna Wadia Richards.[4] Curious as to what a picture-perfect film studies classroom might be, this essay frames such an "alternative discourse" within and beyond traditional modes of teaching film. Framed by these two nontraditional classrooms, this essay affords me the opportunity to focus on the very personal mise-en-scène of my college and home.

Cinephilia, Teaching, and the Personal

Inspiring my essay's own synthesis of personal reflection and pedagogical method, literary scholar Jane Tompkins describes her desire to collapse the personal and professional in her writing: "The criticism I would like to write would always take off from personal experience, would always be in some way a chronicle of my hours and days, would speak in a voice which can talk about everything, would reach out to a reader like me and touch me where I want to be touched."[5] Tompkins reads the scholarly disdain for "words like *love* and *giv-ing*" as "part of the police action that academic intellectuals wage ceaselessly against feeling, against women, against what is personal. The ridiculing of the 'touchy-feely,' of the 'Mickey Mouse,' of the sentimental (often associated with teaching that takes students' concerns into account), belongs to the tradition [of] . . . founding knowledge in the denial of emotion."[6] Ignited by emotion instead of denying it, writing about cinephilia and especially about teaching (as it "takes students' concerns into account") allows if not beckons us to "take off from per-sonal experience." Certain theories of film (especially as they implicitly include ways of *teaching* film) seem to answer feminist critiques of scholarly detachment. Especially a cinephilic approach to film study conflates the personal and professional.

Arguing elegantly for a rejuvenated film history that takes root in our lives, Christian Keathley explains how cinephilia incorporates the personal:

> Much film theory and history of the past twenty-five years has been preoccupied with articulating and exposing the means by which dominant narrative cinema creates a world of drama, adventure, and enchantment that we can step into and lose ourselves in. The cinephiliac anecdote, by contrast, seeks to illuminate the ways in which movies—especially moments from movies—displace themselves out of their original contexts and step into our lives.[7]

Tracing a history of cinephilia-inclined film theory, Keathley establishes a method that privileges not the *loss* of self but rather a sharpening of subjectivity that emerges from the interaction *between* spectator and film. Further emphasizing the dual nature of film study as a visible yet inward experience of images, D. N. Rodowick claims that "revisiting classical film theory today is also a way of revivifying a kind of questioning that explores our sensuous contact with images and recharacterizes their (visible and outward) perceptual density in a way that also leads us inward—a self-examination of our relation to time, memory, and history."[8] Teaching and studying film involves asking why and how we have interacted with moving images as they change over time. Attention to moving images "leads us toward" an inward reflection on how and why we're *moved* to experience such sensuous contact; studying film theory involves studying our perception in relation to personal experience.

Championing the personal in phenomenological film theory, Vivian Sobchack describes the density of film experience: "The film experience not only *represents* and reflects upon the prior direct perceptual experience of the filmmaker *by means of* the modes and structures of direct and reflective perceptual experience, but also *presents* the direct and reflective experience of a perceptual and expressive existence *as* the film."[9] If film conveys the filmmaker's senses, a record of sight that invites us to see; if film conveys both "direct experience and existential presence" of both filmmaker and viewer; if film constitutes a "mutually lived space . . . an intersection and connection of visual activity"; then *teaching* film dramatizes if not amplifies both our subjective embodied vision and our collective experience of learning together.[10] Phenomenological film theory insists upon the reciprocity of film and viewer, and theories of cinephilia emphasize the dynamism *among* spectators (as teachers and students together). Increasingly over the years, my experience of film pedagogy conflates with my own personal ontology, in ways that make inextricable—for better and worse—my worlds within and beyond the classroom. As a new mother recently returned to teaching film and buoyed by Tompkins, Keathley, Rodowick, and Sobchack, I acknowledge the intertwining of my cinephilic, pedagogical, and maternal reflections. I proposed this essay while in the early stages of pregnancy, and I now revise my final essay as the mother of the spectacular nine-month-old Henry Robert. Structured by moments and revelations that connect the classroom with my home, this essay combines fleeting experiences of teaching and mothering into an argument about pedagogy and experience.

One afternoon, in Henry's first month, he and I stepped onto the back porch to look at the light. I talked with him about the light he'd already encountered: the light that defined and created every color and shadow he'd experienced; the light that healed him from jaundice in his phototherapy box at the hospital; the sunlight that made him squint on our neighborhood strolls; the visible changes in light as we walked through our house in front of and past shadeless windows; the light that shone through the homemade patchwork curtains in his nursery; the light that emanated from our camera flash; the light that wrote his image into photographic and video form; and the light that moves on a screen, such that—one day—he would see motion pictures. As a new mother and cinephile, I tried to imagine—and, well-meaningly, to shape—my son's inchoate appreciation of light's changes. Such projection—tied together with my newfound maternal love and my more familiar cinephilia—became part of my new perception as a motherly cinephile or a cinephilic mother, avidly collecting moments: Henry's steady gulps as he feeds, his simultaneous forward thrust of his head and quizzical raising of his eyebrows, his (and my) visible elation in his recognizing a familiar song, his tiny fingers pressed in the palm of my hand or curled around my thumb, his soft full face as I burp him on my shoulder, his cozy burrowing into the nape of my neck, his warm milky breath as it pulses against my cheek as he sleeps in my arms, and his smiles and laughter that sometimes fade into bewilderment upon introducing a camera to the scene.

Returning to the college classroom after maternity leave involved leaving home to teach students who were not my children, yet both home and school remained places where we learned together how to see. Before and now after Henry's birth, I teach as if my life depends on it. Though such a phrase perhaps overstates the contingency of my life to teaching, I almost entirely intend such boldness, insofar as I try to build each syllabus and approach every class with an urgency and clarity: an urgency that respects my students and our course material by asking intense and serious questions; a clarity that tries to pare and focus complex ideas into their most concentrated form. I try to teach my students that our work matters, and I feel responsible for creating an environment within which we collectively feel charged and motivated to learn hard and beautiful things together. Every class, I try to approach with this level of dedication and commitment, turning to the curriculum and our ways of reading as my professional challenge and personal catharsis. I've thus never taught a course detached from my personal life.

Teaching Non-Fiction Film, Nonfictionally

In my first semester after my maternity leave, I taught a focused iteration of Non-Fiction Film titled Cinematic Lives, which I described on the syllabus as follows:

> Showcasing a range of relationships among cinema, self, family, and community, the films of this screening-intensive course feature subjects who look at or hear themselves cinematically, people who learn more about themselves and their world via the screens and cameras in their environment. What makes you pay attention to films that aren't about you? What makes you care about someone else's family, conflict, struggle, trauma, or joy? . . . How and why do we expect film to relate to our lives, in ways beyond merely going to the movies or screening them for entertainment? In the most abstract and urgent of senses, then, why do we watch, make, talk about, film? How can the study of these particular examples of non-fiction films help us to better clarify and articulate these desires and relationships?

I strove to create a course that felt honest and close to my personal life, with urgency and meaning enough that I could justify leaving my son at home to have conversations with students about what's at stake in the world. I was, after all, interested in nonfiction film, in how to read the course films, in how films impact our lives, in how students might read the films in relation to their own experiences; but I also was curious about my own compulsion to photograph Henry. I approached the course as an exercise in why and how we make and view images; talking about these questions with bright, engaged students felt like one way of finding answers.

The syllabus required that students post a weekly paragraph-long "pointed question" or "nuanced reflection" about each feature film to a class blog. Beginning with our first week of studying Vivian Sobchack's "Toward a Phenomenology of Nonfictional Film Experience" with *Grey Gardens* (Albert Maysles and David Maysles, 1975), I became bowled over with the care, sensitivity, and vulnerability these students revealed in their writing, more substantive and lengthy than I'd anticipated. As I completed my reading assignment for our first week of class, I felt further astonished at the surprise I'd unwittingly given myself, as Sobchack writes sensitively of her son Christopher in relation to the *film-souvenir*:

> (However unfulfilled it may be, my desire is to evoke my son as he was in his existence as a baby, not just as he was in this one moment of crawling toward the camera; similarly, I want to re-experience his first birthday party not only in the fragmented space and moments imaged specifically for me, but as a whole coherent and affective event merely suggested by the balloons and cake

in the image). . . . I do not 'intend' the specific image of my son crawling toward the camera, and thus I do not scrutinize the image intensely. Rather I see my son through the image—his smile evoking an ensemble of gestures and looks in excess of the image's specificity, evoking the person I know whose existence and comportment form a general whole that I try to re-member from this image fragment of him.[11]

How grateful I felt for this essay that collapsed my professional and personal worlds in ways that Tompkins would have wished, that Sobchack could lend her own precise phenomenal sensitivity to not only film but also her growing son. Her phrase "I see my son through the image" acutely defines my newfound perception. In this Non-Fiction Film course, my semester after maternity leave, I saw my Henry everywhere; my students gave me permission, as we gave each other permission, to talk through the shifting experiences of film as a site of personal projection and meaning. We kept each other honest and asked for clarification; we challenged, listened, and studied compassionately the ways that, for example, *Sherman's March* (Ross McElwee, 1985) or *The Beaches of Agnès* (Agnès Varda, 2009) could yield equally strong yet divergent reactions.

The course grew strong in proportion to students' willingness to work through sensitive material together in writing and discussion. In a deliberate decision more rewarding than I could have anticipated, framing the course with Sobchack's essay foregrounded our course's methodology and introduced film as an *experience* more than a thing, genre, or category.[12] Enriched by Sobchack's theories of the *film-souvenir*—the home movie in which we recognize "places we've been . . . things we've done . . . as images on the screen"—and students' dedication, the course films transformed into our very own *film-souvenirs*, which grew into our own pedagogical screen upon which we projected our emotional attachment.[13] The last premotherhood film I saw in the movie theater, as I sat sprawled out in nine months of pregnant discomfort, was *Stories We Tell* (Sarah Polley, 2013). That I taught *Stories We Tell* in this course; that I prepared for class while Henry spiritedly bounced in his jumper beside me; that I could seek and find ways to teach and mother that felt personally rewarding and professionally responsible: I credit my brilliant, big-hearted, brave, willing-to-be-vulnerable students with this realization of a pedagogical dream. This nonfiction film class yielded a variety of "cinephiliac anecdotes," in Keathley's terms, which "illuminate the ways in which movies—especially moments from movies—displace themselves out of their original contexts and step into our lives."[14] Teaching my nonfiction film class "nonfictionally" meant being particularly mindful of the many possible cinephiliac anecdotes we together were creating.

After our group discussion of *Silverlake Life: The View From Here* (Tom Joslin and Peter Friedman, 1993), I returned to my office, closed the door, and took time to write about how I had just experienced one of the best classes of my life. Students responded to this difficult diary film—chronicling two filmmakers' love, illness, and death from AIDS—with some of the most mature, reflective, careful, and well-written undergraduate film writing that I've ever encountered. Inspired by students' tender and smart blog posts, I opened class by foregrounding my pedagogical challenge in straddling two approaches to discussion: at one extreme, I could treat this provocative, tender film as a cinematic object like any other, as we shift between texts and screen to arrive at some academic revelation via interrogation of death and cinematic representation; at the other extreme, I could turn the class into a group therapy session, wherein I expect students to offer personal reflections about grief—in ways that I'm hardly equipped to handle professionally. I wanted to err on neither of those sides, hoping instead to strike a balance both professional and humane, neither weepy nor cold but feeling and meaningful. During these opening remarks and subsequent discussion, students' faces looked more beautiful to me than ever before, all warm-eyed and soft-expressioned, all thoughtful and deliberate, all listening and contributing with benevolence and smarts. I told them that, if our class goal were to arrive at some collective and individual balance of intelligence and feeling, that we'd be finished in our time together, given how accomplished their written blog posts and class contributions proved to be.

We began discussion by studying the closing "Bye, Bye, Baby" scene and what ended and continued in relation with what had come before, such as in the scene of Joslin's partner, Mark, dancing joyfully to "Take My Heart Away" in their living room. Students carefully responded to the film's sensitive subject, its inclusion of the audience in their love story in ways that make us feel their loss, its connection with Virginia Woolf's "On Being Ill" and Sobchack's "Inscribing Ethical Space," its conflation of shot duration with life, its wobbly camera as both animating the deceased Tom and conveying Mark's grief.[15] We as a class seemed exceptionally vibrant in this discussion; I personally felt exceedingly alive, as if it were the discussion for which I'd been preparing all my life. My student Kelly Johnson, whose mother had recently died of cancer, talked with me after class about how our discussion of the film's ending spawned her realization that, even though her mother has passed, she will always have existed once in this world (an existence that's irrefutable, unchangeable). She said this film was the first experience of death she'd encountered aside from that of her mother, how her mother's death was "like that," in terms of her eyes not closing; she described how she couldn't watch her mother's lifeless body being prepared, but that this film gave her a way to demystify what those moments might have been like. We talked tearfully about her loss, this film, and our connectedness: my pregnancy advanced during the months that her mother's health declined; Henry was born just weeks before her mother passed away (I held my tiny son in my arms while I wept to watch a video of Kelly reading Billy Collins's "The Lanyard" at her mother's funeral); in the Hendrix press photos taken during my fourth month of pregnancy Kelly sits prominently in the front of the class, her face one of the few visible faces in the shot. Another student, Caiti Rolfes-Haase, after our *Silverlake Life* class finished, posted on our blog, "I just wanted to thank you guys for the discussion today. I won't try and put into words how much I think our class environment facilitates empathy and creative thought, but I will say that I feel really lucky to have the opportunity to share this class with you all." Two other students, Adelia Shiffraw and Rane Peerson, incorporated *Silverlake Life*'s "Take My Heart Away" sequence into their final project *Do You Remember How We Met?*, a tender short film that chronicles their friendship in relation to memorable film sequences; they describe in voice-over the remarkable way that they'd both sought out the song, individually, after our class, so charged it had become. In these ways, film— particularly references to *Silverlake Life*—connected us, giving us ways to talk about and bear witness to what we lose and keep in our lives.

When recent graduates Lance St. Laurent and William Repass visited my class to lead discussion on *The Act of Killing*, we talked afterward about the course; they asked how my being a mother changed my relationship with film. Grateful for the question yet daunted by the challenge of responding, I briefly described my increased sensitivity to any intimation of screened children who fall ill or worse, as with a most recent class discussion of *The Thin Blue Line*'s (Errol Morris, 1988) David Harris, how his childhood photos with his brother who drowned led me to swallow hard, to teach the film within the context of our conversation about luck and justice, all the while that I thought, *Henry, please be careful; please stay alive; please be good.* Moreover, film felt all the more fleeting and ephemeral with my solid learning-to-hug heavy beloved son miles away at home. Films further sensitized me to Henry's fragility, yet Henry felt substantial in contrast with moving images.

After an in-class screening of *Sink or Swim* (Su Friedrich, 1990), the young girl's voice-over accompanying discordant and harmonious images—a young girl's reflection on her early childhood, her parents, her loss, her desire—made all new sense to me. That morning, as I held Henry close in my arms, I ached to appreciate a moment I could know only in its passing, which is the same for *every* moment, of course—every embrace, conversation, fleeting light, and ephemeral sensation. As I watched *Sink or Swim*, I felt renewed love for the spiritual, meditative, and reflective ritual of sitting alongside fellow spectators, wondering what they see and hear, wondering how my own imagination roams and focuses as it does. In that quiet and darkness, in the light of the screen, I thought about how my body felt, which is to say that I realized the extremes of my physical attachment to Henry when my arms felt empty without him, my body lighter, my torso only half there, without his heft and squirming all entwined within my arms and hair, neck and face, chest and waist. My arms now know this growing measure of love that I try and never can wholly hold, as if shifting from Ptolemaic to Copernican worldviews, or from weightlessness to gravity, an orientation toward my family in ways that both pull me from and enrich all that I do and think.

Preparing for class one afternoon at home, I screened Ross McElwee's *Bright Leaves* (2003) on my computer. As I leaned down to laugh with Henry as he played on the floor, *Bright Leaves* shifted to a scene of McElwee's son Adrian, in a startling montage of home video footage, as McElwee offers in voice-over the following: "As if the weight of all these accumulated images could keep him from growing up so fast . . . [or] slow the process down. But, of course, filming doesn't slow anything down." McElwee's words, his longing to slow change and whimsical wonderment as to how filmed images might help, rang familiar. I derive pleasure from and become enthralled with seeing Henry in his various ages. I love looking at older photos and discovering traces of the person I'm now finding him to be; I love looking at newer photos as they make manifest his changes. As Siegfried Kracauer claims, films have the capacity to reveal the world (to reveal my son).[16] After I spend time studying his photos and videos, I look from the screen with more sensitive expansive perception, momentarily carrying Henry's multiple ages as an afterimage of sorts, a heightening that also feels like a weakening for the vulnerability I feel in perceiving his growth. In this course, teaching Joris Ivens's *Rain* (1929)—a film I've studied at length—most fully amplified and underscored what I've elsewhere intimated, how cinematic rain—or *film*—hasn't changed, for all the ways that my world (that each of our worlds) in fact has.[17]

Details and Moments of Revelation

As motherhood impacts my teaching, so too does cinephilia impact my motherhood: that I've recalled Laura Mulvey's championing the pensive engagement *with* a subject over obsessive possession *of* it, as I navigate how I physically see this person to whom I gave birth; that Mary Ann Doane's detailing the intricacies of temporal passage—film as an archive, all the while that we presently behold these moments within a myriad of temporal experiences—informs how I behold my changing son; that Willemen's serialized revelatory moments likewise define my memory of Henry's birth, his early fragile days, our poignant interaction; that I see Varda's benevolent close-ups of her beloved Jacques Demy's aged hands in mortal contrast with Henry's new delicate features; that I hear Jean Epstein's description of a smile's emergence in close-up as I note the slight changes in Henry's expression, building toward his first and now frequent smiles.[18] Henry's growing in the world, so new and wondrous to me, I can liken to what I know as film theory and movement. Like any good genre film, I have a vague idea of what to expect, yet I feel nonetheless thrilled at how he conforms to or defies these patterns. Crawling, pulling up, sitting independently—these accomplishments epitomize suspense, as we can expect that they'll suddenly occur, though we can't say exactly when or how. Henry thus defines my very favorite genre, the utterly singular category: my son. I want to be careful not to turn Henry into my screen, in all its mirroring and framing implications, though I would be naïve to disregard the ways that my cinephilia evolves from worldly interactions, as has my teaching shaped and emerged from my cinephilia. For all the ways that I have been achingly moved by ephemerality (of loved ones, seedlings, friendships, light, moments, all of it), I've never loved so intensely a living organism who changes so dramatically. His swift growth combines with my sensitivity to change to further amplify this love. Epstein writes the following about the cinematic close-up, in ways that enrich my appreciation of Henry's newness in the world:

> Even more beautiful than a laugh is the face preparing for it. . . . I love the mouth which is about to speak and holds back, the gesture which hesitates between right and left, the recoil before the leap, and the moment before landing, the becoming, the hesitation, the taut spring, the prelude, and even more than all these, the piano being tuned before the overture. The photogenic is conjugated in the future and in the imperative. It does not allow for stasis.[19]

Straddling an irrefutable immediacy (his hunger, *now*; his wide-eyed gaze, *now*) and a hesitant becoming (his careful assessment and gentle discovery of how he might move his body; his tentative then vibrant vocalizing; his soft licking his hands as if a kitten grooming; his almost-sitting; his widening smile), an infant seems physically to embody the photogenic, as "conjugated in the future" and defined by potential. Lending images to this inchoate time of beholding Henry's changes, Epstein gives me words for how I love, which is to say that he *teaches* me not only how to see but also how to convey this sensitivity.

Teaching film involves teaching students—and ourselves—how to *find* something to love, whether the long poignant takes of *Rules of the Game* (Jean Renoir, 1939), the audiovisual layering of Witt's (Jim Caviezel's) death in *The Thin Red Line* (Terrence Malick, 1998), the empty spaces in *Tokyo Story* (Yasujirō Ozu, 1953), or the shifting light in *Meek's Cutoff* (Kelly Reichardt, 2010). In film classes, we learn and teach how to see with both intelligence and benevolence—an attention that invites more chances to fall in love. My Non-Fiction Film class explicitly revealed to me the precious meaning that arises from teaching film, how every film has occasion to become a *film-souvenir* after being taught, screened, and shared. As film students and teachers, we together make a multitude of *film-souvenirs*; as we teach and learn throughout our careers, these personal attachments multiply. Slow close analysis of a sequence during class invokes the film's own context (in production, in history, in scholarly contexts) but also our personal subjective memory of our previous lectures and discussions about the scene, the echoes of past students whose contributions polyphonically enrich our own perception, our discovery of new ways to pose questions and rephrase comments that compounds over the years. Teaching film transforms the films that we teach, as collective interpretations honor and collapse our unique perceptions. Some of my best classroom moments have arisen from such occasions: a debate in French New Wave as to whether *Shoot the Piano Player*'s (François Truffaut, 1960) Charlie (Charles Aznavour) had a tear in his eye in the final scene; a meeting of Film Theory that exuberantly close-read, for the entirety of the class, the credit sequence of *Imitation of Life* (Douglas Sirk, 1959); the poignancy of first-year students in Introduction to Film who keep teaching me new ways of reading *Rushmore*'s (Wes Anderson, 1998) closing long take in light of The Faces' "I wish I knew what I know now when I was younger" and the Latin phrase *sic transit gloria*. My cinephilia thus conflates with my teaching method.

Sobchack explains that "even as [*film-souvenirs*] retain the specificity from which their motivational power emerges, the images of the *film-souvenir* are not apprehended for themselves, but rather as the catalyst to a primarily constitutive and generalizing activity that transcends their specificity."[20] In the classroom, these films that we screen "retain [their] specificity" even as they catalyze the "constitutive and generalizing activity that transcends their specificity"; in other words, our daily conversations about a film—our attention to form and details, our interest in broader contexts and affect—grow into a semester's shared collection that "transcends [any one film's] specificity." Created through classroom dialogue, this "generalizing activity" within the film classroom further transforms a film's ephemerality—like shifting states of matter—into a class experience that takes the form of memory, class notes, or audio record. Furthermore, in teaching film, we learn more about the extent to which our cinephilia can in fact be *teachable*. Teaching a film—in ways comparable to what Mulvey claims of the remote control and pause button—mixes up and disrupts the forward momentum of narrative progress, thus creating a classroom of "pensive spectators" who—through scene analysis and incorporation of subjective experience—challenge, frame, and counteract a film's one-way beginning-to-end temporal movement.[21] This temporal reconfiguring happens existentially through our memories and projections, our anticipation and nostalgia.

At our last meeting of the Non-Fiction Film course described earlier, I closed by referencing Sobchack's essay on nonfictional film experience and suddenly realized the connection between pedagogy and *film-souvenirs* that I've tried to explain in this essay. In a seemingly ephemeral moment, I praised the students for our exceptional semester and celebrated the community we'd become. My student Caiti surreptitiously recorded these final remarks to the class, which she then incorporated over the end credits to her final documentary film project, *The*

Hurricane Weather. That a fleeting moment of my teaching now enjoys cinematic permanence or archival status of a sort attests to how the combination of students and film together make the ephemeral more permanent. I somehow want to say that this fascination with the ephemeral defines our relationship not only with moving images but also with our past, in ways that take root in our childhood, in ways that again bring Henry to mind.

In her autobiographical essay "A Sketch of the Past," Virginia Woolf fondly recalls a defining experience in her infancy:

> If life has a base that it stands upon, if it is a bowl that one fills and fills and fills—then my bowl without a doubt stands upon this memory. It is of lying half asleep, half awake, in bed in the nursery at St Ives. It is of hearing waves breaking, one, two, one, two, and sending a splash of water over the beach; and then breaking, one, two, one, two, behind a yellow blind. It is of hearing the blind draw its little acorn across the floor as the wind blew the blind out. It is of lying and hearing this splash and seeing this light, and feeling, it is almost impossible that I should be here; of feeling the purest ecstasy I can conceive.
>
> I could spend hours trying to write that as it should be written, in order to give the feeling which is even at this moment very strong in me. But I should fail (unless I had some wonderful luck).[22]

Woolf writes the light-infused sleep-hazed details of her nursery, the rhythmic sound of water and sight of light, as they enable her ecstatic infantile bliss. Her second paragraph humbly points to the excess of such an ecstasy, as her words fall short of her aspiration; she crystalizes feeling within tangible light-drenched reminiscence. Every time Henry cranes his neck to fixate upon the light streaming through his nursery windows, I recall Woolf's recollection. Or I think of *After Life*'s (Hirokazu Kore-eda, 1999) Bundo San, who recalls his earliest memory at five or six months old: "I was naked, lying on the futon, when I was bathed in this amazing sunlight, an autumn light, not too hot." Ascribing ecstatic and rapturous feeling to this sensation from her past, Woolf idealizes childhood's simple defining experiences. Her language evokes what we might cast in cinephilic terms as excess, as entrenchment in the isolated detail, as interest in revelatory moments themselves impossible to write though inciting one's impassioned attempt nonetheless.

An Archival Impulse: Writing Pedagogical, Cinephilic, and Maternal Experience

In "Leaving the Movie Theater," Barthes expresses his desirable experience of moviegoing as being "fascinated *twice over*, by the image and by its surroundings—as if I had two bodies at the same time: a narcissistic body which gazes, lost, into the engulfing mirror, and a perverse body, ready to fetishize not the image but precisely what exceeds it . . . in short, in order to distance, in order to 'take off,' I complicate a 'relation' by a 'situation.'"[23] By introducing my "situation" of motherhood to my cinephilic relationship with teaching, I seek to introduce the *teaching* body as a subject who does more than enter and leave the movie theater; the *teaching* body includes both of Barthes's modes of spectatorship, as the classroom affords a critical corollary to the seductive hall of the cinema. Within these remembered spaces of both cinema and classroom, it is *my* body, in its recent pregnancy and new motherhood that "gazes, lost" into the screen and fetishizes "not the image but precisely what exceeds it": how every screen is and is not my son; how I can know my new relationship with Henry in the language of cinephilia and teaching; and how, in its revelation of details and fascination with what exceeds representation, my motherhood enriches the classroom and cinema, in ways that help me—as my students have taught, in their *Film Matters* dossier and in every class—to love film, to love teaching, and to love teaching film.

This essay's cinephilia-fueled reflections might betray the obvious (i.e., what we see and how we teach change in accordance with how *we* change, and vice versa); nothing here is remarkable beyond the fact that I had longed to but could not find an essay that connected cinephilia with motherhood and teaching. As I have been startled and inspired by the affinities among these ways of loving and learning, I have thus aspired, however ineffably, to write such an essay. In trying to voice these unwritten connections, I realize that my writing abides what art historian Hal Foster has described as an "archival impulse," which "is as much preproduction as it is postproduction: concerned less with absolute origins than with obscure traces . . . drawn to unfulfilled beginnings or incomplete projects . . . that might offer points of departure again."[24]

Writing about documentaries of film archivists, Rowena Santos Aquino appreciates how the "archival impulse . . . begins with emotional resonance, which is not the opposite of intellectual or educational engagement."[25] She describes the archival impulse as "not just about the technical and technological aspect of acquiring, preserving, and restoring films . . . [but] also about an affective, physical experience."[26]

Though all teaching would ideally be generative, the archival impulse incites a kind of cinephilic and nonfictional pedagogy: one that harnesses reflection, that privileges and develops impressions, that peels back suppositions, that asks questions (generously, supportively, empathetically, rigorously) of every claim, and that ultimately transforms impressions and experiences into something more lasting and substantive. Teaching film cinephilically and nonfictionally layers upon cinema's own archival capacity an additional archive of pedagogical and existential experience: a layering so dense and urgent that it has driven this very essay, which "begins with emotional resonance" and entails "an affective, physical experience," not only of screening and research but also of teaching and mothering. This writing becomes its own archive: of classroom serendipity, of maternal love, of festival experience, of moments and conversations by definition ephemeral.

In an interview regarding her book about writing and motherhood, Rivka Galchen considers her child as a future reader of her work: "I think the book was maybe addressed to her, or had a future her in mind, but not because it would be able to tell her something specific, more like . . . a collection of leaves gathered in the year of her birth and pressed into a book."[27] Galchen casts her reflections about her daughter's first year as indexical—like leaves collected and pressed— more than revelatory; she describes her book as an assemblage of notes, some about experiences she'd otherwise forgotten. I think of my own work here as a combination of the cinephilic archive (of moments of teaching, motherhood, and film experience) and a "collection of leaves," bearing their indexical trace of having existed. The experiences for which there are no indices—the ways by which moving images become *film-souvenirs*, the ways in which I have taught and learned with my students and my son—might here gain shape and structure; the writing itself—the making time, the shaping and revising, the remembering and forgetting, the attempts to render qualities such as breath, weight, texture— has become an index of these experiences.

I think back to this essay's opening detail: the chair tapping the wall in *Küf*, as Basri learns of his son's death. At the New Directors/New Films Festival, I screened that film while three months pregnant, when I surely could imagine but had yet to physically know a parental love so encompassing that to grieve a child would be to lose a world entirely. My students and I celebrated the resonant subtlety of this sonic detail, which now I understand anew: the sound an index of *his* loss, and my memory of this festival moment a trace of all the love and learning that I've discovered—with students and with my son, through writing and speaking about what we love as it passes. In the cinephilic detail rests a history of revelations, the collection of which creates archives of not only our films but also our lives. Woolf "could spend hours trying to write that as it should be written, in order to give the feeling which is even at this moment very strong in [her]"; that even she claims she "should fail" conveys something of my own shortcomings, even as her light-infused childhood recollection has fueled my own attempt to give shape to what I never otherwise can hold. I have gravitated toward my profession for exactly its recognition of the movement and change that we try unwittingly to arrest; and—in teaching and motherhood both—it is this requisite space for reflection upon these changes that makes the most meaning and sense.

KRISTI MCKIM is Associate Professor of English and Chair of Film Studies at Hendrix College. She is the author of *Love in the Time of Cinema* and *Cinema as Weather: Stylistic Screens and Atmospheric Change*.

Notes

1. See Walter Benjamin, "On Some Motifs in Baudelaire," in *Illuminations*, trans. Harry Zohn (New York: Schocken Books, 1968), 155–200; and Paul Willemen, *Looks and Frictions: Essays in Cultural Studies and Film Theory* (Bloomington: Indiana University Press, 1994), 233.

2. Vincent Gammill, Catelyn Gibbs, Rane Peerson, William Repass, Adelia Shiffraw, Emily Smith, and Lance St. Laurent, "Introduction" to New Directors/New Films dossier, *Film Matters*, 4, no. 3 (2013): 48.

3. Ibid., 48–49.

4. Barthes defines *punctum* as a "sting, speck, cut, little hole—and also a cast of the dice. A photograph's *punctum* is that accident which pricks me (but also bruises me, is poignant to me)." Barthes further connects the *punctum* with subjective experience: "Very often the *Punctum* is a 'detail,' *i.e.*, a partial object. Hence to give examples of *punctum* is, in a certain fashion, to *give myself up*." Roland Barthes, *Camera Lucida*, trans. Richard Howard (New York: Hill and Wang, 1980), 27, 43; Rashna Wadia Richards, *Cinematic Flashes: Cinephilia and Classical Hollywood*, (Bloomington: Indiana University Press, 2013), 24.

5. Jane Tompkins, "Me and My Shadow," *New Literary History* 19 (1987): 173.

6. Ibid., 178.

7. Christian Keathley, *Cinephilia and History, or the Wind in the Trees* (Bloomington: Indiana University Press, 2006, 152.

8. D. N. Rodowick, *The Virtual Life of Film* (Cambridge, MA: Harvard University Press, 2007), 75.

9. Vivian Sobchack, *The Address of the Eye: A Phenomenology of Film Experience* (Princeton, NJ: Princeton University Press, 1992), 9.

10. Ibid., 25.

11. Vivian Sobchack, "Toward a Phenomenology of Nonfictional Film Experience," in *Collecting Visible Evidence*, eds. Michael Renov and Jane Gaines (Minneapolis: University of Minnesota Press, 1999), 247–248.

12. Ibid., 241. Sobchack opens by stating that "documentary is less a *thing* than an *experience*."

13. Ibid., 243.

14. Keathley, *Cinephilia and History*, 152.

15. See Virginia Woolf, *On Being Ill* (Ashfield, MA: Paris Press, 2012); and Vivian Sobchack, "Inscribing Ethical Space: Ten Propositions on Death, Representation, and Documentary," *Quarterly Review of Film Studies* 9 (1984): 283–300.

16. See Siegfried Kracauer, *Theory of Film: The Redemption of Physical Reality*, introduction by Miriam Bratu Hansen (Princeton, NJ: Princeton University Press, 1997).

17. See Kristi McKim, *Cinema as Weather: Stylistic Screens and Atmospheric Change* (New York: Routledge, 2013).

18. See Laura Mulvey, *Death 24x a Second: Stillness and the Moving Image* (London: Reaktion Books, 2006); see also Mary Ann Doane, *The Emergence of Cinematic Time: Modernity, Contingency, the Archive* (Cambridge, MA: Harvard University Press, 2003). I refer to Agnès Varda's *Jacquot de Nantes* (1991), of which I write in *Love in the Time of Cinema* (London:

Palgrave Macmillan, 2011). See also Jean Epstein, "Magnification," trans. Stuart Liebman, in *French Film Theory and Criticism: A History/Anthology, Vol. 1: 1907–1929,* ed. Richard Abel (Princeton, NJ: Princeton University Press, 1988), 235–236.

19. Epstein, "Magnification," 236.

20. Sobchack, "Toward a Phenomenology of Nonfictional Film Experience," 247.

21. See Mulvey, *Death 24x a Second,* 181–196.

22. Virginia Woolf, *Moments of Being,* ed. Jeanne Schulkind (New York: Harcourt Brace, 1985), 64–65.

23. Roland Barthes, "Leaving the Movie Theater," in *The Rustle of Language,* trans. Richard Howard (New York: Farrar, Straus, and Giroux, 1986), 349.

24. Hal Foster, "An Archival Impulse," *October* 110 (2004): 5.

25. Rowena Santos Aquino, "To Live (with) Cinema: Documenting Cinephilia and the Archival Impulse," *LOLA* 4 (2013), http://www.lolajournal.com/4/cinephilia.html.

26. Ibid.

27. David Gordon, "Rivka Galchen & David Gordon Discuss Children, Japanese Culture and Writing as a Conversation with a Friend," Electric Literature 2016, http://electriclitera ture.com/rivka-galchen-david-gordon-discuss-children-japanese-culture-and-writing-as-a -conversation-with-a-friend/.

8 Loving Performance

Cinephilia, Teaching, and the Stars

Steven Rybin

Every classroom has its mise-en-scène, but unlike the film director, who stands invisible behind the camera, the film professor is in the unique position of always being a performer within the setting she directs. Orchestrating the presentation of film clips, stills, discipline terminology, and historical facts, the teacher of cinema at once conducts the students' engagement with films and is also a performer in their presentation, a part of the classroom's material world. If loving film means responding creatively to the delightful contingencies of a particular film's imagination, teaching film means actively and performatively shaping the classroom as an extension of the cinema one loves. Movies, and ideas about movies, should not merely be conveyed or communicated to students: movies and ideas about movies should come alive, their meaning living in the space of the classroom in unique and unpredictable ways. Teaching movies, then, is always already about the art of performance.

The cinephile-professor's work can be conceptualized as a kind of performance in the teaching of almost any subject related to film. During the first five years of my teaching career, I taught several sections of Introduction to Film at a small liberal arts college. At this institution, Introduction to Film is a course among several others (such as Music Appreciation and Art Appreciation) that students may take to fulfill college-wide education requirements. The students taking this course thus come from a wide variety of demographic backgrounds and differ in their levels of college preparedness and their engagement with the art of film. Almost universally, few have had exposure to film outside immediately available multiplex options and current topical material they may have glimpsed on the Internet or on television. Part of my performance as a professor in Introduction to Film, then, occurs in the act of enthusiastically and creatively contextualizing difficult subjects such as experimental film and art cinema, quite esoteric material for many early twenty-first-century American college students. Take, for example, a classroom presentation of Stan Brakhage's experimental film *Mothlight* (1963), a collage film, made in part from the wings of dead moths, which I have shown several times to puzzled undergraduates (Figure 8.1). My presentation of this film might be accompanied by my own gestures, expressions, and movements that suggest not only something about how the film was made but also about how a viewer might respond to it. When describing how Brakhage made the film, for example, I often find myself (sometimes quite unconsciously) imitating the gestures I imagine the filmmaker might have made in crafting it: pretending to pick up prostrate dead moths, plucking their wings from their torsos, and affixing the wings to an invisible strip of celluloid. (Sometimes, as an expressive prop and support for my pedagogical performance, I bring in several feet of celluloid film to familiarize my class with the sort of materials Brakhage used.) I might also describe, through facial expressions, my reaction to the film the first time I saw it (and while I cannot quite remember, exactly, how I responded the first time I saw the film, I can imagine my younger self, around the age of most of my undergraduates, responding to the textures of Brakhage with a kind of beautiful bafflement). The important thing about my performance that emerges during the teaching of *Mothlight*, or any other film, is that it is in large part not overly rehearsed or carefully scripted out. I know my material, but depending on the contingent mix of students and level of enthusiasm I am encountering at any given moment, or the particular idea I want to get across, my gestures

Figure 8.1. *Mothlight* (Stan Brakhage, 1963).

and movements might change. In other words, while teaching, the professor becomes, for a time, an actor (and one who must improvise).

Understanding teaching as performance, a performance not buried in cinema's past but rather one that is vitally alive in the present-tense space of the classroom, leads to an intervention in cinephilia's ways of teaching and writing about film acting. The recent discursive history of cinephilia often contextualizes the film actor as a ghostly trace, a conjuring of a past presence, rather than a lively, present-tense figure with a life unfolding in the material space of *now*. For example, in Paul Willemen's conception of cinephilia, which takes the "privileged moment" between spectator and screen as the primary unit of cinephilia, the relationship with the actor is imbued with connotations of nostalgia and past time. Willemen, in fact, prefers the term *cinephiliac* to *cinephilic*, "because of its overtones of necrophilia, of relating to something that is dead, past, but alive in memory."[1] Christian Keathley picks up on this conception of cinephilia in his work, keeping with the spelling of *cinephiliac* in placing emphasis on "the indexical quality of the film image" as "the mark or trace of a prior presence" that "can suddenly and unexpectedly make itself felt to the viewer."[2] This theoretical investment in the mark or trace of a prior presence in the cinephile's experience frames the discussions of actors for both authors. For Willemen, when discussing a moment from Marlon Brando's performance in *On the Waterfront* (Elia Kazan, 1954), "What is given to you to see, for example, might be Brando acting in that role. Then suddenly there is a bit of Brando the person, an aspect of his personal biography or subjectivity coming through."[3] What Willemen refers to here is a historical past manifest in the body of the historically existing film actor who once stood on a set in front of a camera in order to inscribe a presence on film; crucial for Willemen is thus not so much Brando's embodiment of particular gestures, movements, and expressions but rather the index of a biography and culturally documented subjectivity that his presence points to. The history of that actor arises in the witnessed film like a ghost, temporarily alive in the viewer's experience but nevertheless dead, gone, past. In Keathley's study, meanwhile, the actor is often a figure who appears in conjunction with certain contingent moments of fascination that inspire a materialist, cinephiliac form of film history. The memory of the red, vivid lipstick Natalie Wood wears in an early scene in *Rebel Without a Cause* (Nicholas Ray, 1955), for example, is a moment that compels Keathley to discuss not so much Wood's performance but rather the relationship of the lipstick in this cherished moment from the film to the figuration of lips in the larger history of Surrealist art.[4] Even cinephiliac work on the figuration of the body in computer-generated cinema continues to conceptualize its discussion of digital performance through reference to traditional cinephilia's necrophiliac undertones. In Scott Balcerzak's work on the digital motion capture "performed" by Andy Serkis in *The Lord of the Rings* (Peter

Jackson, 2001), Willemen's commentary on the "ghosting," or doubling, of the real film actor onto the character witnessed on-screen is used by Balcerzak to think through how the presence of Serkis remains on-screen even after he is digitized by motion-capture technology.[5]

These examples of scholarly cinephiliac work are invaluable contributions to the recent return of cinephilia to the academy, and they provide a collective framework for connecting film pleasure to larger questions of film history, cultural memory, and the craft of writing. Yet in the pride of place these writers give to pastness in thinking about film, and the film actor in particular, we perhaps lose sight of the importance of the vital and present *now* created whenever the teacher becomes a performer in the classroom, a performer alongside the actors whose films form the subject of her pedagogy. In this consideration of the pedagogy of performance, then, I want to shift our focus from the cinephile's engagement with the past in performance and emphasize instead the *living* presence of the actor in the classroom, a material complex of gestures, evolving positions, movements, and expressions that enable the creation of present-tense meaning. The purpose of this shift is not to completely disconnect the actor from film history or narrative context, both important subjects for a cinephilic pedagogy, but rather to situate the encounter with the actor as an event happening in the present-tense space of the classroom, so as to make the students' eventual grappling with narrative and history performatively alive. In doing so, we make the actor less the subject of film pedagogy and more a creative (if only *cinematically* present) collaborator in the teaching of film, a kind of implicit co-teacher and guide into narrative analysis and historical contextualization.

As already suggested, the film professor is a living actor in the present-tense space of the classroom, even if the figures on the screen (reanimated moths) are already quite dead. Because the Brakhage example with which I began—a play of pure light and shape—contains no human actors, our attention is eventually redirected away from the exquisite otherness of reanimated, cinematic moths to the human figures in the classroom. *We* must perform the film's meaning, to inscribe a present-tense human dimension into its ghostly insect figurations. When I teach the performance of a human actor, however, I need not substitute my own performance for the lack of a cinematic one; the mise-en-scène of my classroom necessarily changes. Now, I stand in front of the classroom. My gestures and expressions are less immediately histrionic. I do not need to exaggerate and contort my body to persuade students to watch an unfamiliar experimental work; I am going to show them a scene with actors, something they are familiar with from a healthy diet of (mostly Hollywood) narrative cinema. Now, I efface my presence and turn the classroom over to the cinematic presence of a movie star. But rather than framing this actor as only or primarily an index of a past historical reality, or as a mere adjunct to the contingent encounter between a cinephile and a moment in a film, I now want to place the actor, and her gestures, movements, and expressions, at the center of the encountered moment in film and the presence of this moment in the classroom. Indeed, just as the professor herself must be palpably present in the performance of teaching, so too must the teacher enable the film actor to *live on* in the space of the classroom, and as something more than an index of pastness or an adjunct to fleeting mise-en-scène.

And thus something strange happens here, no less odd, in its way, than Brakhage's experimental intervention into my classroom. What was once familiar becomes strange; what was once immediately consumable "narrative information" becomes filtered through the moment-by-moment grace of an actor's unique imagination. There is a large screen behind me. On it is frozen an image of an actor I want to talk about: in this moment, it is Greta Garbo. In long shot, she is sitting, at the beginning of a clip I have selected from *Queen Christina* (Rouben Mamoulian, 1933), by a fire, next to John Gilbert. She is in the midst of a romantic encounter with her lover; the two are spending the evening in a small, rustic cottage before her departure the next day. The camera will soon begin a slow right-to-left pan across the room, revealing more of the setting and the various objects that decorate this space: a fireplace, wool hanging from a bedpost, a dresser, a spinning wheel, a fur coat and hat, a mirror, a chair, and a canopy bed. In *Queen Christina*, these props ultimately serve as narrative symbols of the pleasure taken by the title character during the final evening she spends with her lover. At the end of the sequence, Queen Christina herself makes this function clear, telling Gilbert's character that she has been "memorizing this room; in the future, in my memory, I shall live a great deal in this room." But in a class on performance and stardom, something else is tantalizingly revealed beyond narrative and dialogue. The class watches as Garbo walks across the room, the camera following her. She touches some of the objects in the setting, sensuously directing our attention to them: a mantel, a mirror, a spinning wheel, the bedpost wool, a bed, a pillow (Figure 8.2). These objects, courtesy of Professor Garbo, now crackle with a *photogénie* they did not possess before she touched them. Charles Affron has written of the affect her performance creates in us, particularly in regard to the objects in the room: "Wool reintroduces texture; its softness establishes the motif for Garbo's imprint upon yielding surfaces. She slithers across the bed with an unnatural turn of the body. . . . After sinking into the softness of her pillow, Garbo touches a religious picture and then consecrates the wooden bedpost with pillowlike tenderness and holy devotion."[6] Crucially, Affron's interest is not primarily with aspects of film form such as character psychology or narrative development. His interest is in the way Garbo herself calls our attention to the palpable surfaces of every object she touches. Every object in a film is potentially expressive, as James Naremore has taught us; as Garbo shows, actorly gesture, movement, and placement can reveal this diffuse expressivity.[7] Indeed, it is only

Figure 8.2. *Queen Christina* (Rouben Mamoulian, 1933).

through this expressivity that a narrative is created; Garbo is, here, not simply a part of mise-en-scène. She reveals mise-en-scène to us, refracts all potential narrative significance through her singular deployment of body and gesture.

In the classroom, what I ultimately want to do with a sequence such as this is demonstrate to students how things like "narrative information" and "symbolic meaning," sometimes dealt with in unproblematic and straightforward ways in introductory film classes, become tantalizingly mysterious and ambiguous when we fix our attention on an actor's way of uniquely moving through a scene. The whole point of showing the sequence is to convey how these other subjects could not but come later: when a film lover becomes transfixed by an actor, that viewer is given a curious sense that everything the film might mean must begin with the way this particular human being moves through space and time on film. (To prompt my students to begin thinking about this particularity, I sometimes compel them to perform the "commutation test," that is, the substitution of one actor for another in the imagination of the viewer and the consideration of how the role would be different if played by someone else.)[8] As a cinephile-teacher, then, what I want are a variety of responses to the vitality of Garbo's gestures. Garbo, once brought back to life by my pressing play on the classroom DVD player, has the power to teach my students to see, rather than see through, performance. Whereas introductory film textbooks tend to limit discussions of the actor to her role as a "figure," or an element of a film's mise-en-scène (as staged and determined by the director), Garbo and I collaborate in a pedagogical performance that enables students to bring the actor front and center and to delight in the various ways she makes the most "invisible" content of a classical Hollywood movie visible, palpable, vital, and alive.[9]

The Place of Performance in Cinephilic Pedagogy

As I suggested earlier, framing the actor in the classroom in this way also refigures contemporary considerations of the performer in cinephilia. Rather than framing the actor as only a *past* presence in cinephilic writing, or as a mere element of contingently encountered mise-en-scène, the actor is now the main point of focus, and contingency is felt less through a director's vision and more through the unpredictable encounter between the viewer and the actor's gestures, movements, and expressions. But regardless of how much the professor's own performative presence collaborates with the presence of the actor on the classroom's screen, to turn our attention to the actor in this way nevertheless poses a challenge for cinephilic pedagogy, and cinephilic scholarship more widely, to find a more salient place for theorizing and historicizing the presence of the actor. In many of the most justly influential cinephilic texts, the actor is something of a footnote. In Keathley's *Cinephilia and History, or the Wind in the Trees*, for example, the actor is dealt with primarily as a *figure*, or an element of mise-en-scène that functions, in a larger sense, as what Keathley calls a director's "way of looking."[10] Within Keathley's study, certain details that affix to the actor may become interesting, but only rarely does the "cinephiliac moment" as defined by his book encompass a *performed* moment as such. For example, Keathley references Gilbert Adair's fascination with Cary Grant's socks in Alfred Hitchcock's *North by Northwest* (1959), a film I have assigned to my upper-level students in a Special Topics course on Film Performance, a marginal visual detail in the film that the perceptually nimble cinephile can fetishize without losing sight of the important narrative details. Of course, cinephiles such as Adair and Keathley are not simply ignoring Grant in order to focus on the color of his socks; as David Ehrenstein writes of Adair's piece (a quote Keathley also includes), "what it proves isn't that Adair is nodding at the switch—not paying attention during one of the most famous set pieces in movie history—but rather that he's really on the ball."[11] And because he's on the ball, I think we are safe in assuming that Adair, in his viewing, has not failed to note the work of one of the most famous actors in movie history. Nevertheless, whatever Adair might have noticed about Grant's performance, he does not note it at length *in his writing*. This is curious, for what

I find challenging and pleasurable in both my writing about and my teaching of the sequence in question is the man wearing the socks, rather than, or in addition to, the socks themselves. What else was Grant doing, I ask my class, besides wearing those socks? Lots of things, all marvelous, all worthy of description and analysis on the page: the way Grant alternately removes and places his hands in his jacket pockets and around his hips, maintaining a pose of calculated calm as his character scopes out the situation (Figure 8.3); how these hands become quietly demonstrative as Grant walks across the dirt road to ask a passerby about the situation; how his hands shield the back of his head when the crop duster makes its first descent near him; and how, after the plane swoops down above Grant a second time, these same hands clutch dirt as if the earth itself were the only protection the character had against this mysterious assailant.[12]

In other words, what we are discussing in my class when we are discussing *North by Northwest,* or *Queen Christina,* or virtually any film, and what I find endlessly mysterious, endlessly worthy of poring over through perceptually nimble viewing and the ensuing contemplation of the filmic moment—and what I want to open up for my students—is Cary Grant himself. And by "Cary Grant himself," I mean not the index of the historically existing actor (who remains, regardless of the numerous popular biographies that have been written about him, beyond our grasp) but rather the man who moves on-screen, who says lines in a certain way, and who gets from point A to B and, in the performance of that A to B, fundamentally refigures what we might come to think of as the scene's "narrative content." (Of course, the socks are a part of this delicious bundle. But

Figure 8.3. *North by Northwest* (Alfred Hitchcock, 1959).

only a part.) After all, in watching this scene from *North by Northwest*, we have not just watched a crop duster chase down Roger Thornhill in a cornfield. We have watched Cary Grant create, through the way he moves, and through what his hands suggest of his relationship to a suddenly threatening space, a sense of what filmic space is at this moment and what its experience might mean to us.

Another key reason why Cary Grant, or any other actor, is not often salient in many academic discussions of cinephilia is also that as a subject position and way of viewing, cinephilia traditionally prides itself on a certain distinction that sets the cinephile apart from ordinary filmgoers (even as the distinguished cinephile desires to teach to those filmgoers). This distinction is often usefully conveyed in pedagogical terms; Keathley, for example, memorably describes the cinephile-critic as "a viewer who had special knowledge or skill, one who could see and show to others."[13] Occasionally, though, the distinction of the cinephile is prized for its more elusive and ineffable social position rather than its pedagogical reach. Jason Sperb, for example, has noted how traditional conceptions of cinephilia "seem rooted in the pursuit of hard-to-find, elusive films as well as in particular reception practices" as well as "the cult value of things not yet seen by many."[14] Although a pedagogical urge remains implicit in most of these considerations of the cinephile's special status, to frame the cinephile's position and methods of viewing as distinctive from popular reception practices is problematic in terms of performance pedagogy. This is because star studies deals with subject matter of which students, in some sense, already have some knowledge. My students were well equipped to love stars from the first day of class, as was evident from the Leonardo DiCaprio wallpaper decorating the background of one student's laptop to another student's loving anecdote about once meeting Mickey Rooney. Indeed, the fact that *I* like talking about actors affords me no special distinction among my colleagues: in addition to the growing number of film scholars I have met who are also interested in performance, I have also met a number of other professors outside my own discipline who were passionate fans of various stars and could recite entire filmographies and career anecdotes of certain beloved figures. However, even though stardom is something all of my students (and many of my colleagues) are conversant with, the terms of acting analysis are not, and therein lies a special cinephilic skill that, far from simply or only qualifying me as an especially distinctive or special figure, can be used to teach my students to "see and show to others." In teaching how to see and show, I think, the point is not only to show them how to *find* pleasurable and significant moments of acting (many of them already have favorite actors and have thus already found such moments) but rather to show them how to write about the pleasure of these moments in larger critical and discursive contexts.

Thus, where the distinction of the cinephile-professor *can* become pedagogically useful is in the very establishment of this discursive context; by taking the actor seriously—by distinguishing the cinephile's interest in the actor from the other various ways our culture has of discoursing about movie stars—the cinephile-professor can shift the student's focus away from the popular cult of celebrity that tends to inflect most conversations about actors conducted by students new to cinema studies and toward a more nuanced focus on performance itself. Of course, celebrity culture is itself a worthy subject of study for students and scholars. However, one of the negative impacts of that widespread culture for a cinephilic pedagogy of performance is that it makes the actor overly familiar, an ever-present entity whose presence in gossip and news media threatens to overdetermine the contingent encounter with an actor's means of characterization in particular movies. When we watch *North by Northwest*, do we see the Cary Grant of popular biography and mythology, the one who experimented with LSD and had a tortuous late-life relationship with Dyan Cannon, and who was perhaps the lover of Randolph Scott; or do we turn our attention to the more material gestures of Grant on the screen, as we collaborate with him, as viewers, by watching him? Biography and mythology, of course, need not be entirely stricken from cinephilic discussions of performance. But it seems to me best to at least initially set gossip aside in favor of a pedagogy that focuses first on what the actor actually does on-screen; *this* insistence on the performer's material presence might be the most lasting source of the professor's distinctive contribution to cinephilic performance studies. What makes the cinephile-professor's pedagogical performance distinctive is not the *fact* of one's interest in the star (who *doesn't* like movie stars?) but rather the seriousness of her enchantment with the movie actor and her belief that to focus on an actor is to grapple with something central to our experience of film. In my teaching, then, I seek to emphasize how special and ongoingly mysterious the effects the actor has on us are, despite the fact that our celebrity culture frames actors and stars as immediately consumable and understandable figures.

In part, I arrive at this through my own performative passion for certain actors as the semester progresses: I cannot be detached and distanced when discussing personal favorites like Grant or Garbo but rather must be demonstrative, in my role as professor, of my love for their achievements on the screen. My enthusiasm, however, is not meant to simply convey my love for the subject, nor does it ask the student to mimic the specific subjects of my passions or my manner. Instead, I view the performance of enthusiasm in the classroom as a sort of gauntlet thrown down to the class, an implicit challenge for students to answer in kind with their own passionate creations of knowledge. Indeed, at the beginning of my Special Topics course on Film Performance, most of my students felt they more or less understood what a star, and an actor, was, even as their descriptions of performance, in the early weeks of the seminar, tended to conflate the psychological content of the character with the work performed by the actor.

What I want, then, is to encourage my students to consider more closely the details of acting that emerge as significant in their viewing. They cannot simply be consumers of narrative content: they have to, using the actor as an avatar, exist within the film, feeling the movements through story and space via an affective engagement with performative gesture and pose. Murray Pomerance articulates his concern with the liminal affects actors might generate in our experience, asking how our engagements with the actor constitute a giving over of the viewer's self, a virtual *inhabitation* of the film through sensuous, close attention to qualities of performance in a given figure. Pomerance, in his own analysis of the affective dimensions of Janet Leigh's performance in *Psycho*, asks two interrelated questions: "How is the special mode of relationship established that permits intimacy without commitment, revelation without implication? What surrender of the viewer's self is implicit in every acceptance of acted reality?"[15] These are the sort of questions I would like my students to ask.

In initiating my students into how to think through this "special mode of relationship," I first direct their attention to the liminal details of performance, using close description as a key method. To fulfill this part of my course, I assign Andrew Klevan's *Film Performance*, which offers my students a master class in the art of performance description. Of contemporary scholars, Klevan has risen to the challenge of perceiving and describing the present-tense richness of being and manner in a variety of performers most directly. Klevan, dialoguing with the work of Charles Affron and Lesley Stern, persuades us to consider the act of writing on performance as a "process of evocation," in which privileged moments from cinematic works "disclose themselves with equal vivacity"; and, crucially, Klevan centers on the role of duration at play in this act of appreciation and description, writing further that "our effort to appreciate will forever be in process, in pursuit, there will always be more of their achievement to emerge."[16] By emphasizing the act of description that follows and answers the challenge of perceiving performance, we place criticism on film acting squarely in the history of *ekphrasis*, which in the traditional arts means the description, in writing, of a scene painted in a picture.[17] For Lesley Stern and George Kouvaros, likewise, such questions of *ekphrasis* are intimately linked to the writer's desire to evoke the shape of the performance in writing, involving a certain degree of what Stern calls "fictionalization" (the creation of a new narrative, in criticism, as the writer strings a series of privileged moments together), calling upon the student's effort to evoke, in writing, the experience of performance in all of its complexity.[18]

Structuring the Course on Performance

Moving from these larger theoretical issues regarding cinephilia's pedagogical treatment of film acting to more concrete examples of pedagogy, it is useful to discuss how my class on film performance is structured as well as offer some thoughts about the writing produced by my students in the course. I assign a number of screenings and articles on individual actors in my course; beyond Grant and Garbo, the class also explores styles of acting and themes of performance in actors such as Denzel Washington, Julianne Moore, Viola Davis, Nicole Kidman, Katharine Hepburn, Marilyn Monroe, Robert De Niro, Marlon Brando, and various actors from Pedro Almodóvar's films.[19] Later in the course, we touch on issues of performance capture in digital cinema and also discuss the potential democratization of performance by looking closely at what Erving Goffman calls "the performance of everyday life," as depicted in a range of YouTube videos.[20] The heart of the course is a series of Actor Journals assigned to students halfway through the semester. In each of these journals, the student reflects on moments of performance in four different films by the same actor, an actor who means something personal to the student but in ways that perhaps the student has not yet fully reflected upon. By charting patterns of performance across four films, the student not only maps certain themes and tropes in a single actor's unfolding career but also, on a more autobiographical level, reflects, for an extended duration of four weeks, upon why the actor has come to matter to her and how this significance might be put into words. Through this method I aim for students to discover subjects of historical and critical interest through their descriptive engagement with the actor's presence.

While many students, in my experience, exhibit a slightly uniform taste in performers—mostly white, male Method actors—a variety of delightful descriptions of these actors nevertheless emerges. One student studied the films of Gary Oldman, finding that the most fascinating moments of his reserved performance in *Tinker Tailor Soldier Spy* (Tomas Alfredson, 2011) resisted the viewer's efforts to project meaning: "His face is thoughtful; brow furrowed and mouth pursed. His worry over [the situation] is in no way explosive or overly obvious . . . he is calm and controlled . . . standing still, no movement in his arms or neck. Smiley is a character of little expression and movement, making an analysis problematic."[21] Another student wanted to account for her interest in Philip Seymour Hoffman and did so in a series of fascinating entries that, in contrast to my other student's work on Oldman, located psychological content in memorable gestures and expressions. In writing about Hoffman's turn as a drag queen in *Flawless* (Joel Schumacher, 1999), the student wrote: "In most of all the scenes in *Flawless*, [Hoffman's] hands are available for the audience to see, and they typically play a vital role in establishing who Rusty is as a person; Rusty often fidgets with her rings, earrings, or simply just touches her hands a lot when she talks."[22] In general, psychological content is usually not difficult for students to find: the challenge, which the student writer on Hoffman met admirably, is to show how character traits emerge through descriptions of moments of performance worthy of discussion and attention.

If description is necessary for the student to account for, in writing, the memorable affects of performance, the next step is to place those seized moments of "acted reality" into larger critical and historical contexts. Here the aforementioned idea of fictionalization comes into play, wherein each cinephile strings moments of pleasure taken from pockets of cinematic performance into a critical narrative. In other words, what I want my students to do is take the pleasure found in the liminal textures of performance and let it find a home in critical discussions of acting's history. Throughout the course, then, I present film clips and case studies not only as examples of various acting styles produced throughout the twentieth century but as affective barometers of what these various methods mean to us today as a variety of actors, using a variety of techniques and methods, step into my classroom in different ways. The design of my Performance course takes students not only through a series of case studies focused on individual actors but also on a journey through the history of acting styles and the history of methods keyed to the analysis of those styles. In the first two weeks, we discuss the ontology of film acting itself. Guided by Klevan's first chapter in *Film Appreciation* and Cynthia Baron and Sharon Carnicke's discussion of performance elements, we discuss the distinction between acting in cinema and acting in the theater and the various ways in which certain genres (such as melodrama) problematize this distinction.[23] My students soon discover that the intensely emotional style of performance in the family melodrama—a historical genre with which few of them are familiar; in my course, *Far from Heaven* (Todd Haynes, 2002) is our example—produces performances that not only depart from the traditional understanding of cinematic performance as less histrionic but also affect them in ways that are quite distinct from what they consider a "good" performance to be. Using a contemporary melodramatic performance such as Julianne Moore's in *Far from Heaven* ensures that my students cannot simply dismiss the family melodrama as a genre that was relevant "back then" (i.e., in the 1950s) but as one containing moments of acted reality that are still quite relevant to today's society. Indeed, even some of my heterosexual male students, many of whom are initially resistant to the viewing of melodrama, admit a fondness for Moore's performance and the genre of melodrama before the semester is over.

After we establish the ontological groundwork, a series of case studies emphasizes changes in acting style across the twentieth century. With every example, scenes selected from certain films not only illustrate critical points made in assigned writings but also refract these ideas through gesture, movement, and expression—in other words, every step of the way, the actor herself, and my students' responses to her, intervenes in our ensuing discussions of the film.

In discussing François Delsarte's gestural methods, we look at Charlie Chaplin.[24] We examine closely a variety of moments in his performance in *City Lights* (Charlie Chaplin, 1931) and, using the final scene from the aforementioned film, study the way gesture and movement generate unpredictable moments of affect that leave both character and viewer suspended over a variety of narrative and existential possibilities.[25] Discussions of the meaning of gestures and bodily movement are deepened later in the course by looking at Rudolf Laban's movement analysis (as discussed by Cynthia Baron in her piece on Denzel Washington), using *Training Day* (Antoine Fuqua, 2001) as an example.[26] *Training Day*, perhaps because of its familiarity and allegiance to the crime genre (beloved by several of my students), often remains a favorite of my class during the semester, and the sense in which Washington's and co-star Ethan Hawke's performances could be contrasted through Laban becomes an example we return to in later case studies whenever comparisons of different affects generated by two different actors are brought up in discussion. Then, I expose my students to the historical debates between adherents of Konstantin Stanislavski and followers of Bertolt Brecht and use these debates to deepen my students' sense of how stardom functions in film by using another contemporary example, Stanley Kubrick's *Eyes Wide Shut* (1999). Were Nicole Kidman and Tom Cruise "playing themselves" in Kubrick's film, thus "baring the device" in a Brechtian manner and redirecting our attention to the reality of star production? Or were they playing psychologically and realistically consistent characters, named Alice and Bill, with whom we can identify and in whose performances we can immerse ourselves? In our class discussions, we explore these questions by looking closely and repeatedly at the scene in which Alice (Kidman) confronts Bill (Cruise) about his possible affair, all the while smoking pot and sharing her own fantasies about an affair with a pilot. Some students read the performances as fairly conventional depictions of character subjectivity, framed by their understanding of Kubrick's intensive methods of retakes and rehearsal.[27] Others read the scene as Nicole Kidman and Tom Cruise performing themselves, in which our knowledge of their marriage and star personas impact our reading of the films. Of course, these responses are not mutually exclusive, and our class usually settles on a combination of Stanislavskian and Brechtian methods as the best tools to work through our experience of Kidman's and Cruise's performances. Throughout the discussion, we return to scenes of performance from the film itself, using film clips to ensure that the actor herself has a role in the development of our ensuing conversation.

The capstone of the course is a term paper and in-class presentation in which the student weaves descriptions of performance style into a larger reflection on a topic in the history of acting. The paper component of the assignment encourages the student to continue to articulate the relationship between viewer and actor, begun in the journals, and the presentation component ensures that the student's personal relationship with performance becomes publicly useful in the context of an oral report given to the class. Topics tackled by my students vary, but the most intriguing essays and presentations successfully combine description of memorable moments of acting with larger-scale theoretical and historical commentary. One student, for example, looked closely at the performances of Kirsten Dunst in Sofia Coppola's *The Virgin Suicides* (1999) and *Marie Antoinette* (2006), contextualizing a description of Dunst's gestures within an analysis of Coppola's film style, arguing that this synthesis achieved an intervention whereby the female director came to objectify the female body in creative and unpredictable ways. Another student closely described Tom Hardy's turn as Bane in *The Dark Knight Rises* (Christopher Nolan, 2012), situating Hardy's intensely physical performance within the film's own creative sound design, itself a key component of a performance that relies heavily on the deep bass of the soundtrack for the character's threatening vocal effects. My most successful students, in their various papers and presentations, admirably marry memorable pockets of "acted reality" to larger-scale reflections on the place of the actor and the pleasure of watching acting, informed by their newly acquired knowledge of the history of performance and performance studies.

Conclusion

I began by suggesting that the pedagogy of performance must move beyond conceptions of the actor as part of the indexical past reality "pointed to" by the cinema. My motivation in shifting this emphasis is not ultimately because of the problematic nature of the "index" in the digital era of cinema but rather because of my interest in positioning the actor as a living presence in the space of the classroom. In shifting emphasis to performative presence, I acknowledge a certain loss in distinction between my students and myself; although many of my students may not self-identify as "cinephiles," all of us are interested in stars. Nevertheless, I request that my students redirect their interest in stardom toward a more nuanced descriptive analysis of the encountered contingencies of gesture and movement at play in an actor's work, description that in turn engages larger questions of history and criticism in which the actor always retains central presence. This demand makes the cinephile's work as professor in the classroom distinctive from the usual consideration of the movie star, outside the classroom, as a disposable product of popular culture. My critical map for teaching a love of performance thus focuses on two things: a description of the performed moment that has mattered to the student and an effort by the class as a whole to show how these moments of memorably acted realities intervene in and contribute to larger contexts of historical and theoretical study.

What are the benefits of the critical map and method I have provided? For one, encouraging students to describe moments of performance holds them accountable, beyond plot summary and an inventory of a film's stylistic tropes, for what has mattered in their cinematic experience. Teaching them to see rather than see through the actor inscribes them as part of the flow of a film's ongoing experience and challenges them to reflect further on what more they might come to love in viewing film performance (and why). Second, I ensure that my students do not remain within the realm of personal preference and taste. If cinephilia is to matter as it lives on in the twenty-first century, it must make its passion useful for others, and let it become animated within larger histories, critiques, and theoretical reflections that will prove intriguing to a larger community. Thus, through the development of historical case studies and in-class oral presentations, I challenge my students to find appropriate theoretical and historical contexts into which their enthusiasm for a particular performer can intervene.

My approach seeks to carve out a place for the actor, in terms of both pedagogy and writing, in twenty-first-century cinephilia. As twentieth-century cinema becomes more and more an object of the past, contemporary pedagogical methods must work to preserve and, repeatedly, reignite the vitality of that past cinema for our students. Pedagogy on film performance has a crucial role to play in compelling new students of film to think through, moment by moment, the meaning of the present-tense film experience they are enjoying and the larger questions that might emerge from this viewing. To view the actor first as part of the ongoing and unfolding *now* is not to lose sight of larger questions of narrative and history but rather to put students and future scholars in a position of discovering those questions through the pleasure of firsthand experience. Once they are in this position, they too become performers, discovering and conveying, in speaking and in writing, the meaning they have found in the stars.

STEVEN RYBIN is Assistant Professor of Film Studies at Minnesota State University, Mankato. He is the author of *Gestures of Love: Romancing Performance in Classical Hollywood Cinema*, editor of *The Cinema of Hal Hartley: Flirting with Formalism*, and co-editor (with Will Scheibel) of *Lonely Places, Dangerous Ground: Nicholas Ray in American Cinema*.

Notes

1. Paul Willemen, *Looks and Frictions: Essays in Cultural Studies and Film Theory* (Bloomington: Indiana University Press, 1994), 227.

2. Christian Keathley, *Cinephilia and History, or the Wind in the Trees* (Bloomington: Indiana University Press, 1994), 37–38.

3. Willemen, *Looks and Frictions*, 240.

4. Keathley, *Cinephilia and History*, 168–177.

5. Scott Balcerzak, "Andy Serkis as Actor, Body and Gorilla: Motion Capture and the Presence of Performance," in *Cinephilia in the Age of Digital Reproduction: Film, Pleasure and Digital Culture, Vol. 1*, eds. Scott Balcerzak and Jason Sperb (London: Wallflower Press, 2009), 195–213.

6. Charles Affron, *Star Acting: Gish, Garbo, Davis* (New York: Dutton, 1977), 178, 182.

7. See discussion of "expressive objects" in James Naremore, *Acting in the Cinema* (Berkeley: University of California Press, 1988), 83–96.

8. See John O. Thompson, "Screen Acting and the Commutation Test," *Screen* 19, no. 2 (1978): 55–70.

9. For an example of the typical presentation of acting in an introductory film textbook, see David Bordwell and Kristin Thompson, *Film Art: An Introduction*, 10th ed. (New York: McGraw-Hill, 2012), 131–140.

10. Keathley, *Cinephilia and History*, 95.

11. Quoted in ibid., 45.

12. Much of what Cary Grant does in this scene, and other scenes in this film, has been ably described by Naremore in *Acting in the Cinema*, 213–235.

13. Keathley, *Cinephilia and History*, 95.

14. Jason Sperb, "Sensing an Intellectual Nemesis," in *Cinephilia in the Age of Digital Reproduction: Film, Pleasure and Digital Culture, Vol. 1*, eds. Scott Balcerzak and Jason Sperb (London: Wallflower Press, 2009), 96.

15. Murray Pomerance, *The Eyes Have It: Cinema and the Reality Effect* (New Brunswick, NJ: Rutgers University Press, 2013), 128.

16. Andrew Klevan, *Film Performance: From Achievement to Appreciation* (London: Wallflower Press, 2005), 16–17.

17. See Murray Krieger, *Ekphrasis* (Baltimore, MD: Johns Hopkins University Press, 1992), especially 3–21.

18. Lesley Stern and George Kouvaros, "Descriptive Acts: Introduction," in *Falling for You: Essays on Cinema and Performance*, eds. Lesley Stern and George Kouvaros (Sydney: Power Publications, 1999), 16–17.

19. Many of these case studies were complemented by assigned readings from Naremore, *Acting in the Cinema*.

20. Erving Goffman, *The Presentation of Self in Everyday Life* (Woodstock, NY: Overlook Press, 1973).

21. Lauren Yawn, student journal, Special Topics: Film Performance and Star Studies class, fall 2012, Georgia Gwinnett College.

22. Julie McMillian, student journal, Special Topics: Film Performance and Star Studies class, fall 2012, Georgia Gwinnett College.

23. Cynthia Baron and Sharon Marie Carnicke, "Giving Performance Elements Their Due," in *Reframing Screen Performance*, eds. Cynthia Baron and Sharon Marie Carnicke (Ann Arbor: University of Michigan Press, 2008), 33–61.

24. Cynthia Baron and Sharon Marie Carnicke, "Delsarte and the Dynamics of Human Expression," in *Reframing Screen Performance*, eds. Cynthia Baron and Sharon Marie Carnicke (Ann Arbor: University of Michigan Press, 2008), 165–187.

25. Klevan, *Film Performance*, 19–25.

26. Cynthia Baron and Sharon Marie Carnicke, "Laban: Temporal and Spatial Dimensions of Movement," in *Reframing Screen Performance*, eds. Cynthia Baron and Sharon Marie Carnicke (Ann Arbor: University of Michigan Press, 2008), 188–207.

27. See Dennis Bingham, "Kidman, Cruise, and Kubrick: A Brechtian Pastiche," in *More Than a Method: Trends and Traditions in Contemporary Film Performance* (Detroit, MI: Wayne State University Press, 2004), 247–274.

9 Go to the Movies!

Cinephilia, Exhibition, and the Cinema Studies Classroom

Allison Whitney

MANY ELEMENTS OF CINEMA STUDIES curricula either proceed from or seek to instill forms of cinephilia, whether by training students to discern the smallest details of image and sound, or by cultivating a fascination with the interlocking histories of films, filmmakers, audiences, the theatrical spaces they occupy, and the physical apparatus of the cinema's materials and machines. At the same time, academic film study and cinephilia, while never monolithic discourses, are currently in a state of flux and redefinition, in large part because of technological changes in the production, distribution, and exhibition of moving pictures, all of which transform the ways film texts can be enjoyed, critiqued, collected, and studied. These shifts, both in films themselves and in the discourses of those who love them, have considerable implications for academic study and instruction. As Robert C. Allen explains in his 2011 essay "Reimagining the History of the Experience of Cinema in a Post-Moviegoing Age," for most undergraduate students, born in the 1990s, the theatrical experience is not, and perhaps never was, the singular or definitive way of engaging with a film text. Using his own daughter as an example, he explains that her "earliest and formative experiences of cinema occurred not in a movie theater, but in front of a television set connected to a VCR."[1] Meanwhile, even students who remember the days before the VCR now engage with the history of cinema almost entirely through digital media and often via streaming services and online archives. While such systems can be a boon to cinema studies by making great quantities of material available to researchers and teachers, they also have the side effect of further decentering exhibition contexts from students' conception of film history.

The tendency to forget the cinema as a physical and social space can make it difficult for students to grasp the artistic, political, and social implications of the films we study and even to understand the conceptual frameworks of film theory and criticism. For example, as Jenna Ng notes in her essay "The Myth of Total Cinephilia," the classical moments associated with cinephilia were the product of a specific film culture of the 1950s and 1960s, one that is as contingent on the circumstances of spectatorship as a valorization of unique moments in particular films:

> The core of this cinephilia was an all-encompassing film culture in those decades and particularly in France, one which points not only to the movies and art, but also to politics, ideology, community, and social practices. Yet cinephilia was also the *physical* act of viewing films, invariably in the cinema hall.[2]

She goes on to explain how this combination of conceptual and embodied cinephilia generated the "film clubs, the magazines, the cross-continental admirations, the genealogies, the politics" that continue to inform the ways we theorize and historicize the cinema.[3] In my experience, students' comparative lack of experience with the act of theatrical spectatorship can make it more difficult for them to grasp many of the concepts they encounter in the cinema studies classroom. In this essay, I will explain how I have worked to overcome this difficulty by designing assignments that draw attention to subjective experiences of spectatorship in both public and private spaces and by using students' accounts and critiques of their own cinephilia, and that of their contemporaries, to open up a more holistic way of thinking about the importance of the cinema as an art form, a social space, and a cultural institution as well as encourage a more holistic way of conceptualizing cinephilia itself as not just a disposition toward certain moments and details from cinema but a "*physical* act of viewing" deeply tied to the exhibition context.

While teaching undergraduate cinema studies classes at Texas Tech University in Lubbock, Texas, I have developed two assignments focusing on film exhibition in both public and private realms. In the first, I ask students to attend a public film screening in order to observe the relationship between the built environment and audience behavior, while in the second, students interview their elders about early experiences of film viewing in the home. In both cases, the assignments encourage students to contemplate spaces and practices they may take for granted and help open up classroom dialogue about the personal and political implications of spectatorship. Students become mindful of the circumstances of exhibition, while their written and verbal reports offer varying, and often conflicting, accounts of cinephilia—a love of not only the movies but also the phenomenology of both theatrical and home cinemas. For example, in their reflections, students reveal personal narratives of spectatorship and how evocative moments in particular films, ritualized elements of film going, and feelings of nostalgia figure in their experiences and those of the audiences around them. As students remark on everything from the smell of popcorn and the texture of theater seats to family memories of the neighborhood's first television, they can better comprehend cinephilia as a historical phenomenon and therefore understand the critical and scholarly discourses that emerge from it. At the same time, they are also able to generate their own critiques of cinephilia, particularly concerning issues of race and social class, which in turn help them better appreciate film scholarship that resists cinephilia. Finally, students also begin to identify what we might term a regional cinephilia—using specifically local frames of reference to describe their film culture.

Exhibition Study

The exhibition study assignment asks students to attend a screening and to conduct a detailed analysis, not of the film, but of the exhibition space, the behavior of the people within it, and their own experience of the physical and social environment. Allen explains that as "theatrical moviegoing becomes a thing more remembered than experienced, we will be reminded that one of the most striking features of the experience of cinema for a hundred years was its sociality," and it is this sociality where I want the students to direct their attention.[4] Students may choose to attend any movie, at any time of day, and at any cinema, provided that it is a public screening, and I am careful to assure students that even a "bad" movie can provide an excellent opportunity for this exercise. Indeed, I remind students to remain open to the possibility that watching the most unremarkable film can still catch "you in the net of the audience's togetherness; ultimately, you have to give it the time of day."[5] Focusing students' attention on the social dynamics of the cinema, regardless of the quality of the film being projected, is particularly important in an introductory course, where one's syllabus is usually populated by films with "masterpiece" status. Obviously, such films warrant our attention, but the history of film is not only the history of great films, and class discussions tend to benefit from students having observed that even a "bad" movie can generate cinephiliac moments, whether they be personal revelations or powerful collective experiences, experiences that have played a significant role in the cinema's functions as an art form, a medium of mass communication, and an object of academic study.

When I introduce this assignment, many students express a concern that nothing interesting will happen at the theater and that there will be nothing to talk about. In order to focus their attention, I offer an extended list of questions to ask themselves throughout their visit. I remind them not to treat it as a checklist but rather to use the questions to pique their curiosity and make them challenge received ideas. First, I recommend that they arrive at the theater early so that they have time to observe the architecture, the exterior and interior décor, and the behavior of fellow audience members in the lobby, at the concession stand, in the hallways, and in the auditorium itself.[6] Other questions to consider include:

- Where is the theater located? Which neighborhoods are nearby?
- How do you get to the theater? Is it accessible on foot or via public transportation, or do you need a car to get there? What are the parking arrangements? What do these things tell you about what kind of customers the theater is catering to?
- Look at the exterior of the theater. Is it a stand-alone structure or part of a larger complex? What are the neighboring buildings and businesses? How is the exterior decorated? Does it provide space for people to congregate? Are these spaces indoors or outdoors?
- Is the box office automated, or do you buy your ticket from a person? What do the tickets cost? Are there discounts available, and what kind? Do they try to promote concessions or other products during your transaction?
- Note signs throughout the theater, including the exterior walls, the box office area, the lobby, and so forth. What do the signs say?
- What kind of contact do you have with theater staff? Do they seem to initiate contact with customers? Are there visible security personnel?
- Think about the architectural layout of the theater. Where are the concession stands, restrooms, and exits? Are there appointed spaces for people to mingle? How does the architecture influence the way you move through the space?
- Notice the interior design features including lighting (light levels and light fixtures), color schemes, flooring materials, seating areas, artworks, or other elements of the décor. How do these elements make you think and feel? Why do you think they were selected?
- Does the theater identify itself with a particular brand or corporate entity? Is this an "art" or "independent" cinema? How do you know?
- What are the acoustic qualities of the space? Do different areas of the theater sound louder than or different from others? What factors come into play in determining the sounds you do (or do not) hear throughout the building?
- Are there other kinds of activities available such as displays, game arcades, or play areas? Who is using them, and what purposes do they serve?
- What kinds of products are advertised (including other movies), and in which media (posters, pamphlets, coupons, samples, etc.)?
- What kinds of food and drink are for sale? Where is the concession stand located relative to the auditorium and the main entrance? Do the seats have cup holders or other accommodations for snacks?
- What facilities or services are available for people with disabilities? Are these services advertised, and how?
- Observe audience behavior both inside and outside the auditorium. Do people appear to be on dates? Out with friends or family? Alone? What

kinds of assessments or judgments do you find yourself making about people based on the company they keep at the movies?

- Consider the layout of the auditorium (i.e., the room where you watch the movie). What are the seating options? How is the theater decorated? What kind of lighting is available, and when do the light levels change?
- Are the armrests adjustable?
- Are people socializing inside the auditorium before and after the film?
- Where do people choose to sit? What kinds of factors seem to influence their decisions about seating?
- Does the theater offer instruction on audience behavior, such as reminding you to turn off your cell phone? What are these instructions, and how are they delivered and enforced? What kind of appeals do they make to customers (i.e., do they appeal to their politeness, to their respect for the cinema as an art form, to the threat of public embarrassment)?
- What kinds of goods or services are advertised before the movie? What kinds of trailers precede the film? What do the advertisements suggest about the expected audience for this film? How do your fellow audience members react to the advertisements?
- How do people behave during the film? Do they talk, text, laugh, scream, or respond in other ways? If so, do others find these behaviors disruptive, or is it "part of the fun"?
- How do you think the time of day, the type of film being shown, and the gender, race, and age of the audience members influence our expectations of audience behavior? Does the audience meet, or defy, these expectations?
- Does the audience stay seated to watch the credits at the end of the film?

I also instruct students that this is an exercise in unobtrusive observation, so they are not to interview people or otherwise interfere with their activities.[7]

While mainstream commercial cinemas are certainly appropriate venues, I also remind students of other film facilities in the city, including, in Lubbock, the Louise Hopkins Underwood Center for the Arts, which hosts the Flatland Film Festival, or the Science Spectrum, a museum that houses a 15/70mm large-format dome theater. In these cases, I remind them to contemplate the institutional context of the facility and, if applicable, the "special event" status of the screening, as they often host film festivals, educational events, and so forth. Further, one of the local cinemas is a drive-in, which provides fascinating opportunities for observation but also requires a different set of parameters from the conventional cinemas. For example, the drive-in defines interior and exterior spaces in quite different terms from a conventional cinema, since car interiors are private spaces that occupy public space. Meanwhile, the culture of the drive-in generates distinct norms for audience behavior.

In order to prepare for their theater visit, I ask the students to analyze our classroom—another carefully engineered space they have likely taken for granted. I ask them to get up and move around the room, noting the colors, textures, materials, lighting, and other attributes of the space. Students sometimes find this exercise confusing but quickly begin to appreciate the room's powerful influence on their behavior. The classroom where I teach was designed for cinema studies classes, so it is configured very much like a traditional cinema, with no windows, wall and floor materials that moderate reflection and echo, a raked floor, fixed seating, a large screen, an elaborate sound system, and a small chamber at the back for projection equipment. Not only do these elements reflect a particular tradition of cinephilia, where focused, undivided attention to the film yields the kinds of close readings and detailed observation that underpin so much of both film criticism as a cultural practice and cinema studies as a scholarly field, but the room also has significant pedagogical consequences.

As the students point out how the instructor stands on a raised platform, behind a lectern housing the A/V equipment controls, and that the seating is in fixed rows, they realize that the space accommodates a hierarchical power structure, one where the teacher is the primary source of knowledge, and where dialogue among students is physically, acoustically, and socially awkward. I then explain how the room's design is in fact at odds with my educational philosophy, since I would prefer a space that was more conducive to discussion and debate among students. I also remind them how on the few occasions when I have used small-group exercises, the room quickly becomes uncomfortable, as someone invariably has to sit backward on their chair while the people on the outer edges of a row find it more difficult to participate. We continue the exercise outdoors, looking at the exterior of the building and considering how its architectural styles, its landscape design, and even the sound of a neighboring fountain inform the space and our behavior in it. While this attention to university infrastructure may seem like an unnecessary diversion into pedagogical theory, I use it to make the point that the classroom itself is an educational technology and that our behavior in it is heavily influenced by the ideologies that underlie its design. While one can make choices to defy the expectations built into a space, to do so requires strategic thinking and significant expenditures of time and energy, and such activity produces friction and discomfort that may ultimately compromise the learning process. These preparatory activities help students understand what to look for, so that they may discern what kinds of behaviors and experiences the cinema expects of its audiences, while also encouraging them to contemplate how the built environment may enhance, or impede, their personal learning experience in the university.

Domestic Media Interview

While developing a senior-level seminar on film and technology, I devised an exercise where students would interview a person, ideally someone who is older, about his or her earliest memories of watching movies in the home. The films in question could be commercial productions and/or home movies, and the technologies might include 16mm, 8mm, or Super 8 projectors; VCRs; DVD players; LaserDiscs; and television broadcasts. In addition to questions about the technological specificities of their systems, subjects were also asked to speak about their experience more holistically, to describe the intellectual and emotional impact of seeing movies in the home. As with the exhibition study, I offer the students a list of potential questions, but with the caveat that they should allow the interview to flow like a conversation, and that they need not cover every question. Suggestions include the following:

- Was it expensive? Ask subjects for an explanation of the price, that is, what else could they have bought at that time for that amount of money?
- Do they remember the first person they knew who had this technology?
- Was it a "big deal" to acquire this technology? Was it a status symbol?
- How did they access content? A retail/rental store? A mail catalog? What do they remember about the process?
- Did they notice a change in their viewing/reading/listening habits with regard to other media?
- What kinds of movies did they watch at home? Were they different from the types of movies they would watch in a cinema?
- What did they notice about the differences between watching a film at home versus a public cinema? Note that this could include both the aesthetic qualities of the film and the social experience of going to the movies.
- Did this technology influence their ideas about what children should watch? How was children's access to "unsuitable" material controlled?
- Was it a social event to use this technology, that is, would they invite people over?
- Did they ever make or watch home movies? What kinds of equipment did they use? Which family members were the "filmmakers"? What kinds of movies did they make? When and where did they watch these films?

My plan was to discuss the results of these interviews alongside our reading of Charles Toshiro's "Videophilia: What Happens When You Wait for It on Video," an essay that explores the implications of video transfer for our understanding of film aesthetics, criticism, and historiography.[8] Indeed, the interview exercise certainly did allow for a more nuanced take on how cinephilia might extend to, and through, other media, but I was pleasantly surprised at the great diversity in people's accounts and in the way they would challenge received ideas about domestic media exhibition. I will detail those challenges later in this essay, but with both assignments, several key themes emerged, including nostalgia, spectatorship as performance, the potential for cinephilia to inspire and inform critical discourse, and also the discernment of a regional cinephilia that uses uniquely Texan social, economic, and geographical frames of reference to describe filmgoing experiences.

Nostalgia

Cinephilia is inextricable from nostalgia, and in students' responses to these assignments, nostalgia was an omnipresent theme. While I made no direct reference to nostalgia in either the assignment instructions or preparatory class discussions, students would discuss the phenomenon at length, often including the word in their paper titles. In our subsequent discussions, this focus on nostalgia allowed us to contemplate its significance as a factor in cinephilia, and the cinema studies discourses dependent on it, as well as the uses of nostalgia in culture more broadly. Discourses on cinephilia were especially useful in helping students to comprehend nostalgia as a component of their personal experience, as a phenomenon cultivated by the film exhibition spaces and practices, and even as a kind of performance in audience members' public displays of filmgoing preferences. In *The Persistence of Hollywood*, Thomas Elsaesser notes that cinephilia has "always been a gesture towards cinema framed by nostalgia and other retroactive temporalities. . . . Cinephiles were always ready to give in to the anxiety of possible loss, to mourn the once sensuous-sensory plenitude of the celluloid image, its architectural envelope the movie theater, and to insist on the irrecoverably fleeting nature of a film's experience."[9] Many students structured their written work around such moments of mourning, recounting stories about the now-closed cinemas they attended in childhood, or recalling the place of cinephilia in long-lost family ritual. For example, one student began her paper:

> Before my parents divorced, we, as a family, would go see films about twice a month. My father, mother, little brother, and I enjoyed these excursions and our parents would ask us about the films after the movie, which always made our opinions feel important.

Many students state that their continued pleasure in filmgoing combines nostalgia with a sense of ritual, noting how the smell of popcorn (even if they never eat it) or the lights on the marquee remind them of childhood experiences of wonder at the movies. These recollections are also supported by ritualized practices, such as sitting in a favorite seat or buying particular snacks: "Every (and I do mean every) time I go to the theater, I must have a Dr. Pepper to drink before I go into the auditorium. You can call it a ritual if you like." These stories prove useful in class discussion because once students understand that cinephilia has always been tied to nostalgia and the unique temporal properties of ritual, even when the cinema (or a discrete formal or technological element of the cinema) was new, they can better challenge some of the commonsense ideas about technological, industrial, and stylistic change (or stasis) in film history, from "It was a good movie for its time" to "They don't make them like they used to."

In addition to observing their own nostalgia, students also became mindful of how exhibitors evoke nostalgia, particularly in cinema design. For example, one student shared this anecdote about his trip to a cinema where the decorations included reproductions of vintage movie posters:

> One child was asking his dad . . . about why they had a poster for a movie called *Singin' in the Rain*. The dad began explaining that it was a movie that was "very old." Because of our conversation in this class [*Singin' in the Rain* was on the syllabus], I stuck around for a couple minutes to see how the conversation went. The son had asked why they had a poster from such an old movie since it was not a movie that would be played in the cinema. The father explained that he thought it was because many people enjoyed the nostalgia of the older movies. The child then asked his dad what nostalgia was. At that point I simply chuckled and walked away to the auditorium to prepare to see my movie.

In addition to this discovery that parent-child lectures on nostalgia are, it seems, part of everyday moviegoing, students observe how cinema design continually reminds audiences of extinct forms of architecture, vanishing media, and long-deceased stars. For example, in one of the Lubbock cinemas, framed photographs of 1920s movie palaces and Hollywood actors of the 1940s and 1950s are interspersed among the posters for coming attractions. One student described a cinema's design, combining streamlined, neon-illuminated forms with elaborate chandeliers and red carpets, as "*The Jetsons* meets *The Phantom of the Opera*," while others used the filmgoing scenes in *Singin' in the Rain* (Gene Kelly and Stanley Donen, 1952) as a reference point for describing light fixtures and curtains. Further, several students talked about how one of the city's newer cinemas, which opened with all-digital projection and continually reminds visitors of its high-tech features, including advanced sound systems, D-Box motion-simulation seats, a digital IMAX theater, and a glass-walled room facing the lobby where audiences can admire the array of computer hardware housing the digital prints, simultaneously evokes the "old days" by using images of now-obsolete celluloid prints in everything from its paint details to its carpet design.

Strategic uses of nostalgia are even more emphatic at the drive-in. In Lubbock, the Stars and Stripes Drive-In, a three-screen facility on the outskirts of town, is a popular destination, defying the commonsense narrative of the drive-in as a dying institution while also deliberately presenting itself as a relic of the past. One student remarked that it "cheats time by lying about its age"—the cinema opened in 2003, but its design aesthetics, including the aptly named 50's Café, the logo featuring a 1930s model vehicle, screenings of vintage intermission announcements between features (such as animated films of dancing snack bar treats), and even the increasingly obsolete incandescent lighting at the ticket booths, imply a long and continuous history. One student astutely observed that evocations of the 1950s are especially common in this region because of the memorialization of Lubbock native Buddy Holly, and that the drive-in is but one of the institutions that draws upon that history. This impression of the local landscape also emerges in students' observations that as one drives to this cinema, one passes old buildings and gas stations that set the tone for a kind of time travel, or as one student put it, "these elements combine to create a scene that is straight out of *Grease*." Meanwhile, the drive-in also proudly reminds audiences that it was the first cinema in the area to convert to digital projection.

These continual convergences of the old and the new, of nostalgic and futuristic discourses, provide us with insights about how the film industry's marketing practices cultivate cinephilia, while also allowing us to think about how at any moment in film history, or in the history of any medium, there is always a tension between the past and future. From the *film d'art* movement to "classic" film screenings in contemporary digital cinemas, both artists and industries seek to differentiate their productions from the past while aligning themselves with esteemed traditions in order to draw upon their popular appeal, artistic gravitas, and nostalgic sentiment. At the same time, our conceptions of history are invariably shaped by nostalgic discourse. In fact, I find it especially productive to point out to my classes that almost all the films and television shows they reference in their papers, including *Singin' in the Rain*, *The Phantom of the Opera* (Joel Schumacher, 2004), *Grease* (Randal Kleiser, 1978), or *The Jetsons* (ABC, 1962–1963), are themselves either exercises in nostalgia or imaginings of the future. Similarly, when students cite films as reference points for the history of design, the texts that come to mind are not those produced in that period (i.e., films from the 1950s that look like the 1950s) but rather those that reimagine the past for nostalgic ends.

As interesting as these exercises may be, one might wonder if students could gain comparable insights from studying the history of theater design. Indeed, comparing the architectural, acoustic, and design properties of nickelodeons, movie palaces, and multiplexes while also consulting historical accounts of filmgoing as a cultural practice would yield a nuanced understanding of film history. And yet, historical accounts of movie theaters usually only hint at the experiences of the spectators therein, and even high-quality photographs, architectural plans, and biographical anecdotes may not transmit the complex interplay of physical, sensory, and social experiences in those spaces. Allen explains that cinema studies education rarely takes the social elements of film experience into account, and when it does, it tends to focus on relatively narrow groups and historical moments. He describes how a "largely unspoken and unexamined assumption of most film studies scholarship has been that the experience of cinema could be made uneventful, inconsequential and reproducible by reducing it to the abstracted, individual act of textual engagement: the only events that mattered were taking place on the screen."[10] This view ignores the "event" status of the act of communal filmgoing itself and the fact that each of these events is created out of a unique combination of factors, from the macro level of the historical moment to the micro level of the composition of the audience on a given day. To be fair, the unique and transitory nature of each filmgoing experience makes it very difficult to document and reconstruct, but these exercises and our accompanying discussions of cinephilia and its valorization of lived experiences allow students to contemplate the particularities of each screening, each act of going to the cinema, as an event in itself.

Spectatorship and the Performance of Cinephilia

As students contemplate their own spectatorship experiences, particularly within the framework of cinephilia, they also come to understand how one's relationship to the medium, and to concepts like nostalgia, is not just evoked by the theatrical setting but also performed by its occupants. For example, a week before the exhibition study was due, a student came to my office hours to discuss her paper and confessed that this was the first time she had ever gone to a film by herself. She found the prospect so frightening that on the way to the theater, she turned her car around to go home, only proceeding to the cinema when she reminded herself that her grade was on the line. Going to the movie alone is not required for the assignment, but those who do often echo this student's anxiety. When I ask why it seems so daunting, they express worries about how others will perceive them, suggesting that people will think they are sad or lonely (although students who are mothers suggest it might be nice to have a few hours to themselves). Not only does this self-consciousness reveal the assumptions they make about fellow audience members' personal lives, but it also demonstrates how public film spectatorship is a highly expressive act, revealing one's interests, tastes, and social identities. Students come to realize how purchasing a ticket, reacting to the texts on-screen, and interacting with the people and spaces around them are all subject to public interpretation. The activity of filmgoing, which most students initially regard as primarily an act of personal media consumption, suddenly becomes a performance—and often a performance of cinephilia.

Students offer numerous accounts of audiences actively and vocally performing their cinephilia before, after, and during screenings. For example, several of the local cinemas feature slide shows before the feature where movie trivia questions are interspersed with advertisements. While these slide shows have the practical effect of retaining audience attention so they will look at the commercials, they also allow people to demonstrate, not only to their friends or dates but also to everyone around them, the extent of their film knowledge. Some students observed people declaring that they did not know the answers, not because they were admitting their ignorance, but because the films were too lowbrow, implying that "I don't watch *that* kind of movie." Students who attended festival screenings at the local arts center noticed quite demonstrative performances of cinephilia, noting how the social events before and after screenings are perhaps even more about being seen as a cinephile than about the films themselves. In one case, in describing a multiplex housing a restaurant and bar called The Scene, a student noted how the establishment's slogan makes personal visibility an attraction in itself: "Before, after or during the movie . . . see and be seen at The Scene."

In order to improve their opportunities for observation, I recommend to students that they arrive at the cinema early and that they sit at the back of the auditorium so they can watch where people decide to sit. Not only do they observe people's reluctance to sit next to a stranger, but they also tend to notice the performance of gender roles. For example, when heterosexual couples who appear to be on dates enter the auditorium, the men seem to select the seats, and when men attend a film together, they often leave a seat between them, making it clear that they are not on a date (even, arguably, if they are).[11] Others note that when men accompany women to films targeted at female audiences, such as romantic comedies or other "chick flicks," or when trailers for such films are screened, male viewers often make a point of sighing audibly, or otherwise making dismissive comments to distance themselves from the film. Of course, female audience members also make audible comments during trailers to express their interest level, and students also observe people nodding or shaking their heads to indicate their preferences. In our class discussion, I ask if students had ever felt the need to comment on other forms of advertising, and they agree that it would seem strange to respond to a billboard by declaring to passersby, "I have no intention of purchasing that brand of chewing gum." One student suggested that declaring your interest in films during the trailers "serves as a mechanism for the audience to socialize and find common ground with their friends and family," while others noted that individuals might want to distance themselves from films that seem incompatible with their personal self-presentation, regardless of their actual interests and tastes. Therefore, the public element of film spectatorship may affect one's ability to experience, or at least express, one's pleasure (or displeasure) in viewing a film, particularly when the film's genre, style, cast, or story seems incompatible with the expectations for one's gender or other social identities. These classroom discussions are fascinating in themselves, but they also provide a useful reference point throughout the semester, to remind students of the spectator's own visibility as part of the social dynamics of filmgoing. Further, it allows for critiques of dominant ideas about the value, be it artistic or historical, of given films or film traditions when we consider how much is at stake in publicly acknowledging one's cinephilia and the particular forms it may take. Meanwhile, the fact that many of the most notable moments of performance occur before the screening, or during the trailers and commercials—that is, elements that are not the feature film itself—help remind students that when we study the history of cinema, our tendency to focus on films in isolation from their accompanying texts may create inaccurate impressions of viewer experience.

Telephilia, Videophilia, and the Home Front

Performances of cinephilia, or rather telephilia/videophilia, figured in many of the narratives from the domestic media exercise, as several of the interview subjects talked about the relationships among video and television exhibition in the home, the performance of hospitality, and both family and community values. These anecdotes provided rich material for class discussions of how media in domestic settings are at once distinct from and informed by narratives and traditions of cinephilia, and also how those narratives connect with larger social questions. For example, a student interviewed his uncle, who had been one of the first television salespeople in Lubbock, and he detailed not only the technical complexities of early TV installation and operation but also the social implications of television ownership. Several interview subjects shared anecdotes about their neighborhood's first television and how the owner would invite people over to experience not just TV shows but the physical presence of the television set. In one case, since broadcasts were limited, people would come over to watch the test pattern—a scene that almost perfectly illustrates the fascination with technology that underlies much of cinephiliac discourse while also demonstrating the power of new technology as a status symbol. In another student's interview about the family's first VCR, it became clear that her grandmother appreciated the machine not only for continually reviewing favorite films but also because it allowed her to stage screenings as social events in her home. She would devote as much attention to food preparation as to video selection, and she was very conscious of creating an environment for her friends and family that was as "special" as visiting the cinema, while also demonstrating her skills as a homemaker.

Furthermore, other anecdotes revealed how public visibility at the cinema, and as a cinephile, are in many respects contingent on social privilege. For example, a student who interviewed his African American relatives explained how their stories would begin with accounts of cinephilia, such as his aunt's detailed recollections of Grace Kelly films, but they also recalled a level of tension; since she had lived in a region with racially segregated theaters, going to the movies was fraught with fears of humiliation, alienation, and threats to personal safety. While students who had interviewed white subjects spoke about their excitement at seeing television for the first time, this woman's story provided a powerful alternate history. When her family friend acquired the neighborhood's first television set and invited everyone over to watch, it was a revelation for her and for the black community to see a movie in a private space and thus to set the terms for their own film appreciation. This story allowed us not only to discuss the history of segregation in cinemas but also to question how narratives of spectatorship and the pleasures of cinephilia so often operate on the premise of a white, male, middle-class subject, who has the privilege of feeling welcome and secure in most public spaces. In many respects, these moments resonate with Christian Keathley's discussion of "cinephiliac history," where anecdotes attest to the powers and properties of cinema while also challenging traditional historical discourses.[12] Students admitted that even as they read up on early television history, they tended to assume a white suburban subject, while this student's stories made them question that premise.

Regional Cinephilia

Students' diverse accounts of domestic spectatorship also illustrate another advantage of drawing upon the discourse of cinephilia, as it affirms the importance of regional specificity in media history. Texas Tech University is located in the Texas panhandle, where a significant number of students come from rural areas or are only one or two generations away from agricultural livelihoods. In many instances, these students employ agricultural analogies, such as noting how theaters' strategies for controlling the behavior of customers, including shifts in scale from large foyers to smaller hallways, or changes in lighting and floor materials to produce a calming, quieting effect on the viewer, are similar to those used on livestock. Students have explained further how theaters' capitalist infrastructure interpellates customers by comparing the systems intended to maximize audience throughput to those used in slaughterhouses. They also notice that restrooms are located close to the exits, encouraging patrons who use the facilities after the screening to then leave the building, having exhausted their usefulness as purchasing agents. Of course, all architectural and interior design strategies are mindful of how people will move through space, but students are taken aback at how elements of the cinema that make them feel comfortable and attended to are those that render them most like cattle. These observations inspire vibrant debates about audience agency, for while one might enjoy feelings of communal experience, that experience is also dictated by external interests. Once students have the opportunity to think about how audiences operate both within and against the cinema, or how mechanisms of capitalism and social control are embedded in the theatrical space, and to articulate these dynamics in terms that are meaningful in their local culture, they are better able to appreciate why critics might challenge cinephilia or why filmmakers might resist convention in the formal structure and exhibition of their work.

Once students are able to articulate critiques of cinephilia that stem from their own experiences, they are better prepared to understand how critiques of this discourse have been integral to cinema studies as a discipline. For example, one of the most influential works of film scholarship emerging from such a critique is Laura Mulvey's "Visual Pleasure and Narrative Cinema," but Mulvey herself offers an important nuance on the origins of that discourse in an edited conversation with Peter Wollen and Lee Grieveson, where she explains:

> But if it had not been for the background of cinephilia, the "Visual Pleasure" critique would never have been possible. It was a critique that was enabled by cinephilia and a deep love of Hollywood.[13]

The notion of a critique enabled by cinephilia resonates with students, for while the exercises lead them to remark on and valorize their own cinephilia, they also produce some troubling discoveries. For example, in the exhibition study, many students notice how cinema infrastructure both reflects and contributes to social divisions within the city. When asked to consider the theater's location and how accessible it is via public transit and sidewalks, students remark on how it is difficult, even hazardous, to access the theaters on foot, as getting to the cinema often requires walking through expansive parking lots or areas that would not feel safe at night. Some students notice the types of cars in those parking lots, pointing out that the makes and models suggest middle-class ownership, while others observe that the audiences are, in some instances, more white and middle-class than would be expected given the demographics of surrounding neighborhoods. These observations allow us to discuss how segregating practices persist in American public spaces and how these practices might shape public expressions of cinephilia in their own communities.

Students' commentary on the drive-in movie experience also provides an ideal opportunity to explore regional cinephilia. Texas has a long history of drive-in restaurants and cinemas, attesting to the importance of car culture in the region, and for decades the drive-in was often the only cinema available to rural communities. Indeed, many students mention their parents' and grandparents' accounts of going to the drive-in and its vitality as a social space. Students invariably note that on an aesthetic level, the drive-in offers a substandard viewing and listening experience, as ambient light from headlights, the moon, and your neighbor's car, combined with watching through one's windshield, do not necessarily cultivate close reading of the image, while listening to a film through a car radio does no favors to the sound design. And yet students consistently describe the drive-in as a space of "magical" experience whose pleasures are as contingent on the social elements of cinephilia as on the films themselves, if not more so. As one student described it, the drive-in "produces a kind of generational movie magic that I observed firsthand: as children reenacted scenes from the movies, adults enjoyed a romantic date with sweet chatter in a veil of privacy, and as elders relived and told stories about their younger days at the cinema."

While one might have similarly enchanting experiences at a drive-in anywhere in the country, many students also observe that being outdoors allows them to contemplate the natural environment, noting the surrounding landscape; preshow sunsets; the moon and stars; the sights and sounds of birds, bats, and insects; and even the sublimity of watching a lightning storm move across the horizon as the film plays in the foreground. Students notice how the drive-in, with its direct connections to Texas car culture and rural infrastructure, combined with the ecological specificity of the outdoor space, makes them conscious of film culture as a part of local history, while also realizing that their own practices of cinephilia may not be as universal as they had assumed. These opportunities to discuss film culture as a local phenomenon are particularly useful in an introductory class, where discussions of global cinema culture can leave some students feeling distanced from the "great moments" in cinema history.

Personal/History

As students begin to write about their observations, they often ask if they are permitted to use the first person in their papers, as most writing instructors have forbidden them from using anything but the seemingly objective position of the third person. I assure them that "I" is appropriate for this assignment, which not only allows for a discussion about the significance of voice in writing but also gives me the opportunity to question the premise of a truly universal or objective perspective. Of course, while encouraging them to use the first person, one must also be wary that assignments built around the subjective experience of individual students may inadvertently affirm students' solipsism rather than broadening their knowledge and perspective. However, by framing students' discussions in relation to cinephilia, they are able to extrapolate from their experience in ways that are productive, allowing them to better appreciate how the cinema might have created intensely meaningful experiences for people across cultures and historical periods, for good or for ill. Furthermore, Marijke de Valck explains that the difficulty in distinguishing cinephilia as a concept from cinephilia as an individual experience is actually productive, because

> cinephilia has proven to be so enduring precisely because it forms a bridge between the biographical and the theoretical, the singular and the general, the fragment and the whole, the incomplete and the complete, and the individual and the collective.[14]

As students become attuned to the specificity of the film experience, it affords them a healthy skepticism about generalized accounts of film reception and spectatorship practices while they also discover that they are themselves part of cinema history.

Conclusion

While many accounts of cinephilia focus on moments when a viewer is struck by details in the image or soundtrack, cinephilia's various permutations are also contingent on the circumstances of exhibition. From the social scene at the art house theater, to the collector's enthusiasm for VHS and other "extinct" media, to blog debates on the merits of one DVD transfer over another, the technologies, economies, and social contexts of viewing are always formative in cinephilia and in the study of film in the academy. The exercises I have described here, based in the lived experience of film cultures, past and present, help students build a critical framework to examine their own assumptions about film history and criticism, to comprehend the cinema as a compelling and powerful cultural force and social space, and to appreciate how a love of cinema can inspire critical consciousness.

ALLISON WHITNEY is Associate Professor of Film and Media Studies at Texas Tech University. Her research interests include the history of media technology, oral histories of film culture in Texas, studies of film genre, and film and media studies pedagogy.

Notes

1. Robert C. Allen, "Reimagining the History of the Experience of Cinema in a Post-Moviegoing Age," in *Explorations in New Cinema History: Approaches and Case Studies*, eds. Richard Maltby, Daniel Biltereyst, and Philippe Meers (Exeter, UK: University of Exeter Press, 2007), 43.

2. Jenna Ng, "The Myth of Total Cinephilia," *Cinema Journal* 49, no. 2 (2010): 147.

3. Ibid.

4. Allen, "Reimagining the History," 44.

5. Nataša Durovičová and Jonathan Rosenbaum, "Movies Go Multinational," in *Movie Mutations: The Changing Face of World Cinephilia*, eds. Jonathan Rosenbaum and Adrian Martin (London: British Film Institute, 2003), 146.

6. For the sake of clarity, I instruct students to refer to the room where the screening takes place as the *auditorium*, while reserving *theater* and *cinema* for the building (or in the case of the drive-in, the outdoor space) that houses the auditorium.

7. As both the exhibition study and the domestic media exercise involve human subjects, I made inquiries with my university's Institutional Review Board (IRB). Their decision was that the exhibition study did not require IRB review provided that students did not document identifying details, even if they observed people they knew, and that they did not interview people at the cinemas about their experiences. While normal social interactions were acceptable, students were instructed not to ask people direct questions, even if they were curious about, for example, if a couple was on a date, or how old they were, or why a person who seemed to be outside the target demographic for a given film had chosen to attend. Students were also advised that while they could and should take notes during their visit (and in fact, using one's cell phone to do this would likely go unnoticed), taking photos or audio/video recordings would get them kicked out of the theater, or worse, accused of piracy. Meanwhile, before conducting their domestic media interviews, I made it clear that subjects were to be informed that the interview would be recorded and shared with classmates. If subjects did not feel comfortable with this arrangement, they had the option of remaining anonymous.

8. Charles Shiro Tashiro, "Videophilia: What Happens When You Wait for It on Video," *Film Quarterly* 54, no. 1 (1991): 7–17.

9. Thomas Elsaesser, *The Persistence of Hollywood* (New York: Routledge, 2012), 63.

10. Allen, "Reimagining the History," 51.

11. Of course, students could not always hear what couples were saying to one another, nor could they be certain about the romantic and/or familial status of couples or groups of any gender. And yet the outward appearance of agency or leadership in these instances, and the assumptions that audience members make about one another, are important parts of the cinema experience.

12. Christian Keathley, *Cinephilia and History, or the Wind in the Trees* (Bloomington: Indiana University Press, 2006), 138–139.

13. Laura Mulvey and Peter Wollen with Lee Grieveson, "From Cinephilia to Film Studies," in *Inventing Film Studies*, eds. Lee Grieveson and Haidee Wasson (Durham, NC: Duke University Press, 2008), 228.

14. Marijke de Valck, "Reflections on the Recent Cinephilia Debates," *Cinema Journal* 49, no. 2 (2010): 138–139. Note that in this paragraph, de Valck is referring to an earlier essay with Malte Hagener, "Cinephilia in Transition," in *Mind the Screen: Media Concepts According to Thomas Elsaesser*, eds. Jaap Kooijman, Patricia Pisters, and Wanda Strauven (Amsterdam: Amsterdam University Press, 2008), 19–31.

10   Cinephilia and Paratexts

DVD Pedagogy in the Era of Instant Streaming

Lisa Patti

In 2013, the "What Netflix Does" Tumblr began to upload screenshots comparing an image from a film in its original aspect ratio with the "same" image as it appeared when it was streamed on Netflix.[1] Having amassed an impressive archive of these shot comparisons, the site attempted to draw attention to the radical transformations of the filmic image generated by altered aspect ratios. When I shared examples from "What Netflix Does" with the students in one of my media studies classes, they responded with less consternation than I had expected (and hoped) they would. The students acknowledged the significance of the differences between the paired shots but resisted my assertion that this stealthy slicing of the film by Netflix (or the content providers who supply Netflix with their films) constitutes a vital breach of the filmmaker's and film viewer's trust. Their ambivalence underscores the importance of combining an introduction to film style (with its attendant reverence for the cinematic image in its original form) with an investigation of contemporary film exhibition. Cinema studies pedagogy, historically tethered to the theatrical exhibition of film and the replication of those exhibition conditions in the classroom, must grapple with the relocation of cinema to virtual spaces and the new forms of cinephilia produced by that migration. This chapter examines the shifts from theatrical cinephilia to DVD cinephilia to virtual cinephilia and the consequences of these shifts for teaching.

I program the syllabi for my media studies classes with Netflix as a primary (although not exclusive) screening resource. For example, one semester my Introduction to Media and Society syllabus included a series of films available at the time on Netflix—*Clueless* (Amy Heckerling, 1995), *This Is Not a Film* (Jafar Panahi, 2011), *The Act of Killing* (Joshua Oppenheimer, 2013), *Imitation of Life* (Douglas Sirk, 1959), *Paris Is Burning* (Jennie Livingston, 1990), and *Black Girl* (Ousmane Sembène, 1966)—in addition to a selection of television shows. A range of media texts (films, television shows, short films, and music videos) located in other online venues, including Hulu, YouTube, iTunes, Amazon Instant

Video, and UbuWeb, supplemented this Netflix filmography. In order to expand the range of exhibition experiences offered in the course, I co-organized one public film screening at a historic downtown theater in collaboration with other faculty teaching media studies courses, and throughout the semester I scheduled screenings in class of documentaries and experimental films that are unavailable online. For all of the films on the syllabus from Netflix and other online distributors, DVD copies were available on reserve at the library both to accommodate students who prefer to watch films on DVD or who do not have easy access to Netflix and to provide a backup resource in the event that films disappeared from Netflix before their screening date on the syllabus.

Netflix's contracts with its content providers have expiration dates, so films and television shows disappear. As an introduction to the unstable nature of online distribution (experienced not only through disappearing content but also through various technological glitches), these moments are productive in the classroom. As programming obstacles, however, they generate difficult choices. Each film on a syllabus interacts with a specific matrix of critical concerns. There is no even exchange between two films, and the limited depth and breadth of Netflix's catalog further complicate attempts to design a streaming-centered syllabus. The need to adjust course filmographies, often with very little notice, is not a new issue. Instructors have grappled with broken film reels, scratched DVDs, and other material nuisances great and small for decades, and instructors replace films on their syllabi for many reasons—shifting the critical concerns in a course, updating a filmography to reflect changes in the field, or simply responding to boredom with films that have been taught multiple times. The programming difficulties generated by the unpredictable archives housed by Netflix and other online distributors, however, activate a series of questions about the agency of online distributors in cinema studies courses that rely on them. Programming film screenings from a range of distributors and across multiple platforms brings attention to the material and social impact of different modes of film exhibition, inviting students to analyze film texts in relation to the contexts of distribution and exhibition. In a single week, students may watch a film via Netflix on laptops or other devices, attend a public film screening at a large downtown theater, and watch a documentary on DVD in our classroom. Our discussion of these films always involves comparative assessments of these scenes of exhibition, and the role of Netflix as a retail intermediary is a central critical concern.

While Netflix thus serves as both a primary programming resource and a generative distribution case study, I am struck by the relevance to Netflix of an observation about Facebook made by the novelist Zadie Smith in her review of the film *The Social Network* (David Fincher, 2010): "We know what we are doing 'in' the software. But do we know, are we alert to, what the software is doing to

us? . . . [S]oftware is not neutral. Different software embeds different philosophies, and these philosophies, as they become ubiquitous, become invisible."[2]
Can we ask the same questions of Netflix that Smith asks of Facebook? What is
Netflix doing to us? Is Netflix shaping contemporary cinephilia? And, if so, what
form does contemporary cinephilia take? What are the implications of attaching
cinephilia to a corporation? How do the financial transactions embedded in this
model (between Netflix and its content providers, between students and Netflix)
define cinephilia for students?

Smith's reflections on the architecture of Facebook and its impact on personal identities and social interactions anticipate the algorithmic machinations
of Netflix and its imagination of each of us as a cinephile. This new formula-
tion of cinephilia (in both the philosophical and mathematical senses) distances
cinephilia from its most resonant associations with theatrical exhibition—the
valorization of the theatrical event, the projected image, and the materiality of
film. Susan Sontag's frequently cited elegy for the "death of cinema," and in turn
cinephilia, cements these associations:

> Even more than what you appropriated for yourself was the experience of sur-
> render to, of being transported by, what was on the screen. You wanted to be
> kidnapped by the movie—and to be kidnapped was to be overwhelmed by
> the physical presence of the image. The experience of "going to the movies"
> was part of it. To see a great film only on television isn't to have really seen
> that film. It's not only a question of the dimensions of the image: the disparity
> between a larger-than-you image in the theater and the little image on the box
> at home. The conditions of paying attention in a domestic space are radically
> disrespectful of film. Now that a film no longer has a standard size, home
> screens can be as big as living room or bedroom walls. But you are still in a
> living room or a bedroom. To be kidnapped, you have to be in a movie theater,
> seated in the dark among anonymous strangers.[3]

For Sontag, cinephilia requires an immersive "surrender" to the filmic image that
can only be experienced when facing the towering screen in a dark theater; even
the most rigorously designed home viewing environment is vulnerable to the
intrusions of the quotidian details that inform domestic life. Sontag's pronounce-
ment of the death of cinephilia is both prescient and premature. The cinematic
spectator may still be "kidnapped" by the image, but this moment of seizure pro-
vokes not stillness but mobility, as cinephiles move among physical and virtual
spaces to pursue new cinematic experiences.

The unique public and collective event described by Sontag still exists but
in fewer and fewer locations, as film itself is replaced by digital projection, as
many independent theaters close, and as the ranks of theatrical cinephiles become increasingly concentrated in the (usually urban) locations of independent

theaters or film festivals. The primary space of cinephilia is now the home, and instant streaming increasingly mediates domestic access to film. After a rather brief period of DVD cinephilia (and the longer period of video cinephilia that preceded and overlaps it), when the acquisition of private film collections and home theater installations offered cinephiles an opportunity to cultivate a domestic film culture, instant streaming has now shifted cinephilia's framing of collection from the private back to the public. While the screening location may be the home (or any of the other private or public spaces where a viewer might choose to watch a streaming video), the screening archive is once again a shared space, albeit a virtual one. Personal film libraries exist not on a shelf but in a cloud-based personal archive or in a corporate archive accessible through a membership or subscription.

This virtual cinephilia permits promiscuous, idiosyncratic itineraries through film history. If theatrical cinephilia and DVD cinephilia were both marked by an investment in the image—fleeting yet unforgettable in the theater, ensnaring and freezable at home—virtual cinephilia is defined not by the passionate investment in cinematic images but by the lines of flight from these images. Virtual cinephilia exposes and explores the vectors of attachment that extend from a film to its various genealogical affiliates—for example, films by the same director, belonging to the same genre, or featuring the same language, to name only a few categories of affinity. Virtual cinephilia also leads to the various paratexts that surround and support films, including reviews, posters, trailers, title sequences, and commentaries. Earlier iterations and generations of cinephilia privileged cinema's moments; virtual cinephilia privileges cinema's map.

Streaming sites like Netflix rely on algorithms to classify films and generate suggested itineraries for navigating their map of cinema. A comprehensive 2013 investigation of Netflix's tagging practices revealed that the company's database included a staggering 76,897 microgenres or "altgenres."[4] Users of Netflix and other algorithm-based media distribution sites will recognize the "If you liked *x*, you might also like *y*" announcements that frequently appear. Netflix's algorithm harnesses a combination of human and computational tagging "to create genres, but also to increase the level of personalization in all the movies a user is shown. So, if Netflix knows you love Action Adventure movies with high romantic ratings (on their 1–5 scale), it might show you that kind of movie, without ever saying, 'Romantic Action Adventure Movies.'"[5] In other words, behind Netflix's catalog of films lies an invisible cinematic map, one that guides viewers along preferred routes. This computationally dense cartography of cinema applies to both streaming and DVD, but streaming enables the instant exploration of these tagged pathways, eliminating the delay of a day or two as the next disc travels to you by mail. Virtual cinephilia thus builds on the immediacy of online exhibition and research.

DVD Pedagogy

Not all students (and perhaps very few) enter cinema studies classes as virtual cinephiles, but many of them have experience both watching movies online and searching through sites that contain general information about contemporary cinema (for example, Fandango and Rotten Tomatoes). In fact, watching movies (and television shows) online is often their primary form of accessing cinema; DVDs are much less relevant to students as consumers than they are to instructors. I have circulated questionnaires to students in classes at several institutions where I have taught, asking them to describe their engagement with DVD culture. Students consistently report that they own few, if any, DVDs. The DVDs they do own are almost exclusively gifts from family and friends. Students also indicate that they rarely rent DVDs, and their DVD rental experiences are usually confined to the time that they spend living with their families and friends during university breaks. While they are on campus, most students do not buy, rent, or watch films on DVD. For students studying film in the era of instant streaming, the DVD is an artifact of the exhibition habits of their childhoods, when they visited the local Blockbuster store on the weekends to rent the newest releases.

DVD cinephilia belonged to a previous generation, tied to a trend in home exhibition when, for some cinephiles, DVD viewing could create a private utopia of cinema, an individualized film theater without the unpredictable and obtrusive distractions of public spaces—the chattering patrons in the row behind you, an errant cell phone ringing, or the projectionist's clumsy reel change. Barbara Klinger describes the DVD cinephile's fascination with cinema, collection, and technology, united through a "hardware aesthetic" that "conceives of value according to imperatives drawn from technological considerations" and leads to the "enshrinement of the action and/or special effects film, a reversal in aesthetic fortune for titles regarded as either classics or failures, a rereading of films through the ideology of the spectacular, and the triumph of a particular notion of form over content."[6] This version of cinephilia is not extinct. The years since the publication of Klinger's book have witnessed the introduction of new home theater hardware (including 3D television screens and Blu-ray discs) and the expansion of DVD and Blu-ray catalogs. While the cinephiles that Klinger profiled may continue to refine their home theaters and expand their film collections, this version of cinephilia is remote from the experience of many of today's university students. They cite cost and space as the factors that discourage their development of a DVD or Blu-ray collection. Subscription-based sites like Netflix and cloud-based systems like iTunes allow students to access thousands of films and television shows from their laptops, tablets, and mobile phones. They acknowledge that they may not be able to find legal copies of every film they may want to see through these distributors, but many report that they are very comfortable with the options of either downloading an illegal copy or simply watching something else.

While few students have DVD or Blu-ray collections (or watch films at all on DVD or Blu-ray), most cinema studies instructors have at least a modest personal collection of films on DVD and in other formats such as VHS. I have more DVDs than books on the shelves in my campus office, and I have colleagues whose offices resemble video stores. Many instructors supplement their personal collections with institutional collections maintained by departments or libraries. The storage of films on 16mm and 35mm (still a preferred format for some instructors) requires more care, and the projection of these films requires more expertise (and much more expensive equipment) than the storage and projection of films on DVD. While the screening of a film in a film format may be ideal in many cases, DVD collections have allowed teachers to design rich syllabi at a minimal cost, a nontrivial consideration when many program budgets are contracting and film rentals from archives and museums may be prohibitively expensive. By noting that DVDs are flexible, efficient, and affordable programming resources for cinema studies classes, I am not suggesting that 16mm, 35mm, and other film and video formats are no longer valuable or implying that DVD exhibition is superior or even equivalent to film exhibition. Rather, while recognizing the aesthetic richness of film formats and the urgency of film preservation efforts, I argue that the shift to DVD exhibition has generated pedagogical benefits.

The widespread use of DVDs as teaching resources in university classrooms initiates new pedagogies that raise and respond to urgent questions about teaching film in the age of new media. Wheeler Winston Dixon and Gwendolyn Audrey Foster ask, "How has our students' visual consciousness been shaped by the tidal wave of imagery from competing sources that sweeps over them, often two and three layers deep? . . . How can we make the works of the past resonant in an atmosphere of constant mutability?"[7] Dixon and Foster cite several advantages of DVDs, including portability, visual clarity, and flexibility (with menus for selecting subtitles and screen formats, among other options). Moreover, DVDs enable students to explore film style by analyzing individual frames and to research film history by listening to scene commentaries, watching other bonus features, and reading the critical essays included with some DVD editions.

As pedagogical objects, DVDs also chronicle film history and production and capture the industrial, formal, and cultural variability and instability of film. For example, the Criterion Collection edition of Vittorio De Sica's *Terminal Station* (1954) also includes producer David Selznick's aggressive re-edit of the film for its American release under the new title *Indiscretion of an American Wife* (1954). The DVD includes new digital transfers of both versions of the film and presents a selection of marketing paratexts as bonus features. *New York Times* film critic Dave Kehr's essay in the printed booklet that accompanies the DVD notes the "rare opportunity to compare and contrast Hollywood and European sensibilities as they existed in the early 1950s. . . . [I]t is fascinating to see how identical material can be pushed and pulled, wholly through the postproduction process, in two radically different directions."[8] The critical possibilities afforded by this DVD edition may not restore the losses lamented by cinephiles who regret the shifts to new modes of exhibition, but they enable a productive form of DVD cinephilia, illustrated in its most critically and technically accomplished form by the online video essay "What is neorealism?" produced by the artist kogonada to compare De Sica's work and Selznick's in order to demonstrate the aesthetic, narrative, and political force of neorealist style. As an interim step in the move from theatrical cinephilia to virtual cinephilia, DVD cinephilia promotes a fascination with the material object, its variability, and its mutability.

Virtual Cinephilia

The virtual cinephile may revel both in the thousands of films available online in exhibition portals as diverse as Netflix, Viki, and the Internet Archive and in the sites that enable interactive engagements with cinema. The proliferation of online journals and blogs where professional and amateur critics discuss cinema has expanded the locations of cinephiliac discourse. From the launch of the online edition of the journal *Film Criticism* to the Tumblr *Cinephilia and Beyond* to the user reviews on Metacritic published alongside reviews from major newspapers and magazines, online venues for film criticism and commentary make possible a robust interactive film culture.[9] In addition to these spaces for film criticism, virtual cinephilia traverses other sites and forms of interactivity: participating in Kickstarter campaigns to fund the production and distribution of new (usually independent) films, sharing remix videos on YouTube that perform loving and/ or critical readings of favorite films, and shopping for rare and out-of-print films in old and new, legal and illegal formats. Virtual cinephilia is an experience not only of reception but also of production, distribution, and exhibition.

Chuck Tryon locates the crux of this new mode of cinephilia in the concept of "platform mobility" or "the ongoing shift toward ubiquitous, mobile access to a wide range of entertainment choices . . . and the social, political, and economic changes that make mobile access more desirable."[10] For Tryon, platform mobility creates a new cinematic spectator "who is ostensibly capable of controlling his or her viewing experience, whether that entails starting a movie in one platform and continuing it on another, watching a movie on a mobile device, or accessing digital libraries through various streaming platforms and digital downloads from anywhere an internet connection is available."[11] The autonomy and interactivity enabled by platform mobility blur the boundaries that separate distribution regions, formats, and cultures. The erosion of these boundaries makes possible new modes of production and reception, but platform mobility also threatens some films and film formats. In a pointed introduction to his book-length study of streaming, Wheeler Winston Dixon charges, "Amazon and Netflix seem poised to do away with all vestiges of the real and enter the digital-only domain. What will be lost in the process is not only the physical reality of books and DVDs; many titles won't make it to Kindle or streaming video, simply because they're not popular enough."[12]

The observations offered by Tryon and Winston Dixon apply forcefully to the shift from DVD exhibition to online exhibition in (or out of) the classroom. The adoption of a streaming syllabus entails loss—the loss of public, collective viewing and the revelations produced by moments of shared awe, laughter, or boredom; the loss of grand exhibition spaces, whether a university auditorium or a theater; and the loss of control over the film's projection, particularly in the rare circumstances when films were screened in pristine 35mm visual plenitude but even in the more common instances of DVD projection when at least the size of the image, the darkness of the room, and the modulation of the sound could be perfected as much as the DVD, the projector, and the room would allow. By inviting students to watch films via instant streaming outside the classroom, instructors cede control over the social, spatial, and aesthetic conditions of film exhibition.

The streaming syllabus could enable students to watch films in exhibition environments we can only (if we dare) imagine. Would a student watch *Lawrence of Arabia* (David Lean, 1962) on a cell phone? with headphones? on a bus? in short installations in between other commitments, like an epic web series? And if all of these conditions converge in a viewing experience, has that student seen *Lawrence of Arabia* at all or merely a fragmented digital simulation of the film? Confronting these anxious questions leads to nostalgia for traditional classroom screening practices, those that approximate the conditions of seeing the film in a theater as closely as possible. While I share that nostalgia, I have found that streaming syllabi present a series of opportunities for encouraging virtual cinephilia. Viewing films online provides students with immediate opportunities for formal analysis (through repeat viewings), extensive research (from superficial perusals of a film's Internet Movie Database (IMDb) page to rigorous reviews of scholarly articles, production histories, and other critical artifacts), and creative engagement (by curating and producing remix videos, GIFs, scene commentaries, and other interactive and appropriative responses.) Caetlin Benson-Allott recuperates the productive potential of the "platform agnosticism" derided by film critic David Denby, explaining that platform agnosticism "denaturalizes the connection between technological forms and narrative genres, which helps the critic see their historic imbrication. Thus, and seemingly against all odds, platform agnosticism can make us better historians, theorists, and critics."[13] Platform agnosticism can also make us better teachers.

Sites like In Media Res offer many accessible and reproducible examples of the critical value of both platform mobility and virtual cinephilia. For example, a "theme week" curated by the editors of *Cinema Journal* showcased five short reflections on the film *Clueless*.[14] Individual posts analyzed a magazine cover, a GIF, a subtitled still, a music video, and a remix video, demonstrating for student readers the ways that new media objects that are accessible online (via YouTube, Tumblr, and other popular venues) generate new critical possibilities for film analysis. Inviting students to select a media object and then write a short post analyzing it in the style of In Media Res is a productive introductory assignment, sharpening their skills as curators and writers before a more involved research and production project might be launched (as described shortly).

These vertical forms of cinephiliac engagement with a film promote the cultivation of cinematic depth—learning as much as possible about a film and then, if one is inclined (or assigned), producing new knowledge to contribute to the expanding archive of information about the film. Lynne Stahl argues that "even an act as minute as *clicking* begets a sense of discovery and agency and adds a component of self-determination" to student research.[15] These critical and creative explorations were possible long before the advent of instant streaming or even of the Internet itself, but the process of viewing a film online and then meandering along the critical vectors that extend from it exploits the virtual proximity of films to their online critical counterparts.

Vertical cinephilia in virtual space is complemented by horizontal cinephilia—the viewing relay that extends from one film to the next according to both predictable (and, at times, algorithmically outlined) paths and original itineraries. Much has been written, particularly in the popular press, about binge viewing and new protocols of television exhibition. Netflix has been at the center of many of these discussions, as its library makes possible not only the quick consumption of entire television series but also the viewing of original television series produced by Netflix and released one season at a time rather than one episode at a time. Television critics puzzle over the euphoria and anxiety of this abundance of available content and the ideal way to consume it.[16] While binge viewing may not be as common a mode of consumption for film as it is for television—viewers may be less likely to watch ten uninterrupted hours of Fellini films than they are to watch *Battlestar Galactica* episodes for the same marathon viewing period—some of my students have shared that watching Sirk's *Imitation of Life* led them to watch his other films—*All That Heaven Allows* (1955) and then *Written on the Wind* (1956) and so on. Not all of cinephilia's vectors, however, are auteurist. Students may discover a love of specific stars, genres, national cinemas, cinematographers, or composers. While the Netflix algorithm may lead students to contemplate whether they would like to watch another "drama featuring a strong female lead set in the Midwest," students are just as likely to use other on-line resources, like IMDb, to chart their own cinephiliac course. Their authorship of these routes through film history produces an active, improvisational cine-philia that repositions individual films as installments in a series.

The opportunities for the exploration of vertical and horizontal cinephilia online may be most intriguing to students who already identify as cinephiles and for whom the films introduced in any classroom context would likely lead to independent exploration. For these students, virtual cinephilia extends and in-tensifies their existing investment in cinema. Thus, the incorporation of stream-ing into cinema studies classes may be most transformative for students who are ambivalent about cinema. Some of these initially resistant students may develop a curiosity about particular films screened for the course that leads them to addi-tional screenings and research online. However, just as an instructor cannot rely on a course attracting a group of students who arrive on the first day as devoted cinephiles, neither can she presume that the course will convert every student into a cinephile. One strategy for engaging students as cinephiles is to adapt DVD pedagogy for courses based on streaming. A focus on the media paratext as both an object of study and a model for student work enables a productive fusion of DVD pedagogy and new modes of exhibition and production.

Paratextual Pedagogy

Jonathan Gray has argued for the value of the paratext as a text in its own right:

> The study of paratexts is the study of how meaning is created, and of how texts begin. Moreover, precisely because paratexts help us decide which texts to consume, we often know many texts only at the paratextual level. Everyone consumes many more paratexts than films or programs. When we move on-ward to the film or program, those paratexts help frame our consumption; but when we do not move onward, all we are left with is the paratext.[17]

Paratexts, the small, short, or shifting texts that orbit or support a film, have historically been overlooked as objects of study, but this oversight has been cor-rected due in large part to the widespread introduction of DVDs in the classroom. The digital bonus features and other components included in DVD packages (from glossy booklets to blurbs on the back cover) offer valuable ways to frame the analysis of the films they introduce, market, and analyze. One dominant ef-fect of DVD packaging has been to reassert the centrality of directors as auteurs, established through the circulation of "director's editions" and the prominent inclusion of interviews, audio commentaries, and other features that privilege the director's authorship and analysis of the film. However, DVD paratexts may also introduce students to other critical frameworks, including industrial history, fandom and reception, and global distribution.[18]

Paratexts have been an important marketing tool for DVD distributors, but they are also valuable pedagogical tools. For example, Monika Mehta explains how she uses DVD paratexts to introduce her students to the industrial and textual history of Hindi-Urdu film songs. In a video essay that adopts the form of a DVD commentary, Mehta argues that the cover of *Lata: A Journey*, a DVD compilation of songs by the prolific playback singer Lata Mangeshkar, who voiced songs for over one thousand Bombay films, offers students an access point into understanding the relationships between and among intergenerational cinephilia, stardom, performance, and music in Bombay cinema. The front cover of the DVD features an image of Mangeshkar, and the back cover features an array of photos of the many film stars whose screen performances fused their bodies with Mangeshkar's voice. All of the stars pictured on the back cover are young, while the image on the front cover presents a much older Mangeshkar, who was seventy-nine at the time the DVD was published. Her invisibility on-screen allowed her to have a much longer career than most female Bombay film stars whose careers ebbed as they aged. Furthermore, her aural presence in a long filmography of Bombay cinema provides a cinephiliac continuity that unites generations of spectators. Mehta notes, "More often than not, each generation has its favorite screen stars. . . . In spanning seven decades, Mangeshkar's voice accomplishes a feat difficult for most visual stars: it becomes an aural bridge connecting generations and thereby producing intergenerational audiophilia."[19] When she discusses stardom in courses on Bombay cinema, Mehta complements her analyses of individual song-and-dance sequences from the films featuring Mangeshkar's voice with a close reading of the cover of the compilation DVD, producing a comprehensive analysis that foregrounds the value of paratexts as central elements of film study in the university classroom.

DVD Pedagogy in the Era of Instant Streaming

An emphasis on paratexts accommodates the incorporation of DVD pedagogy into courses that rely on streaming. In effect, the DVD maintains a significant presence as both an industrial and a pedagogical object. For my Introduction to Media and Society class, I have designed a multimodal research and production assignment that involves paratexts as both the objects and the products of research. (A sample set of guidelines for this assignment is included at the end of the chapter.) Working in small groups, students select a film from a specific institutional canon—for example, the lists of the "greatest" films published by the American Film Institute. During the first half of the semester, the students watch the film several times and begin a two-pronged exploration. They produce a textual analysis of the film, focusing on the close reading of individual scenes and shots, and they conduct extensive research about the film, gathering information about the film's production history, critical reception, and cultural significance. The research dimension of the project is framed within a research dossier assignment that the students complete as a prelude to the project.[20]

Their research leads to the production of a set of paratexts for a proposed DVD or Blu-ray edition of the group's selected film for the Criterion Collection. While each group independently investigates their film through the critical contexts introduced in the course (for example, genres, directors, narrative structures, stardom and fandom, the politics of representation, and industrial histories), as a class we explore the institutional identities of the Criterion Collection and the American Film Institute. The Criterion Collection maintains a commitment to releasing meticulously restored versions of the films in their catalog, enhanced by extensive menus of bonus features and lush packages. Thus Criterion Collection DVDs serve as ideal models of the pedagogical (and industrial) value of DVD paratexts. We watch films distributed by the Criterion Collection (streaming on Netflix or Hulu), and then we examine the DVD or Blu-ray editions of the films, screening bonus features, analyzing cover art, and reading catalog essays.[21] The Criterion paratexts (which are usually excluded from the presentation of Criterion films online) are resources for understanding the films in new historical and theoretical contexts, and they acquaint students with the Criterion brand in preparation for their projects. We also study the shifting canons of cinema defined by institutions like the American Film Institute, debating the criteria for including films on their lists and contemplating the impact of these lists on the academic study of film.

By the time students begin the production phase of their projects, they have established an understanding of their selected film and of the institutions that frame their project. Armed with this information, each group produces a set of paratexts for their planned Criterion Collection release. They create several original paratexts—a front and back cover for the DVD, a critical essay, a trailer, and a scene commentary—using a variety of digital programs. They also curate a set of print and digital bonus features discovered during their research, converting them from citations in their bibliographies into bonus features. For example, one group of students designed a Criterion Collection edition of *Singin' in the Rain* (Stanley Donen and Gene Kelly, 1952), producing an original commentary track for the scene featuring Debbie Reynolds's performance of "Would You." Their commentary combines a formal analysis of the cinematography and sound design in the scene with an exegesis of Hollywood's transition to sound. They also proposed the inclusion of several bonus features that they discovered during their research, including a deleted scene featuring Debbie Reynolds performing "You Are My Lucky Star," a video tutorial that breaks down each step in Gene

Kelly's legendary tap performance in the "Singin' in the Rain" scene, and a short documentary about Kelly's career.[22] The project as a whole offers viewers a comprehensive account of the film's critical, historical, and popular value, providing information about Hollywood musicals, sound design, dance, and stardom in a multimodal public format.

By designing paratexts for the Criterion Collection through practices of curation and appropriation, the students immerse themselves in the discourses of cinephilia. The detailed formal analyses of striking images presented in their scene commentaries, the archival discoveries they include as bonus features, and their original cover art present their selected film to an imagined audience of cinephiles and to the corporate intermediary that most explicitly embodies and markets cinephilia. In doing so, the students approach each film *as cinephiles* even if they do not identify as cinephiles beyond the boundaries of the project. In this limited pedagogical context, cinephilia thus serves as a mode of scholarly engagement rather than a personal identity or affiliation.

The promotion of virtual cinephilia in the classroom shifts film analysis beyond the image, focusing on three related forms of cinephiliac investment: the vector, the series, and the archive. The vector traces the virtual paths from a film to other texts and paratexts; the series transforms film viewing into an ongoing enterprise, with one film leading to another; and the archive invites students to explore independently the material collected in online venues. Each of these new objects or forms of virtual cinephilia extends from the film into another sphere of exhibition or reflection. The cinematic image contracts the film into an essential moment, rewarding the attentive cinephile with the revelation of an enigmatic or elegant or haunting detail, one often concealed from the casual spectator. The vector, the series, and the archive reward the distracted cinephile who follows the film to another film or image or text, who produces from one film a series of films as if curating a private film festival, and who tracks the film into multiple archives, often contributing new paratextual material to those archives. Virtual cinephilia is mobile, interactive, and restless, an approach to film that students recognize, welcome, and sometimes even love.

Appendix I: Sample Assignment

Group Project Guidelines

OVERVIEW

For the final project, each group of students will produce a set of bonus features for a proposed Criterion Collection DVD/Blu-Ray edition of one of the films included on the American Film Institute's 100 Years . . . 100 Movies list. The Criterion Collection is a prestigious distribution company that releases DVD and Blu-ray editions of "important classic and contemporary films." Their DVD/Blu-ray editions feature both pristine technological restorations and original bonus features produced and curated by leading scholars, critics, artists, and archivists. Your project will reflect an understanding of the value of: your assigned film, the canon of American cinema as defined by the American Film Institute, and the Criterion Collection brand.

You will use iMovie, Photoshop, Wordpress, and other digital tools to produce and curate a set of bonus features based on extensive research about your assigned film. The project will combine the forms of textual, industrial, and cultural analysis introduced throughout the semester.

I. Wordpress Site

Your group must design a Wordpress site as the venue for the bonus features you will curate and produce. Your Wordpress site should feature (1) a URL and a title that are both informative and creative; (2) a well-organized format for presenting individual posts; and (3) an inviting and professional visual design. When you design your Wordpress site, imagine the consumers who purchase Criterion Collection products as your primary audience.

II. Criterion Collection DVD/Blu-Ray Paratexts

The central focus of the project is the production of a set of bonus features for your film's proposed DVD/Blu-ray release. Each group will: design a front and back cover for the disc case, curate a set of archival bonus features discovered during your research process (interviews, essays, etc.), write an essay about the film and its critical contexts, and produce two original digital bonus features—a trailer for the DVD/Blu-ray release of the film by Criterion and a commentary track for a scene from the film.

Each Element of the Production Process Is Reviewed Below:

- Design a front cover and a back cover for the disc case, incorporating images, the film's title, corporate logos, production details, and so on. You may use Photoshop (or another image-editing program) to design the front and back cover.
- Curate a set of digital bonus features for the disc and a set of print features for the booklet that would be enclosed with the disc. Your curated bonus features may include images, videos, critical essays, interviews, and other archival documents that you discover during your research process. You must include a minimum of three digital bonus features for inclusion on the disc and three print bonus features for inclusion in the booklet. You will post all of these bonus features on your Wordpress site. In addition to the three print features for the booklet, you must

also write a short essay for the booklet providing a critical overview of the entire DVD/Blu-ray package.

- Produce two original digital bonus features: a trailer for the Criterion DVD/Blu-ray release and a commentary track for a scene from the film. You will use iMovie to create both of these paratexts. The trailer may re-mix footage from the film, footage from the original trailers, and material from other image sources into a new trailer for your proposed Criterion release. The trailer should be approximately two minutes long. The commentary track should accompany a single scene from the film and should combine textual, industrial, and cultural analysis in its discussion of the scene. The scene should be approximately four minutes long.

III. Bibliography/Filmography

As a separate post in your Wordpress site, please present a complete bibliography listing all of the sources (books, articles, images, videos, etc.) featured and cited within your project. Please prepare your bibliography with complete citations for each entry formatted according to the *MLA Style Manual*.

LISA PATTI is Assistant Professor of Media and Society at Hobart and William Smith Colleges. She is co-author (with Glyn Davis, Kay Dickinson, and Amy Villarejo) of *Film Studies: A Global Introduction* and co-editor (with Tijana Mamula) of *The Multilingual Screen: New Reflections on Cinema and Linguistic Difference*.

Notes

1. The Tumblr site http://whatnetflixdoes.tumblr.com is no longer active. For an article contemporaneous with "What Netflix Does" that reported on the site when it was active, see Jason Bailey, "Why Is Netflix Secretly Cropping Movies?" *Flavorwire*, July 17, 2013, http://flavor wire.com/404511/why-is-netflix-secretly-cropping-movies.

2. Zadie Smith, "Generation Why?" *New York Review of Books*, November 25, 2010, http://www.nybooks.com/articles/2010/11/25/generation-why/.

3. Susan Sontag, "The Decay of Cinema," *New York Times*, February 25, 1996, http://www.nytimes.com/1996/02/25/magazine/the-decay-of-cinema.html.

4. Alexis C. Madrigal, "How Netflix Reverse Engineered Hollywood," *The Atlantic*, January 2, 2014, http://www.theatlantic.com/technology/archive/2014/01/how-netflix-reverse-engineered-hollywood/282679/.

5. Ibid.

6. Barbara Klinger, *Beyond the Multiplex: Cinema, New Technologies, and the Home* (Berkeley: University of California Press, 2006), 75.

7. Wheeler Winston Dixon and Gwendolyn Audrey Foster, "Teaching Film in the Age of Digital Transformation," in *Teaching Film*, eds. Lucy Fischer and Patrice Petro (New York: Modern Language Association, 2012), 358.

8. Dave Kehr, liner notes, "*Indiscretion of an American Wife & Terminal Station,*" *Indiscretion of an American Wife/Terminal Station*, DVD, dir. Vittorio De Sica (1954; New York: Criterion, 2003.)

9. For a discussion of interactive film cultures, see Chuck Tryon's *Reinventing Cinema: Movies in the Age of Media Convergence* (New Brunswick, NJ: Rutgers University Press, 2009).

10. Chuck Tryon, *On-Demand Culture: Digital Delivery and the Future of Movies* (New Brunswick, NJ: Rutgers University Press, 2013), 4.

11. Ibid.

12. Wheeler Winston Dixon, *Streaming: Movies, Media, and Instant Access* (Lexington: University Press of Kentucky, 2013), 6.

13. Caetlin Benson-Allott, "Confessions of a Platform Agnostic, or Film Criticism After Film," *Film Criticism* 40, no. 1 (2016), doi: 10.3998/fc.13761232.0040.105.

14. For a list of the posts included in the *Clueless* theme week on In Media Res, see http://mediacommons.futureofthebook.org/imr/category/tags/clueless.

15. Lynne Stahl, "Parapedagogy: Teaching Film Analysis from the Digital Periphery," *Cinema Journal Teaching Dossier* 1, no. 3 (2013), http://www.teachingmedia.org/parapedagogy-teaching-film-analysis-digital-periphery/.

16. See, for example, Willa Paskin, "The Dirty Secret of Binge-Watching," *Slate*, November 13, 2013, http://www.slate.com/articles/arts/how_we_watch_tv/2013/11/binge_watching_tv_is_just_another_name_for_being_a_couch_potato.html.

17. Jonathan Gray, *Show Sold Separately: Promos, Spoilers, and Other Media Paratexts* (New York: New York University Press 2010), 26.

18. For extended discussions of the critical and pedagogical value of DVD bonus features, see John Thornton Caldwell, *Production Culture: Industrial Reflexivity and Critical Practice in Film and Television* (Durham, NC: Duke University Press, 2008), and Pat Brereton, *Smart Cinema, DVD Add-Ons, and New Audience Pleasures* (New York: Palgrave, 2012).

19. Monika Mehta, "Teaching Hindi Film Song Sequences," *Cinema Journal Teaching Dossier* 1, no. 3 (2013), http://www.teachingmedia.org/teaching-hindi-film-song-sequences/.

20. For a complete description of the research dossier assignment and sample projects, see Leah Shafer and Lisa Patti, "Extreme Searching: Multi-Modal Media Research," *Journal of Interactive Technology and Pedagogy* 1 (2012), http://jitp.commons.gc.cuny.edu/extreme-searching-multi-modal-media-research-2/.

21. In 2016, the Criterion Collection launched a new streaming site, Filmstruck (www.filmstruck.com), in partnership with Turner Classic Movies. Filmstruck is now the exclusive online location for Criterion films.

22. Peter Kohl, Francesca Pittelli, Xena Pulliam, and Zheng Xu submitted this project for the course Introduction to Media and Society at Hobart and William Smith Colleges during the fall 2013 semester.

11 Lessons of Birth and Death

The Past, Present, and Future of Cinephilia in Martin Scorsese's Hugo *(2011)*

Andrew Utterson

> Cinema's 100 years seem to have the shape of a life cycle: an inevitable birth, the steady accumulation of glories and the onset in the last decade of an ignominious, irreversible decline.
>
> —Susan Sontag, "The Decay of Cinema"

> No matter where the cinema goes, we cannot afford to lose sight of its beginnings.
>
> —Martin Scorsese, "Martin Scorsese: Film Director"

As TEACHERS AND STUDENTS of cinema today, we face the question of how best to understand a medium at the moment of its supposed passing, an extended turning point at which critics, filmmakers, and theorists alike have consistently proclaimed cinema's death or dying. How, in turn, might we address the generational divergences that exist in relation to our experiences of cinema—and cinephilia—especially for an entire generation of students whose encounters succeed the "ignominious, irreversible decline" identified by Susan Sontag and others?[1] In apocalyptic, existential terms, are we teaching and studying a dead medium? How might we approach a century and more of cinema, and a medium in memoriam? And, in a shift from cinema to postcinema, how might we best communicate the essence of cinema to a postcinematic generation?

Cinema itself offers many of the most valuable answers to these questions, in the form of films and filmmakers who consciously reflect on the evolving history and changing status of the moving image. Cinema, in its ability to explore and arguably memorialize this history, is in certain respects its own best teacher, not least as a new generation seeks to negotiate its own understandings of and relationships with this medium.

As one example, approximately 120 years after the so-called birth of cinema, and amid much debate as to its supposed death, Martin Scorsese's *Hugo* represents a revealing case study in changing conceptions of cinema and cinephilia, as mapped in explicitly generational terms.[2] Specifically, it provides a narrativized, media archaeological history of cinema, exploring and archivally recontextualizing the canonical works of the early cinema of the late nineteenth and early twentieth centuries. In turn, *Hugo* reflects on the status of cinema today, and the continuing legacy of a cinephilia whose metaphorical "flame" is passed to a new generation of cinephiles, as symbolized by *Hugo*'s eponymous protagonist and the lessons of his own cinematic discovery.

In exploring early cinema through this late- or postcinematic lens, *Hugo* offers a useful model for how we might teach and study cinema today, not least concerning the potential role of cinephilia in understanding film history.[3] Reflexively exploring the relationship between cinema and that which comes after, Scorsese guides the spectator, via his fictional proxies, on a journey of discovery as to what cinema has been as a means to also explore what it still might be. Indeed, in simultaneously looking backward and forward, that is, to the past as a means to understand the present as well as the future, *Hugo* provides its most illuminating lessons on the value of cinephilia through the taught acts of film history and historiography.

Learning to Love the Past: Cinephilia for a Postcinematic Generation

> Is there a way around this conundrum of the *cinéphile*, who would rather consent to the "death" of cinema than have it bastardized by digital technologies and hybridized by films being shown on all manner of unsuitable surfaces and in all kinds of unseemly places?[4]

In teaching and studying film in the context of the "conundrum" outlined by Thomas Elsaesser, how might we draw on the legacy of cinephilia—most simply defined as a love of cinema   while also recognizing the new screen technologies and associated cultures that have come to exist?

In the context of the classroom (used here as a loose term for which we might also read *lecture hall, auditorium,* etc.), generational divergences exist in our experiences of cinema and the particularities of an entire generation for whom it exists principally, or even exclusively, in the past tense. After all, if we accept the claims of death that circulated so loudly in the mid-1990s—an ironic combination of centenary celebrations and fin de siècle anxieties—and that have continued in the decades since, an intriguing scenario presents itself: for the first time in the history of formal film education, we are encountering a generation of students who were born, and have lived their entire lives, in this postcinematic era. Put simply, we are teaching the first postcinematic generation, one that has only ever experienced cinema—or a particular conception of cinema (one rooted in the primacy of the theatrical experience, the materiality of film, etc.) that prevailed for a century or more but now fades into history—as a combination of received or mediated memories and historical re-creation. Teachers and students sit astride this generational, cultural, cinematic divide, separated by the "year zero" of cinema's death.

Cinephilia, by extension, is likewise historically and culturally contingent. As Christian Keathley has argued, referencing Susan Sontag, it is not cinema that has died but rather cinephilia: "What has in fact faded out is not the cinema itself, but a certain kind of intense loving relationship with the cinema that goes by the name of 'cinephilia.'"[5] Notably, Keathley goes on to argue the generational dimensions of this cultural shift, noting how the

> reluctance on the part of so many young students to seek out the broad range of films that the history of cinema has to offer seems to mimic the changing habits in perception brought on by the conditions of modernity: faced with an abundance of stimuli—or in this case, an abundance of availability, of choices—one closes down, sets up boundaries where none seem to exist, retreats into what one already knows instead of seeking out what is new.[6]

For others, changing perceptions, definitions, and materialities of cinema have led to the relocation of a cinephilic impulse, as opposed to its fundamental erosion. According to Wheeler Winston Dixon and Gwendolyn Audrey Foster,

> for those who live and work in the post-filmic era—that is, those who have come to consciousness in the past 20 years—the digital world is an accomplished fact and the dominant medium of visual discourse. Many of our students remark that the liberation of the moving image from the tyranny of the imperfect medium of film is a technical shift that is not only inevitable but also desirable.[7]

This generational divergence is echoed by Jonathan Rosenbaum:

> It's a strange paradox that about half of my friends and colleagues think that we're currently approaching the end of cinema as an art form . . . while the other half believe that we're enjoying some sort of exciting resurgence and renaissance. . . . How can one account for this discrepancy? One clue is that many of the naysayers tend to be people around my own age (sixty-six) or older, whereas many of the optimistic ones are a good deal younger, most of them under thirty.[8]

In each of these instances, age, and therefore generational specificity, is acknowledged as being fundamental to our relationships with cinema and its history.

Against this backdrop of competing proclamations of death and dying, the question remains: might *any* film, *Hugo* or any other, arouse the type of deep feelings of love—that is, *philia*—that are directly experienced rather than exclusively received via indirect signifiers and memories?

With Scorsese positioned as arch-cinephile, whose life and oeuvre broadly correspond with the postwar generation of heightened cinephilia, *Hugo* is a film that articulates an obsessive love of cinema.[9] Indeed, over a number of decades, Scorsese has assumed a position of cultural patron and protector of our shared cinematic heritage, whose publicly declared cinephilia extends from his own films (from *Hugo* to cine-biographical documentaries such as *A Personal Journey with Martin Scorsese Through American Movies* [1995] and *My Voyage to Italy* [2001]) to archival, curatorial, and other cultural activities—and might even be seen as an authorial signifier. For example, Scorsese founded and chairs the Film Foundation, a nonprofit organization "dedicated to protecting and preserving motion picture history."[10] This remit is paralleled by the affiliated World Cinema Foundation, also chaired by Scorsese, whose mission is likewise framed as being "dedicated to preserving and restoring neglected films from around the world."[11]

Loosely linking fact and fiction, *Hugo*'s exploration of cinema—and cinephilia—is routed via a generational melodrama, in the form of a young boy's discovery of the films of a mysterious man who is revealed to be none other than the great French filmmaker Georges Méliès. In part, *Hugo* is directed toward an audience for whom the passing of cinema is experienced firsthand, that is, those who are old enough to have experienced at least some of the first century of cinema. Yet, at the same time, in channeling a nostalgia that is narratively embedded, it transfers these memories to a generation for whom this experience is more remote, historically and/or culturally, with the cinema of Méliès and others positioned as "neglected films from around the world."

In the context of teaching and studying cinema, *Hugo* is revealing in that it both explicitly narrativizes and represents a process of cinephilic discovery while offering broader historiographic lessons concerning the historical and indeed generational specificity of this process. In narrativizing Hugo (Asa Butterfield) and companion Isabelle's (Chloë Grace Moretz's) encounters with Méliès (Ben Kingsley), Scorsese stresses the importance of our shared cultural heritage and its sites and modes of engagement, including the traces of received cultural memory and the cumulative archive of cinema as a museum of memory, as a number of canonical works of early cinema are excerpted in *Hugo*, archivally embedded as footage that is diegetically motivated in one form or another.

In exploring cinephilia and cultural memory, *Hugo* considers the fundamental questions of whose memories are evoked via the cinematic archive and whether our understandings of this past are universally shared. Svetlana Boym has argued that "nostalgia is about the relationship between individual biography and the biography of groups or nations, between personal and collective memory."[12] In this sense, *Hugo* constructs a complex cinematic nostalgia, bringing past and present into communication, exploring cultural memories that are filtered in the first instance via authorial consciousness (i.e., Scorsese as "auteur"), but that are in turn passed from one generation to the next. Such complexity lies in both the historiographic framing of cinema's death and the idea of a long-lost cinematic essentialism, which exists, in part, as cinephilia for a postcinematic generation, communicating a profound nostalgia for cinema, and channeling its cinephilic potential, but via mnemonic and emotional triggers that in some respects constitute "phantom" signifiers. In generational terms, the fundamental difference is that between a nostalgia for something one has known, loved, and lost (or, is losing) and a nostalgia evoked by an existential awareness of something one has never had the opportunity to experience directly. After all, if cinema is dead, and died many years ago, how else might one be nostalgic for a past one never knew?

Cinema in Memoriam: Mediated Memory and the Ghost of Cinephilia

In looking back, memorializing cinema, much of the essential cinephilia of *Hugo* is bound up in its nostalgic re-creation—a variation on what Christian Metz once described in terms of a tendency "to maintain the cinema in the imaginary enclosures of a pure love"—not just of so-called early cinema but of an entire conception of cinema.[13] That is, *Hugo* evokes the pleasures of a mode of cinema that is arguably already alien to today's students, a type of cinema that captures live action, that stores and exhibits its representations via the physical materiality of celluloid, and whose images are in turn projected in 2D, onto a big screen, within the controlled conditions and collective experience of the movie theater.

In dramatically reconstructing the earliest decades of cinema, *Hugo* exists as a historical re-creation—a history lesson of sorts—albeit one tinged with a reflexively self-conscious historical imaginary, which is found, for example, in the dramatized depictions of cultural figures such as James Joyce (Robert Gill), Django Reinhardt (Emil Lager), and Salvador Dalí (Ben Addis). In the same way that a history teacher seeks to provide a sense of the past through empathy with historical figures and sensory evocation of a period and place, Scorsese evokes the Paris of the late nineteenth and early twentieth centuries (peopled by Méliès, most notably) in order to give contemporary presence to the moment of modernity that saw the emergence of cinema. Yet this is also a history explicitly infused with cinephilia. Rather than drawing on this period in the abstract or with a detached objectivity, the film evokes cinema via an impassioned cinephilia, a subjective sense of the sheer excitement that can come from the discovery of the moving image and a relationship with the films and filmmakers of the past.

As scholars like Jason Sperb and Sandra Annett have argued, in their respective discussions of "new nostalgia" and "nostalgic remediation," *Hugo* returns us to this past from a distinctly contemporary perspective.[14] From the vantage point of its release in 2011, *Hugo* operates, in some respects, according to what Boym has defined as "restorative nostalgia," outlining a mode of looking back that seeks to preserve the past, or at least memorialize it, shoring up a vision of history that might otherwise be forgotten, replaced, and possibly lost forever.[15] In this nostalgic historiography, Scorsese represents the pedagogical models of curator and guide, preserving pivotal works of the past and in turn directing us as a docent does in a gallery or museum. In doing so, *Hugo* explicitly links cinephilia to a number of sites of learning, both traditional and other. In the quest for enigma resolution, that is, unlocking the secret of the mysterious Méliès, the library—that most traditional site of learning—is shown to be an important source of knowledge. After visiting a Parisian bookshop—described by Isabelle as "only the most wonderful place on earth. It is Neverland and Oz and Treasure Island all wrapped into one"—Hugo is directed toward further bibliophilic discovery in a Parisian library.

The *bibliothèque* in question is the fictitious Film Academy Library, a repository of near-Alexandrian proportions in which Hugo encounters fictional film historian Professor René Tabard (Michael Stuhlbarg), author of an equally fictitious volume on silent cinema (*Inventer le rêve: l'Histoire des premiers films* or, in loose translation, *The Invention of Dreams: The History of the First Films*) held within the library. As Hugo and Isabelle read aloud, the films they encounter are intercut, from Méliès to Edwin S. Porter, D. W. Griffith, F. W. Murnau, and beyond. "What began as a sideshow novelty soon grew into something more when the first filmmakers discovered they could use the new medium to tell stories," reads Hugo, to which Isabelle adds, "Méliès was one of the first to realize that films had the power to capture dreams." A deep knowledge of film history, it is demonstrated, can be unlocked via the written word—hardly a revelation for cinema scholars, but instructive for those who are just beginning to learn about cinema's past.

Elsewhere, the objects, tools, and materials of cinema are likewise historically located, as Tabard leads Hugo and Isabelle through his archive of Méliès-related materials, in this fictional scenario, giving presence to the act of filmmaking and the history of cinema. Archival photographs, cameras, and other objects are shown, as a dramatic flashback places these objects in context with Méliès at work in his studio, which is described by Tabard as "like something out of a dream . . . an enchanted castle . . . a palace made of glass." Again, the protagonists—and in turn the spectator—are guided through the history of cinema as if in a museum, with the memory of cinema located in objects as well as words.

In *Hugo*, it is the space of the movie theater—the "kingdom of shadows" or "palace of dreams"—that functions as the most potent site for the discovery of cinema, and for cultivating the pleasures associated with this act. In the context of considerable contemporary anxiety concerning changing cultures of cinema exhibition and reception, Scorsese consciously conjures the specter of the theatrical era, and it is within the space of the cinema that passion for the moving image is most explicitly mobilized. "Do you want to have an adventure?" Hugo asks Isabelle, prompting their visit to a festival of silent cinema, replete with posters of the stars of "*le cinéma muet*," including Douglas Fairbanks, Max Linder, Charles Chaplin, Buster Keaton, Charley Chase, and Harold Lloyd. It is here that the nascent cinephiles attend a screening of *Safety Last!* (Fred C. Newmeyer and Sam Taylor, 1923), a film in which Lloyd famously dangles precariously from a stories-high clock face, just as Hugo will in the course of his own adventures (in an allusion or homage to the earlier work). The movie theater is represented as a still-resonant site and space of shared film history, cultural memory, and discovery and learning (Figure 11.1).

Cinema is celebrated as a projected experience, that is, the moving image on the "big screen," in implicit contrast to the proliferation of alternate screens that have supplanted or at least fundamentally challenged the primacy of this experience.[16] "I would recognize the sound of a movie projector anywhere," notes the dramatized Méliès. Yet in the context of the 2011 theatrical release of *Hugo*, one can reasonably question how most spectators would have encountered such a film and in turn whether theatrical exhibition is already a fundamentally historical re-creation.[17] As Thomas Elsaesser has noted, describing an era pointedly referred to in the past tense,

> Cinephilia meant being sensitive to one's surroundings when watching a movie, carefully picking the place where to sit, fully alert to the quasi-sacral feeling of nervous anticipation that could descend upon a public space,

Figure 11.1. *Hugo* (Martin Scorsese, 2011).

however squalid, smelly or slipshod, as the velvet curtain rose and the studio logo with its fanfares filled the space.[18]

Providing historical perspective, *Hugo* recreates what is arguably the most famous moment in the genesis of cinema, depicting the Salon Indien du Grand Café, Paris, on the evening of December 28, 1895. It is here that the very first public audience of projected films reportedly gasped and recoiled at the advancing train of *L'arrivée d'un train en gare de La Ciotat* (*Arrival of a Train at La Ciotat Station*, Auguste and Louis Lumière, 1895), which the spectators feared would burst through the screen as it advanced as if directly toward them. "When the train came speeding toward the screen, the audience screamed because they thought they were in danger of being run over," Isabelle reads aloud, as an extract from the original film is intercut with Scorsese's dramatic recreation of this illustrative and in some respects originary moment in the power of projected moving images. Even if the version of history Isabelle recounts has been disputed by cinema scholars, the scene nevertheless provides an immersive illustration of theatrical exhibition for an audience that will increasingly associate such exhibition with the past.

Augmenting this history lesson, examples of early cinema are embedded and narrativized via the discovery of Méliès and other key films and filmmakers of the silent era. Excerpted works include *La sortie des usines Lumière* (*Workers Leaving the Lumière Factory*, Auguste and Louis Lumière, 1895), *The Great Train Robbery* (Edwin S. Porter, 1903), *Intolerance* (D. W. Griffith, 1916), *Das Cabinet des Dr. Caligari* (*The Cabinet of Dr. Caligari*, Robert Wiene, 1919), *The Kid* (Charlie Chaplin, 1921), *The General* (Buster Keaton, 1926), and *Die Büchse der Pandora* (*Pandora's Box*, G. W. Pabst, 1929), among others. In this sense, *Hugo* could even be thought of as a straightforward pedagogical tool via which to explore the emergence and evolution of early cinema through anthologized works.

More complexly, the referencing of Méliès and others is embedded within a metafictional context, with original works transplanted into a narrative that reflexively frames this historiography, placed within a context of cinephilic discovery and a nostalgia that engages cultural memory via archival recontextualization of the first decades of cinema. For example, predigital works are relocated within a digital cinematic context, with historical relations charted both between and within periods and texts. In terms of archival practices, Paolo Cherchi Usai has warned of the perils of dematerialized representation of works of cinema whose definition rests, at least in part, on their physical qualities, that is, filmic materiality and projection, arguing that "once resurrected in digital form, early cinema gains in visibility while renouncing its identity as an artwork."[19] In seeking to retain the spirit—if not always the materiality—of early cinematic works, *Hugo* is not just an archival act, seeking to preserve the history of cinema in the context of an evolving technological landscape, but also a pedagogical act, seeking to foster and celebrate the act of cinephilic discovery.[20]

In terms of reflexive historiography, *Hugo* acknowledges its processes of archival repositioning, revealing a series of media archaeological and film historical relations. Mixing "old" and "new" media, analog and digital, and exploring celluloid memory through postfilmic media, *Hugo* renders explicit a cinematic lineage and historiography, exploring, identifying, and redefining the essence of early cinema within a much broader history of what Siegfried Zielinski has termed "hearing and seeing by technical means."[21]

In particular, archival anxieties are at the very core of the film, an expression of Scorsese's deep concerns regarding not just the death of a certain experience of cinema—one that took place in the movie theater—but also the archival degradation and decay of the entire corpus of our shared cinematic heritage, not least in terms of the materiality and mutability of film and the ultimate obsolescence of the medium.

For Cherchi Usai (in a volume titled nothing less than *The Death of Cinema*, for which Scorsese contributed a preface), anticipating the inevitability of this scenario,

> moving image preservation will then be redefined as the science of its gradual loss and the art of coping with its consequences, very much like a physician who has accepted the inevitability of death even when he continues to fight for the patient's life. In monitoring the progress of image decay, the conservator assumes the responsibility of following the process until the image has vanished altogether, or ensures its migration to another kind of visual experience, while interpreting the meaning of the loss for the benefit of future generations.[22]

If cinema exists as a dying "patient," whose ultimate death is acknowledged, Scorsese has yet to give up on the task of caring for the patient, or even the possibility that life might continue beyond the body, to extend this metaphor. In one instance, as Tabard guides Hugo and Isabelle through his archival collection of Méliès materials, Hugo asks, "Could we watch some of his movies?" Tabard's response hints at the precariousness of film preservation in the world beyond this fiction. "I wish you could, but time hasn't been kind to old movies. This is the only one that we know of that survived," the professor laments as he holds a solitary film canister in his hands (Figure 11.2). "Out of hundreds, one—and still, it is a masterpiece." The "it" he speaks of is none other than *Le voyage dans la lune* (*A Trip to the Moon*, 1902), as the films of Méliès and others are placed within a dramatized preservation of real cinematic artifacts. In fact, careful viewers will note that the label on the canister appears to be for another Méliès film, *L'hallucination de l'alchimiste* (*The Alchemist's Hallucination*, 1897), hinting perhaps at the further cinematic discoveries the characters will experience before the film is over.

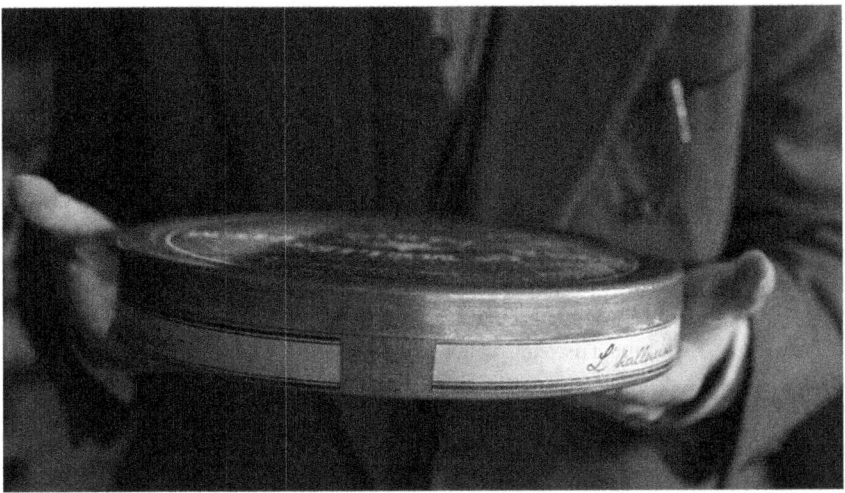

Figure 11.2. *Hugo* (Martin Scorsese, 2011).

In exploring the creative impulse of a dynamic historiography, Domietta Torlasco has gone so far as to describe the act of "'archiving' as intervention—not the systematic preservation of film materials but the creative reelaboration of cinema's aesthetic and ideological complexities."[23] Indeed, for Cherchi Usai, film history, and its archival dimensions, are not altogether incompatible with the idea of narrative:

> Film history comes to exist as such when moving image destruction is described and explained in order to make clear the causes and patterns of decay, . . . film history is quite compatible with a narrating presence and with the goal of deciphering the traces left by each viewing on the relics of an entity recognized as being no longer extant. The imaginary object will then be mirrored in an imaginary account: an exercise in storytelling.[24]

As an example of such "storytelling," playfully suturing past and present, Scorsese even inserts himself—and his iconic directorial presence—into his fictional scenario, as it engages with film history and preservation. In a cameo that sees Scorsese play a photographer who takes a portrait of Méliès, Scorsese travels back in time to physically embody and visually represent the spirit of cinephilia and early photographic and in turn cinematographic invention.

The "story" of the precarious state of our cinematic heritage, in precisely archival as well as more general cultural terms, later finds presence in a scene in which the fragility of film stock is described in relation to the loss of countless Méliès films. The story of the filmmaker's life and career is narrated as archival

World War I footage places this narration in historical context.[25] The materiality of this footage has a textural and in turn intellectual function, in which visibly evident decay signifies the archival status of the footage and the preservation of a moment in history, precisely in the context of the loss of film history, as it is explained that countless Méliès films were melted down so that their chemical constituents could be reused in the manufacture of shoe heels. "The world had no time for magic tricks and movie shows. . . . No one wanted my movies anymore," the dramatized Méliès narrates over images of war. Death, in the most profound of historical settings, forms a backdrop for understanding the fragility of the cinematic corpus, equating the obsolescence of the medium with a death of sorts.

In *Hugo*'s dramatic finale, as the rediscovered Méliès and his works are unveiled at a Parisian gala, the fictional Tabard speaks as if on behalf of Scorsese, and in turn *Hugo*, as archival footage of the real Méliès and his films are intertwined with this dramatization:

> For years, most of his films were thought to be lost. Indeed Monsieur Méliès believed so himself. But we began a search. We looked through vaults, through private collections, barns, and catacombs. Our work was rewarded with old negatives, boxes of prints, and trunks full of decaying film which we were able to save.

If *Hugo* is "an exercise in storytelling" that simultaneously seeks to illuminate the past via an "imaginary account" of early cinema's "imaginary objects," it also seeks to reflexively foreground and detail a material archival process. The period of early cinema becomes the locus for an existential drama playing out more than a century later, implicitly linking historiographic conceptions of birth and death. Cinema is eulogized in a mass for a medium now arguably best considered in memoriam, one whose past glories are celebrated and in turn memorialized, with *Hugo* itself a reflexive archival act and site of preservation.

Whether in the library, movie theater, or elsewhere, *Hugo* represents and culturally frames the pleasures of cinematic discovery, passed from director to spectator, via Hugo and Isabelle, and indeed from one generation to the next, as paralleled by the generational dynamics of the narrative. In framing cinephilia in the context of nostalgia, cultural memory, and a "golden age" symbolized by the films and filmmakers of a bygone era, Scorsese navigates a historical but also mythic path through a century and more of cinema.

The History of Film, the Future of Cinephilia

> I'm writing this letter to you about the future. I'm looking at it through the lens of my world. Through the lens of cinema, which has been at the center of that world. For the last few years, I've realized that the idea of cinema that I

grew up with, that's there in the movies I've been showing you since you were a child, and that was thriving when I started making pictures, is coming to a close. I'm not referring to the films that have already been made. I'm referring to the ones that are to come. I don't mean to be despairing. I'm not writing these words in a spirit of defeat. On the contrary, I think the future is bright.[26]

As one type of cinema fades into the past, Scorsese nevertheless looks forward to suggest that the pursuit of a historically rooted cinephilia might offer a connective tissue in terms of our understanding of cinema today (and indeed tomorrow). Similarly, *Hugo* encourages us to consider not simply whether the medium we teach and study is dead or dying, but whether continuities might be charted between the cinematic and postcinematic, as well as future iterations of a cinephilic impulse. Put another way, if *Hugo* is an afterword to one particular history of cinema, it is also perhaps the foreword to another.

In exploring a nostalgia for the past, *Hugo* utilizes this memory as something that might also reframe contemporary definitions of cinema. Its historical focus is far from what Marshall McLuhan once described in terms of a tendency for people to cling to "the rearview-mirror view of their world," referring to how, "because of the invisibility of any environment during the period of its innovation, man is only consciously aware of the environment that has *preceded* it."[27] In depicting the very first decades of cinema, re-creating an era in which the cinema of the past was "new," explicit connections are drawn between the emergence of cinema in the late nineteenth and early twentieth centuries and its reconfigurations today, which *Hugo* arguably also represents.

Thus, *Hugo* explores the changing contours of cinema via the very technologies that have brought about its supposed death—whether the fact that *Hugo* was shot digitally (in postfilmic contrast to the materiality of early cinema, as explored in *Hugo* via the physicality and archival precariousness of Méliès's work); or the fact that it so extensively employs digital visual effects (in direct comparison to the equivalent sense of illusion and magic of the trickery employed by Méliès); or the fact that it was shot for 3D exhibition (again, in revealing play with the aspects of early cinematic depth and dimensionality explored in the film itself). *Hugo* thus reflects on the nature of cinema and explores the medium's relationship to new imaging technologies precisely as live action, as captured on film and projected to a public audience, becomes a decidedly historical iteration of the medium.

To return to Boym's schema of nostalgic modes, *Hugo* goes beyond the "restorative"—with its implication of being reactionary, conservative, or regressive—imploring us instead to embrace the history of cinema as a way of figuring new technological and aesthetic possibilities. Unlike "restorative nostalgia," for Boym, the twinned notion of a "reflective nostalgia" is one that looks to the past for a progressive purpose.[28] This is a process by which even mourning, memorialization, reminiscence, and remembrance—all of which are associated with historiographic discourses concerning the death of cinema—have the potential to become contemporary acts.

Hugo explores the past in order to articulate a redefinition of cinema by way, in part, of what D. N. Rodowick has defined as the fundamental "turning point . . . wherein the relative positioning of the photographic and the digital was reversed," a model similarly explored in Lev Manovich's equation for a mode of cinema that emerged in the last decade or more: "Digital film = live action material + painting + image processing + compositing + 2-d computer animation + 3-d computer animation."[29] In *Hugo*, these elements are intertwined to the point of often being indistinguishable, and, with regard to lessons concerning how we might approach early cinema, they suggest a series of illuminating parallels with contemporary shifts. In terms of camera technology, for example, the developments in imaging tools by Méliès and the Lumières might be compared to Scorsese's own innovations: *Hugo*, after all, like many recent films, was shot entirely digitally.[30] Thus a film that is ostensibly about early cinema might also be considered, in Manovich's parlance, as "digital film" par excellence.

Ironically, with regard to the materiality of film (or, the immateriality of an absence thereof), the production of *Hugo* represents a shift from the photochemical past that is so cherished in the film itself, including in a scene in which Méliès is shown cutting and reassembling strips of film by hand in what effectively depicts the invention of editing. As Scorsese has noted, "The cinema began with a passionate physical relationship between celluloid and the artists and craftsmen and technicians who handled it, manipulated it, and came to know it the way a lover comes to know every inch of the body of the beloved."[31] In relinquishing this "beloved," while simultaneously narrativizing the pursuit of the "body" of Méliès's films, rescued from metaphorical as well as literal neglect, *Hugo* renegotiates and redefines the essentially cinematic as something not solely based in celluloid precisely in the context of medium and materiality.

Similarly, *Hugo* explores the relationship between live action and animation, including the use of computer-generated objects and the degree to which even live-action imagery is increasingly manipulated on a frame-by-frame basis. In doing so, *Hugo* draws a parallel between the role of visual effects today and the illusionism of the past, not least in the shape of Méliès. In a film that in 2012 won the Academy Awards for Best Cinematography and Best Visual Effects, Scorsese foregrounds the showmanship of Méliès as a magician for whom cinema represented a new "box of tricks," as *Hugo* re-creates the fin de siècle stage magic from which the cinema was partly born. "It was like a new kind of magic," recalls the dramatized Méliès of his stage show and first encounter with cinema at a traveling circus, as his own studio and sets—replete with all manner of elaborate props, costumes, and the wizards, mermaids, travelers, adventurers, magicians, and other exotic characters of his films—are re-created in flashback. "Magic tricks and illusion became my speciality; the world of imagination."

In one scene, the use of hand-painted colorization in *Le voyage dans la lune* is explained as a proto–special effect. "It's in color," exclaims Hugo, to which Madame Méliès (Helen McCrory) responds, "But of course, we tinted the film, we painted it by hand, frame by frame." *Hugo* links the "magic" of early cinema with the illusionism of contemporary visual effects. For the real Méliès, "the scenario, the 'fable,' or 'tale'" was regarded "merely as a pretext for the 'stage effects,' the 'tricks,' or for a nicely arranged tableau."[32] If *Hugo*, by contrast, is clearly a work of narrative, its reliance on the fantastical—in the form of magic, illusionism, and visual effects as sleight of hand—is also seen by Scorsese as essentially cinematic.

Comparisons might also be drawn between the exhibition of early cinema as a "new" technology and contemporary shifts in distribution and exhibition, especially 3D. In one instance, *Hugo* excerpts the famous closing shot of *The Great Train Robbery*, in which an armed man shoots as if directly toward the spectator, "breaking the wall" in a way that was shocking in the context of early cinematic form but has become commonplace in contemporary 3D cinema as a means of establishing an exaggerated sense of depth. Similarly, as re-created in *Hugo*, the wonder with which the Grand Café audience is wowed by the arrival of the Lumières' cinematic train finds parallel in the fact that *Hugo* was shot for today's "new" technology of 3D exhibition (albeit alongside screenings in more traditional sites, as well as other platforms).[33] In its reconstructed

Figure 11.3. *Hugo* (Martin Scorsese, 2011).

screening of *L'arrivée d'un train en gare de La Ciotat*, as the train speeds toward the screen, with a distinct sense of depth established in relation to the audience members and the screen beyond them, there is an emphasis on the sense of perspective that caused such a reaction, apocryphal or not, to the original two-dimensional screening in 1895 (Figure 11.3). If, in *Hugo*, we are privy to a historical re-creation of the first public cinema screening, this is also a film that seeks to reconfigure the mode of exhibition via which this historical re-creation is in turn experienced.

In each of these instances—and there are no doubt others—in bringing past and present into such communication, *Hugo* suggests an aesthetic but also historiographic model for employing cinephilia to chart the history of cinema, from birth to death and beyond. . . .

Conclusion

Reflecting on the development of film studies as a discipline of academic study, Laura Mulvey has argued that "what begins with cinephilia, with the love of Hollywood . . . becomes the theoretical study of Hollywood."[34] As the study of film continues in countless educational institutions throughout the globe, but as cinema itself is characterized by many as being in a state of rigor mortis or otherwise in its dying throes, cinephilia takes on new resonances and meanings, bound up in a complex play of generationally specific responses to the evolving history of cinema and the related mnemonic realms of nostalgia and cultural memory, with considerable ramifications for historiographic approaches to film, and how we teach and study this medium. Cinephilia itself has become one part of the history and theoretical study of film, and, in the hands of the reflective teacher, its legacy retains the power to inspire what Sontag envisaged as "the birth of a new kind of cine-love."[35]

In the context of the postcinematic present, and the postcinematic generation who is at its vanguard, we must acknowledge the necessary plurality of cinephilias, embracing simultaneously new conceptions of cinema and cinephilia alike, as well as the specific relationships with the cinematic archive that constitute the journey of each nascent cinephile—and each generation of cinephiles—as they encounter film history.

As Ian Christie has noted, "One of the key claims made by early film scholars is that understanding the media revolution of the 1890s helps us understand the equivalent revolution we're living through today."[36] Representing these twin "revolutions," *Hugo* offers a model for the study of more than a century of cinema, grappling with conceptions of the cinematic archive, cultural memory, and medium obsolescence. In narrativizing and archivally recontextualizing key works of early cinema, placing them in the context of contemporary technological and aesthetic developments, *Hugo* guides us through the "media revolution" of early cinema and the parallel shifts of today, with the moving image one means of reflecting on its own status and historiography.

How one situates oneself in relation to this historiography, and the modes and tenses of nostalgia invoked, are framed as generationally specific, vis-à-vis the film's eponymous protagonist and his companion Isabelle. For today's students, *Hugo* evokes the history of cinema, and the essential pleasures and passions associated with a historically rooted cinephilia, modes of engagement that are transferred to new cultures, venues, and practices. For today's teachers, meanwhile, *Hugo* simultaneously provides a model for the historicizing of cinema's birth and subsequent death, ways of understanding early cinema—and *all* of cinema—by utilizing cinephilia as a means of illuminating film history across the media archaeological span of an entire "life cycle," to reprise Sontag.

Above all, *Hugo* narrativizes the discoveries that might arise out of an appreciation of our shared cinematic heritage. As *Hugo* navigates film history, it mobilizes the essential pleasures and passions associated with a historical understanding of the medium, demonstrating how the legacy of cinephilia might in turn foster new knowledge and awareness of the moving image, in all of its forms—past, present, and future. In this respect, the memory of cinema becomes a vital element to the future of cinephilia, which becomes a meme that might be learned and transmitted from one generation to the next, and from cinema to that which succeeds it.

ANDREW UTTERSON is Associate Professor of Screen Studies at Ithaca College. He is the author of *From IBM to MGM: Cinema at the Dawn of the Digital Age,* editor of *Technology and Culture: The Film Reader,* and co-editor of the four-volume anthology *Film Theory: Critical Concepts in Media and Cultural Studies.*

Notes

1. Susan Sontag, "The Decay of Cinema," *New York Times Magazine,* February 25, 1996, http://www.nytimes.com/1996/02/25/magazine/the-decay-of-cinema.html. See also Michael Witt, "The Death(s) of Cinema According to Godard," *Screen* 40, no. 3 (1999): 331–346; Paolo Cherchi Usai, *The Death of Cinema: History, Cultural Memory and the Digital Dark Age* (London: British Film Institute, 2001); Laura Mulvey, *Death 24x a Second: Stillness and the Moving Image* (London: Reaktion Books, 2006); André Gaudreault and Philippe Marion, *The End of Cinema? A Medium in Crisis in the Digital Age,* trans. Timothy Barnard (New York: Columbia University Press, 2015).

2. The "so-called birth" refers to the popularly held but theoretically disputed notion of a singular moment of cinema's origin and the typical account of this "birth" as having occurred with the first public screening of projected films by Auguste and Louis Lumière at the Grand Café, Paris, on the evening of December 28, 1895. While claims of the "death" of cinema are not new, and have been postulated at various times throughout its history, especially in the context of moments of significant technological change, what is arguably unique about the discourses that have circulated since the mid-1990s is their sustained and widespread nature, mirroring the pronounced technological and cultural shifts that have led to fundamental changes in how we experience the moving image.

3. In my own "real world" teaching context, *Hugo* has been used as a concluding screening and case study for an undergraduate college course that surveys the history of American film. Indeed, in terms of linear chronology, this course begins with many of the silent-era shorts (including those of Georges Méliès, at a time—pre-Hollywood—when French films constituted a significant proportion of those screened in the United States) that are referenced and excerpted in *Hugo*. In its explicit and reflexive historicizing of cinema, approximately 120 years after its so-called birth, *Hugo* comes full circle, considering the earliest decades of cinema in the context of parallels with its so-called death. In the curricular context of an historical overview of American film, *Hugo* thus exists as a coda of sorts, a suitably summative final gesture.

4. Thomas Elsaesser, "Turn-of-the-Century Epistemes in Film History," in *A Companion to Early Cinema*, eds. André Gaudreault, Nicolas Dulac, and Santiago Hidalgo (Chichester, UK: Wiley, 2012), 603.

5. Christian Keathley, *Cinephilia and History, or The Wind in the Trees* (Bloomington: Indiana University Press, 2006), 2.

6. Ibid., 24.

7. Wheeler Winston Dixon and Gwendolyn Audrey Foster, *21st-Century Hollywood: Movies in the Era of Transformation* (New Brunswick, NJ: Rutgers University Press, 2011), 3.

8. Jonathan Rosenbaum, *Goodbye Cinema, Hello Cinephilia: Film Culture in Transition* (Chicago: University of Chicago Press, 2010), ix.

9. For an account of Scorsese's nascent cinephilia, via the stirrings of a deep love both as a child and as a student at New York University in the mid-1960s, see Ian Christie and David Thompson, eds., *Scorsese on Scorsese* (London: Faber and Faber), 1–22. For diverse perspectives on the histories and theories of cinephilia, see, among others, Marijke de Valck and Malte Hagener, eds., *Cinephilia: Movies, Love and Memory* (Amsterdam: Amsterdam University Press, 2005); Keathley, *Cinephilia*; Jonathan Rosenbaum and Adrian Martin, eds., *Movie Mutations: The Changing Face of World Cinephilia* (London: British Film Institute, 2003); Scott Balcerzak and Jason Sperb, eds., *Cinephilia in the Age of Digital Reproduction: Film, Pleasure and Digital Culture, Vols. 1 and 2* (London: Wallflower Press, 2009, 2012); Rosenbaum, *Goodbye Cinema*; Marijke de Valck, "Reflections on the Recent Cinephilia Debates," *Cinema Journal* 49, no. 2 (2010), 132–139; Rashna Wadia Richards, *Cinematic Flashes: Cinephilia and Classical Hollywood* (Bloomington: Indiana University Press, 2013).

10. "Mission Statement," The Film Foundation, accessed June 27, 2016, http://www.film-foundation.org/mission-statement.

11. "Home," World Cinema Foundation, accessed June 25, 2014, http://worldcinemafoundation.org. Note that the World Cinema Foundation URL is no longer active; it is now the World Cinema Project and can be found at this URL: http://www.film-foundation.org/world-cinema.

12. Svetlana Boym, *The Future of Nostalgia* (New York: Basic, 2001), xvi.

13. Christian Metz, "The Imaginary Signifier," trans. Ben Brewster, *Screen* 16, no. 2 (1975): 23.

14. Jason Sperb, *Flickers of Film: Nostalgia in the Time of Digital Cinema* (New Brunswick, NJ: Rutgers University Press, 2016), 52–70; Sandra Annett, "The Nostalgic Remediation of Cinema in *Hugo* and *Paprika*," *Journal of Adaptation in Film & Performance* 7, no. 2 (2014), 169–80.

15. Boym, *The Future of Nostalgia*, 41–48.

16. As an intriguing example, noted filmmaker—and indeed former Scorsese collaborator (as screenwriter of *Taxi Driver* [1976], for example)—Paul Schrader has argued that "the projected image in a dark room is a very 20th century notion . . . we're entering into the post-theatrical era." Public address at the 53rd Festival Internacional de Cine de Cartagena de Indias (FICCI), February 24, 2013, quoted in Wendy Mitchell, "Paul Schrader: Film Undergoing 'Total Systemic Change,'" *Screen Daily*, February 25, 2013, http://www.screendaily.com/news /paul-schrader-film-undergoing-total-systemic-change/5052354.article.

17. In my own context, in teaching film history, an important pedagogical experience is ensuring that students encounter at least one class screening in a movie theater in order to reflect on the historical dimension of cinema exhibition and the changing sites and ways in which moving images are experienced today.

18. Thomas Elsaesser, "Cinephilia or the Uses of Disenchantment," in Marijke de Valck and Malte Hagener, *Cinephilia: Movies, Love and Memory* (Amsterdam: Amsterdam University Press, 2005), 29.

19. Cherchi Usai, "Early Cinema Recollections," in *A Companion to Early Cinema*, eds. André Gaudreault, Nicolas Dulac, and Santiago Hidalgo (Chichester, UK: Wiley, 2012), 541.

20. For works that describe cinephilic relationships in the specific context of new media recontextualization, see Mulvey, *Death 24x a Second*; Alison Trope, "Footstool Film School: Home Entertainment as Home Education," in *Inventing Film Studies*, eds. Lee Grieveson and Haidee Wasson (Durham, NC: Duke University Press, 2008), 353–374; and Caetlin Benson-Allott, *Killer Tapes and Shattered Screens: Video Spectatorship from VHS to File Sharing* (Berkeley: University of California Press, 2013).

21. Siegfried Zielinski, *Deep Time of the Media: Toward an Archaeology of Hearing and Seeing by Technical Means*, trans. Gloria Custance (Cambridge, MA: MIT Press, 2006).

22. Cherchi Usai, *The Death Of Cinema*, 105.

23. Domietta Torlasco, *The Heretical Archive: Digital Memory at the End of Film* (Minneapolis: University of Minnesota Press, 2013), xiii.

24. Cherchi Usai, *The Death of Cinema*, 91.

25. For general overviews of the life and work of Méliès, see Maurice Bessy and Lo Duca, *Georges Méliès, mage* (Paris: Prisma, 1945); and Georges Sadoul, *Georges Méliès* (Paris: Éditions Seghers, 1961).

26. Scorsese, "A Letter to My Daughter," *l'Espresso*, January 2, 2014, espresso.repubblica.it /visioni/2014/01/02/news/martin-scorsese-a-letter-to-my-daughter-1.147512.

27. Marshall McLuhan, "Playboy Interview: Marshall McLuhan," *Playboy* 16, no. 3 (March 1969): 59.

28. Boym, *The Future of Nostalgia*, 49–56.

29. D. N. Rodowick, *The Virtual Life of Film* (Cambridge, MA: Harvard University Press, 2007), 28; Lev Manovich, *The Language of New Media* (Cambridge, MA: MIT Press, 2001), 254–255.

30. For a general discussion of cinematography in *Hugo*, see Mark Hope-Jones, "Through a Child's Eyes," *American Cinematographer* 92, no. 12 (December 2011), 54–67.

31. Martin Scorsese, "Martin Scorsese: Film Director," in *Tacita Dean: Film*, ed. Nicholas Cullinan (London: Tate, 2011), 117.

32. Georges Méliès, quoted in Tom Gunning, "The Cinema of Attraction: Early Film, Its Spectator and the Avant-Garde," *Wide Angle* 8, nos. 3 and 4 (1986): 64.

33. For a discussion of 3D cinematography in *Hugo,* see Hope-Jones, "Through a Child's Eyes."

34. Laura Mulvey and Peter Wollen, "From Cinephilia to Film Studies," in *Inventing Film Studies,* eds. Lee Grieveson and Haidee Watson (Durham, NC: Duke University Press, 2008), 228.

35. Sontag, "The Decay of Cinema," 61.

36. Ian Christie, "*A Companion to Early Cinema,*" review of *A Companion to Early Cinema,* eds. André Gaudreault, Nicolas Dulac, and Santiago Hidalgo, *Sight and Sound* 23, no. 2 (2013): 124.

12 Cinephilia and Philosophia

Or, Why I Don't Show The Matrix in Philosophy 101

Timothy Yenter

Introduction

Philosophy has discovered film.

More precisely but less pithily, academic philosophers who have not been significantly influenced by French intellectual movements of the last forty years have suddenly begun publishing books and essays about film in unprecedented numbers. Open Court has ninety-nine published volumes in their "Popular Culture and Philosophy" series, with thirteen more volumes announced.[1] Blackwell currently has forty-four titles in their "And Philosophy" series.[2] Not all of these volumes are about films, but, given that these volumes started in 2000, the trend is notable. Additionally, there is a new academic market for philosophy and film. Routledge has a "Philosophers on Film" series, with eight edited volumes focusing mostly on recent films, as well as multiple books introducing "philosophy and film" and "philosophy through film," specifically designed to provide "dependable resources for those studying and teaching philosophy and film."[3] In the last twenty years, at least three journals (*Film-Philosophy* [1996], *Film and Philosophy* [1997], and *Cinema: Journal of Philosophy and the Moving Image* [2010]) and one organization (Society for the Philosophic Study of the Contemporary Visual Arts) specifically devoted to the connections between film and philosophy have appeared. These are in addition to the numerous monographs written by philosophers about films, filmmakers, and genres as well as traditional issues in aesthetics.

These latter resources are primarily geared toward scholars and philosophy-of-film courses. The shelves of film and philosophy books should have made it considerably easier to teach with films in introductory philosophy classes, and certainly many philosophers have found them useful. However, shortcomings of many of these pop culture volumes (which I discuss in the next section) make these works rarely useful in the classroom. I propose instead a new model for how to teach film in a philosophy class. The model develops the virtues inherent in cinephilia and connects these virtues to the good life. Discussions of the good life are some of the oldest recognizably philosophical questions. According to a common taxonomy, the three traditional questions of philosophy are "What is there?," "What can I know?," and "How should I live?" The third question is the question of the good life; it prompts the questioner to reflect on who she is, her place in the world, her values, and how to attain a life that embodies those values. In the third section, I expand and situate this question more fully. This question has been and should continue to be an important part of philosophy, and this opens a space for cinephilia to inform teaching philosophy by posing an appreciable approach to life, love, and art while avoiding some problems with the more popular methods of using films and film clips in philosophy classes. Finally, I address and respond to two objections to my proposal, then conclude by sharing my experiences enacting this pedagogy.

The Problem of "Philosophy Through Film"

The *pop culture and philosophy* books that dominate the philosophy shelves at bookstores have three major shortcomings. These books are written with fans already in mind, so they assume that you already love the Harry Potter books or *Doctor Who* or Woody Allen, and proceed from there to draw out a philosophical point or two. The goal is often minimal (such as to inform fans that some philosophers have also written about the themes or ideas that lurk in their work), so too frequently these book chapters fail to engage their objects in a philosophically sophisticated manner. Many people writing in the pop culture and philosophy books really do love their subjects. Many are knowledgeable about their subjects. Yet few manage to engage with anything else written on the subject and almost never with anything from film or media studies. By setting minimal goals, failing to do interesting philosophy, and failing to engage broadly and reflectively, these essays too often have limited value for the classroom.

More thoughtful and more rigorous work is being done by those interested in *philosophy through film*. In these articles and books, it is claimed that a film does or is philosophy, and it is our role as viewers to discover and evaluate this philosophical idea or argument. *The Man Who Shot Liberty Valance* (John Ford, 1962) prompts a discussion of whether history progresses and has meaning. *Crimes and Misdemeanors* (Woody Allen, 1989) advocates moral relativism. *12 Monkeys* (Terry Gilliam, 1995) contains a thesis about determinism, free will, and time travel. In each case, the philosopher poses either that the film (1) embodies a position or, in some stronger versions of the philosophy through film thesis, (2) presents an argument for a thesis. These approaches share a commitment to treating films as *content-bearers*. The viewer is expected to treat films as advancing, holding, or assuming a theoretical position; in the classroom, we could uncover this meaning through priming in the readings or through classroom discussion.

While this isn't the case in the best of the philosophy-through-film texts, in teaching it is tempting to treat the film as an accessible and less sophisticated text that gently ushers the student into a more complex engagement with written texts or a discussion predetermined by a professor. To pull a common example, say you are teaching skepticism in Philosophy 101. The anthology has a selection from René Descartes's *Meditations on First Philosophy*, David Hume's *Enquiry Concerning Human Understanding*, and G. E. Moore's "Certainty." You're thinking about how to introduce global skepticism to undergraduates, and you decide *The Matrix* (Lana Wachowski and Lilly Wachowski, 1999) would serve nicely. After running through the reasons for doubt from the *Meditations*, you pull up a YouTube clip of Morpheus explaining to Neo how the matrix works, then ask students to consider whether there is any way to tell if they are in the matrix. If students begin to discuss how the film employs déjà vu as a technique to determine that there is a glitch in the matrix, you gently correct them to say that, no, you are not asking how to tell if you are in the matrix according to the rules of the movie but how to tell if you are in a simulation right now. You never considered *The Matrix* as a film but simply as a way of illustrating or highlighting or delaying a point that you wanted to make. One danger of treating films as content-bearers is that students can be too easily contorted away from the film and toward some further point.

Using film clips to make some point beyond what is happening in the film is not a great harm. Films, like written texts, do not have only one legitimate, predetermined use. However, using films only in this way is too limiting. When we consider the possibilities contained within cinephilia to encourage students to develop curiosity, seek out new experiences, and appreciate artistic achievement, we find a way to go further.

A second and related danger is turning films into mere illustrations. Thomas Wartenberg has argued that illustrations can be philosophical, and thus treating films as illustrations can be a way of treating them as philosophical works.[4] In this and other ways, proponents of philosophy through film, screened philosophy, or film-philosophy argue that films should be taken seriously as philosophical texts. I have various concerns about these claims, but we can set those aside for now. Pedagogically, using films as illustrations or thought experiments may have some use, but these are one-off opportunities. Students watch a film clip (or a whole film) and are told that it poses a problem or possible solution; then, the lecture or discussion continues. *La Jetée* (Chris Marker, 1962) or *12 Monkeys* illustrates a coherent theory of time travel, for instance, while discussing what theories of personal identity are consistent with time travel narratives. The film itself is illustrative at best and redundant at worst. If it succeeds at illustrating time travel, or the cost of embracing utilitarianism, or the notion that violent protection of the community inevitably turns back on the community, it does so only by reducing the film to a single example, idea, or argument. Illustrations can easily narrow, simplify, or distort. Furthermore, to have pedagogical value, the instructor may need to introduce sophisticated interpretative techniques that students may not yet possess, a defense of his or her preferred interpretation, and the complex debates that the film can be seen as addressing. The realities of limited time during the semester make this prospect unappealing if the film is doing something that can be done without the film.

In cinephilia we can consider how students might learn to ask their own questions, seek their own problems, and find their own things to appreciate. The long-term value of this is missing from the illustrative model. Put another way, a philosopher could use *Freaky Friday* (Gary Nelson, 1976) to address theories of personal identity, but helping students become intellectually curious will allow them to pose their own questions about *Freaky Friday* or *The Loneliest Planet* (Julia Loktev, 2011) or *Metropolis* (Fritz Lang, 1927). In the next two sections, I develop a model of using film in philosophy classes that connects the cinephile's passionate approach to films with the philosopher's intellectual and lived pursuit of the good life. This model doesn't extinguish the goods of the content-bearer model, but it provides further goods that can justify and enrich the screening and discussing of films.[5]

What Are We Talking About?

I will be arguing that cinephilia provides a model of engaged teaching in philosophy and related disciplines. Before proceeding to the argument, I will introduce the major concepts I'm addressing: cinephilia and the good life.

Cinephilia evolves, yet it is still linked to its etymological origin—the love of film, of cinema. Much of what has been written about cinephilia focuses on its emergence and the related development of the auteur theory among French critics and filmmakers of the 1960s. The debate about cinephilia in the last two decades has often focused on the extent to which the two concepts are separable or should be separated, or whether there is an American cinephilia distinct from French cinephilia (and so on for each nation or region). Rather than return to this topic, about which many others have written ably, I will simply note that a reasonably robust notion of cinephilia can be maintained that does not require the impossible task of turning ourselves into late 1960s cinemagoers. Furthermore, teaching others to be cinephiles does not obviously require turning them into auteurists. My intentionally broad characterization of cinephilia is not meant to dislodge it from any of its historical manifestations but rather to capture a recurring tendency of some people to love film inordinately and find like-minded folks to share that love. Thus, I am not assuming at the outset that there is some late, great period of cinephilia that we should mourn, as Susan Sontag and Andrew O'Hehir have claimed.[6] Nor am I assuming that cinephilia can't ebb and flow or look different over time or be tied to various other historical trends like auteurism or the rise of online film discussion sites. However, if one wants to confine cinephilia to a narrower historical phenomenon, teaching students to be cinephiles will be impossible (because it requires becoming uprooted from one's own historical moment), or one will have to consider whether my claims about cinephilia match the alternative conception of cinephilia that the reader endorses.

Cinephilia, as I will use it, has two aspects: a set of practices and a cluster of virtues that arise out of those practices. For some readers the term *virtues* calls up associations with *purity* and *humility* and other concepts that Friedrich Nietzsche dismissed as "slave morality."[7] However, nothing so narrow or puritanical is intended or warranted. Virtues are the habits necessary to pursue the practices from which they arise or to pursue a life that on reflection seems best.[8] The key point is that to engage in certain practices one must develop character traits to perform well at those practices; these are the virtues.[9]

My approach is grounded in the practices of cinephiles. To be a cinephile one mustn't just watch films or love a particular sort of movie. Someone who only loves musicals or horror movies is not a cinephile. Cinephiles are omnivores, consuming studio and independent features, new and old, domestic and international.[10] They might be academics, but their interest in film is not limited to their academic research. They might not be academics, but they take thoughtful writing on cinema seriously, whether it is based in the academy or not.[11] Recently, many cinephiles have migrated online, prompting reflection about the new era of cinephilia and its relation to technology, criticism, production, and viewing platforms. Historically, cinephiles have valorized the experience of watching a film in a theater, and many continue to support the screening of films in their original format (a projected film print when possible, a carefully restored digital copy when available, and always in the original aspect ratio).[12] In the next section, I will address the virtues that arise out of these practices.

While readers of this volume are likely to have some interest or stake in the definition of cinephilia and be familiar with the many recent volumes discussing it, they might not be as familiar with discussions of the good life, the second concept to play a large role in what follows. So I will briefly lay out a conceptual and historical map to orient readers.

The problem of the good life is the problem of how to live. What should I do? How should I act toward someone who has wronged me? Would I be happier in a bustling city, in the suburbs, or in the country? Should I become a doctor or a professor or a professional snowboarder? To answer these questions (especially the latter two) requires judgments based on knowing particulars about oneself.

To answer these questions also requires making judgments about what *any* person should do, or what *any person with my interests, abilities, and so on* should do. Philosophers typically focus on this second set of judgments. In doing so, we consider whether there are certain features that any life must have to be called *good* (say, close friendships or work one finds fulfilling) or whether there are many different kinds of good life.

A problem with any discussion of the good life is that a number of issues that run together might plausibly be kept distinct. Roughly, we could distinguish among living a morally good life, a happy life, and a meaningful life. A morally good life is one that achieves excellence in developing character, or acting meritoriously, or having good consequences follow from one's attitudes and actions.[13] A happy life is one that has the maximum amount of pleasure and the least amount of pain, or whatever the correct account of well-being is.[14] A meaningful life is harder to define, but the concept is meant to capture a potential third set of questions we might ask about our lives, questions like "Did my life make a difference?" and "Is this the kind of life I want to be living?" One might be happy from moment to moment but still feel that something is missing; whatever is missing is what would make for a meaningful life. For instance, Susan Wolf argues that two popular claims about the meaningfulness of life are that one should live passionately (you should do what you love) and one should be involved in a project larger than oneself (your life should impact others), and she articulates a theory of the meaningfulness of life that combines these two qualities.[15]

In addition to those three axes of evaluation, we could also consider a few historically important questions relating to the good life. First, is happiness an emotion, a mood, or a state of being? The ancient Greek discussion of *eudaimonia*, sometimes translated into English as "happiness," usually focused on this third definition. Beginning with Plato's Socratic dialogues, *eudaimonia* is a life well lived; it is well-being or flourishing. Socrates, Plato, and Aristotle claim that *eudaimonia* includes virtue, so a morally good life is necessary for the happy (eudaimonistic) life. This introduces the second major question: is being virtuous part of what it is to lead a happy life, or could one be virtuous and still be unhappy (in the rich sense of flourishing)? For Plato, the virtuous life is the happy life; the virtuous person is flourishing, even if hated, slandered, and pained. For Aristotle, virtue is required for happiness, but it is not sufficient for it (that is, one cannot be truly happy unless one is virtuous, but being virtuous does not guarantee a happy life).

Returning to the issue of what happiness is, Epicurus is the most famous proponent of hedonism, the view that happiness can be reduced to experiences of pleasure and pain. Virtue allows one to be happy (by allowing one to practice self-control to reach delayed pleasures, for instance), but virtue is not identical to happiness, says Epicurus. Medieval philosophers tended to reorient happiness around knowing God (especially in the beatific vision), and they emphasized mercy, forgiveness, and especially love as virtues, which ancient philosophers (especially the Stoics) tended to downplay or outright disdain.

Starting in the seventeenth century, questions of rightness (how one should act) were typically separated from questions of goodness (what is valuable). This directly affects questions about the nature of the good life, because it was no longer assumed that doing what is right will promote one's own or others' well-being. So for Immanuel Kant, happiness is a fleeting psychological state dependent on external circumstances and thus poorly suited for a universal, necessary theory of right action, which could only be based on rationality. However, for hedonists like John Stuart Mill and Henry Sidgwick, pleasure is valuable and pain is disvaluable, and they argue that right action is promoting pleasure and minimizing pain for all. By explicitly casting moral theory as universal (treating all persons as moral subjects) and independent of one's own well-being, modern ethicists faced a problem of explaining why a person should act for the sake of others when that disadvantages the person's own well-being. That is, "Why be moral?" takes on new importance. (Ancient eudaimonistic theories do not face a strong version of this because it is rational and good to act in one's self-interest, and medieval theists identified one's self-interest with God's plan for one's life.) Additionally, fewer modern than medieval philosophers identify the good life with knowledge or love of God.

Among the critics of modern moral theory (as I've glossed it), Nietzsche opposed its reliance on "slave" virtues, its reliance on a false theory of agency, and its denial of life; Leo Tolstoy opposed its displacement of faith from the core of living; and Elizabeth Anscombe argued that secular, modern moral theories failed to give an adequate basis for their frequent use of "ought" and "right." Tolstoy is particularly interesting because he formulates a question that dominated the twentieth-century discussions. Even if one is in a psychological state of happiness, there seems to be a question that remains: "Is this all there is?" Or in Tolstoy's phrasing, "What is it for? What does it lead to?" Tolstoy's question (and Nietzsche's answer) was picked up by Jean-Paul Sartre, Albert Camus, and others who thought that there was no answer to Tolstoy's question. Sartre, for instance, says existentialism begins with the realization that there is no creator God, and thus there is no design or purpose or human nature that could provide meaning or ground ethics.[16]

Recently there has been an influx of new philosophical writing on the meaning of life, but no obvious trends have emerged.[17]

To summarize, in discussing the good life, we could focus on one of three axes of evaluation: goodness, happiness, and meaningfulness. These might be distinct, or they might be overlapping, or they might be identical. Some define goodness as what leads to one's happiness, some argue that meaningfulness reduces to goodness, and so on. When discussing the connection between cinephilia and the good life, I am using "good life" in the broadest sense, which includes the morally good life, the happy life, and the meaningful life. My pedagogical model posits cinephilia's potential contribution to university instructors' attempts to encourage students to seek lives that are meaningful, happy, and good.

Cinephilia and the Good Life

Let's assume for the moment that one of the goals of instruction in philosophy is to encourage students to reflect on, explore, and attempt to live a life that is happy, meaningful, and good. (I address objections to this assumption in the next section.) What can cinephilia contribute? We don't need to make all students into cinephiles, but by exhibiting our own cinephilia and encouraging it in our students, we can develop transferable virtues, by which I mean character traits that cinephiles exhibit but that would serve anyone well.

Cinephiles take joy in discovering new things. They enjoy not just new films or recognized classics, but forgotten films, actors whose work is no longer appreciated, cinematographers who capture surprising moments, and other talents who contribute to making films. Cinephiles are fond of treading off the beaten path, looking for hidden gems, or simply enjoying the small pleasures of a mediocre film. They wonder why others love what they love, so they pursue new experiences to see if they can love it, too. Curiosity and adventurousness are what I call transferable virtues. People who are curious and adventurous in their tastes are more likely to live lives that are happy, good, and meaningful. So even if our students never fall in love with film, they will have seen what it is like to be curious and adventurous in one's tastes, and with those attributes modeled they can transfer them into their own passions. Other transferable virtues of the cinephile are careful attention, joy in exploration, appreciation of beauty and achievement and innovation in art, and desire for understanding. These are some of the most useful traits to develop because they lead to other valuable goods.

In addition to practicing these virtues, cinephiles form communities to share their discoveries. Cinephilia drives one to seek out like-minded persons, and, as Jonathan Rosenbaum reminds us in his calls for a stronger cinephiliac community, it should also encourage information sharing that crosses affiliations (e.g., academics, journalists, filmmakers).[18] To turn to one of Rosenbaum's *Movie Mutations* correspondents, Adrian Martin advocates a cinephilia that embodies "mutual reflection" and "cross-cultural understanding" and looks "to find certain insights into our own situations whenever we can."[19] I doubt that I am alone in wishing my students would find ways of navigating beyond their own experiences with curiosity and reflection. This is a partial list of the character traits that cinephilia develops, and it doesn't yet include the pursuit of and appreciation of beauty or resonant stories and characters. If we can find a way to have students become cinephiles—or if not become cinephiles, at least see these virtues modeled by cinephiles—then our students have an opportunity to evaluate those traits and decide if they want to pursue them.

Would turning our students into cinephiles make them happier? There's no reason to think that cinephiles are any more or less happy from moment to moment than other people, but we probably don't need to make these interpersonal judgments. Instead, we can demonstrate to students what it is like to have short-term and long-term goals that are united around a conception of the sort of life we want to live. While modeling that life, we need not impose our goals on them, but we can show how a life involving those goals creates benchmarks by which we can measure our pursuit of a happy, meaningful life. Even if our goals are set for purely subjective reasons, our lives are objectively worse when we do not achieve the goals that are important to us.

For instance, I am waiting to watch Jacques Tati's *Playtime* (1967) until I can see it projected in 70mm. However, with the conversion of commercial theaters to digital projectors, the destruction and decay of most of the film prints ever made, and the fact that I probably live a thousand miles from the nearest active, working 70mm projector, it is unlikely that I will ever attain this goal. Now, would my life be some great failure if I never saw this? No, not a great failure. But would it be a little worse? Yes, I think so. That I care about this goal makes it modestly important in a way that it wouldn't be modestly important to someone who didn't have this care. Philosophers often focus on whether there are particular objective goods that all people should have, but I will make only the more modest claim that it is plausible that some things are good for a person at least partly because the individual values them, so we can objectively evaluate lives based on whether they achieve goals that they have set. If someone wants to have children and they do have children, their lives can be judged as better than if they never had children. If someone wants to be remembered as a kind and generous person, but they are remembered as a cruel and selfish person, then their life is worse by a standard that mattered to them.[20]

With this objective standard of meeting subjectively determined goals, we can determine what sort of life would be the most likely to make us happy, help us find meaning, and develop the character traits necessary for this life. When we model this for students, they may become cinephiles who adopt those same goals and virtues, or (more likely) they may find their own communities, practices, and goals that they can use to organize their life. This is a much richer, more long-lasting, and more important set of goals than the content-bearer assumption connected to the philosophy-through-film model. In cinephilia, *what the film says, illustrates, or argues* is but one of many worthwhile ways of engaging with a film. Loving films, searching out new experiences, having transformative aesthetic experiences, appreciating unexpected moments of wonder in otherwise unremarkable films—these and others suggest a more comprehensive approach to films and a more comprehensive approach to life. These further ways of engaging with films are also more in line with the long-term goals we should be considering when we are teaching. If we want students who don't just learn what's on the syllabus but learn to love learning itself; if we want students who don't just read the assignments but seek out new information; if we want students who don't expect to receive passively content provided by the instructor but make their education their own; then we will want to develop character traits like curiosity, ingenuity, humility, self-reliance, and artistic appreciation. These traits aren't just valuable for the cinephile but for everyone.

To clarify, my argument has not been that cinephilia is required to live a good life. One ugly consequence of such a strong view would be that anyone who had lived without access to cinema could not have lived a good life, an absurd thesis that would mean 99 percent of the people ever to have lived could not have lived a good life. My claim is that the qualities distinctive of cinephilia are those that plausibly contribute to a good life or, at least, provide one model for students of how to pursue a life of their choosing. The precise object of those qualities (what is loved, what is appreciated, what arouses curiosity) could be most anything. (I do think there are some restrictions on what one could love in living a good life; loving the torture of animals is off-limits, for instance.) What matters for the argument is (1) that cinephilia exhibits these virtues and (2) that students often arrive in college aware of film, engaged with film, and primed to fall further in love with film, which makes cinephilia an excellent entry point for the discussion of the good life.

The Good Life? Really?

Some readers may be surprised by the emphasis I have placed on the role of the good life within academic philosophy. Many think that such questions are no longer discussed. I am happy to report that the academic study of philosophy, despite recent reports to the contrary, still asks the classical question, "What is a good life?" Despite this, a cottage industry has developed out of the claim that universities in general, and the humanities in particular, have given up on the big questions about humans' place in the universe and the meaning or meanings of the lives we lead.

The urtext for these discussions over the last twenty-five years is Allan Bloom's *The Closing of the American Mind*. In detailing the "decomposition of the university," he claims, "In [the humanities] there is no semblance of order, no serious account of what should and should not belong, or of what its disciplines are trying to accomplish or how."[21] Thus, students are left adrift without the texts or the tools to answer the big questions to which they seek answers. Many more books and articles followed in Bloom's wake, often explicitly political in nature.[22] Roger Kimball's *Tenured Radicals* (which went through three editions) and Dinesh D'Souza's *Illiberal Education* (which launched his public career), to name two prominent examples, combined Bloom's criticism that universities had stopped asking the big questions with the politicized polemics that recalled *God and Man at Yale* by William F. Buckley, Jr.[23] Such jeremiads often focus on perceived threats to established disciplines and methods. Kimball names the purported threats: "It is no secret that the academic study of the humanities in this country is in a state of crisis. Proponents of deconstruction, feminist studies, and other politically motivated challenges to the traditional tenets of humanistic study have by now become the dominant voice in the humanities departments of many of our best colleges and universities."[24] These perceived challenges were often tied to concerns over political correctness, which was said to have a chilling effect on universities.[25]

These stories focus on departments other than philosophy because these trends have been less pronounced in philosophy than in other humanities departments. The decline in writing about the good life in Anglo-American philosophy is largely due to a twentieth-century movement known as analytic philosophy. This family of movements within academic philosophy emphasized conceptual analysis, valorized science as the only route to understanding the world, posed (then later rejected, then still later reconsidered) a deep logical grammar discoverable within language, and dismissed aesthetic, religious, and ethical claims as either without meaning or simply expressions of emotional states with no cognitive content. Elements of this approach live on, particularly in what is increasingly called "naturalist" philosophy. For many of those linked to this family of traditions, questions about the good life appeared meaningless, irresolvable, or (minimally) not philosophy's primary aim. As Scott Soames writes in his important history of the period,

> In general, philosophy done in the analytic tradition aims at truth and knowledge, as opposed to moral or spiritual improvement. There is very little in the way of practical or inspirational guides in the art of living to be found, and very much in the way of philosophical theories that purport to reveal the truth about a given domain of inquiry. In general, the goal in analytic philosophy is to discover what is true, not to provide a useful recipe for living one's life.[26]

Given the philosophers that Soames focuses on (a coterie of very influential German, British, American, and Australian philosophers), this is largely right.[27] Put succinctly, it was not so much the rise of cultural studies, deconstruction, or other late-twentieth-century movements that redirected *philosophy* away from asking about the good life but a commitment to philosophy as a science or as a preparation for a scientific understanding of the world that displaced this question.[28]

Even though this was the major trend in English-language philosophy for much of the twentieth century, it is not as though the question was ever too far from philosophers' minds. Even restricting ourselves to England and America, pragmatists like William James, John Dewey, and Jane Addams, neo-Thomists influenced by Étienne Gilson and Jacques Maritain, and of course the many existentialists, phenomenologists, postmodernists, idealists, and historians of philosophy continued asking the classical questions. Saying that philosophy in the twentieth century ignored questions about the meaning of life conflates analytic philosophy with all of English-language philosophy.

Expanding beyond philosophy again, there is something troubling about these critics' claim that the rise of cultural studies somehow diminished or removed the central questions of how we should live. In fact, one of the recurring themes of cultural studies is that any attempted depiction of the goodness or meaningfulness of life that restricts itself to only a few voices is unlikely to capture what is good or meaningful about people's experiences. Studies of class, sexuality, gender, ethnicity, and more provide new ways of thinking about lives, not the suffocation of the most important questions. Other trends in the humanities, such as deconstruction, are also meant to be individually liberating as one recognizes the problems inherent in the system one receives and employs tools to overcome those problems. Whether one restricts oneself to the trends within philosophy or within the humanities generally, it was never the case that questions of the good life were absent. Perhaps more importantly, so what if they were? They need not be now.

Is This Our Role as Educators?

A second criticism is that, regardless of what has been taught, the good life, or cinephilia, or both *should not* be part of what philosophy departments teach. My focus on laying out the theoretical space and showing that cinephilia has a place in academic pedagogy in philosophy is very odd in a certain way. Cinephilia is, etymologically, historically, and avowedly, a *love* of cinema; perhaps, too, instructing someone in the good life is similarly paternalistic. What I have been advocating is thus something strange: we should teach students to love or tell them how to love. Objections to this idea are of two general sorts: love cannot be taught, and love must not be taught. I'll start with the latter.

On a particular construal of the purpose of education, love has no place. Education exists to create citizens, or future job holders, or future job creators. Or, as it is sometimes more narrowly cast, *publicly funded* education should serve the public good, which is then typically defined in terms of "job skills."[29] On this view of education, teaching students to love anything is off-point at best and counterproductive at worst. I cannot respond adequately to this line of thought, but, although ubiquitous, this view is both false and pernicious. Even on the assumption that this narrow view of education is correct, developing a love of learning, facility with cultural difference, and careful attention are precisely the sort of skills that will make for successful citizens, employees, and entrepreneurs. Furthermore, as some of the considerations of the good life draw out, having a job and participating in society are instrumental goods that bring about those things that are truly valuable: happiness, goodness, meaning. To focus only on those instrumental goods would be a potentially devastating mistake.

On the point that love cannot be taught, surely this is right in some strict sense. It would be very odd for me to evaluate my students at the end of the semester according to how much they love the book we read or God or science or their partner or my partner or *The Court Jester* or Juliette Binoche. We can't both "teach to the test" and require that our students love. We don't list "love" under Course Objectives on the syllabus (although perhaps words like *appreciate*, *deepen*, and *engage* might sneak the idea in surreptitiously). This narrow understanding of teaching, though, is not the only way to teach. We can, to use terms I have repeated throughout, *model* love for our students and *encourage* them to find something they love and pursue it. We are fostering an ability to love and the ability to choose (or be chosen by) what they will love. Many of them, sadly, won't love *films* as we do, but we can show them the benefits of passionately loving something so that your whole person is engaged in the pursuit of it.

Applications and Conclusions

How does teaching philosophy of film in the cinephiliac mode look? In this final section, I will discuss specifics of how I have used this approach in introduction to philosophy (100-level) and philosophy-of-film (300-level) courses. After motivating this approach further, I turn to specifics. Some of what I say here will be relevant to anyone teaching film outside cinema studies departments, who wants to blend their discipline's methods and questions with those from cinema studies. These hurdles are lessened somewhat for departments with strong institutional, historical, and methodological connections to cinema studies, such as communication studies, American studies, and comparative literature; students are more likely to be familiar with the tools, readings, and approaches that often developed in communication among these disciplines. The pedagogical problem, for those of us who teach with films but are not housed in cinema studies departments, is double-edged: to increase students' theoretical and affective engagement with films, while also introducing them to our own discipline's questions and methods. For those of us committed to incorporating the insights and perspectives of cinema studies in our courses, the time constraints of a semester are real. Furthermore, it is pedagogically imprudent to delay the material that students came to study by introducing a lot of theoretical groundwork whose value will only become apparent later.

On these very real teaching concerns, the *philosophy and pop culture* books are little help. *Philosophy-through-film* essays and books rarely engage with writing from outside philosophy, so teaching from them does little to introduce students to the questions and methods of other disciplines. Those who teach and write with the *philosophy-of-film* approach often downplay or dismiss scholarship in cinema studies, which has created an information silo, with philosophical writing separated from historical and theoretical writing about film.

One option would be to leave films out of the curriculum. However, it is not in the best interests of our students or ourselves to teach films only in cinema studies courses. No discipline should have exclusive claim to a set of texts or cultural objects, even if the discipline is as methodologically diverse as cinema studies. Additionally, cinema studies thrives on interdisciplinarity. The field benefits from the work done in adjacent disciplines to illuminate concepts, generate ideas, and refine approaches. Finally, students are often very familiar with filmic texts, even if their filmic literacy is underdeveloped, so other disciplines can provide richer educational experiences by incorporating films. The ubiquity of films, their affective potential, their social importance, their interest to students—there are simply too many pedagogical reasons to teach with films for us to ignore them completely.

As a potential solution for philosophers who love film and want to use films in our teaching but are wary of or disappointed in the existing methods, I have suggested that modeling cinephilia encourages students to reflect on practices and character traits that are possibly constitutive of a life that is happy, meaningful, and good. In connecting cinephilia to the good life, we offer a richer approach to the use of films in the philosophy classroom and connect the theoretical questions of the good life to a practical instantiation of one answer to them. How might the model I have described work in the classroom? To extend and apply the approach I have described and defended to this point, I will lay out two examples from my own teaching. The first is from a 300-level Philosophy of Film course; the second is from a 100-level Introduction to Philosophy course.

Early in my 300-level Philosophy of Film course, taught at a state university to students who often have little or no background in either philosophy or cinema studies, we watch an entire film together. For the last two years, I have screened *Coherence*, a 2013 microbudget narrative feature from writer-director James Ward Byrkit and producer Lene Bausager. After giving students the title and no further information, after the opening credits sequence, at approximately the twenty-minute mark, at the forty-minute mark, and at the end of the film, I pause the film and ask students to write down every question they can think of. I then collect their questions (usually by e-mail), collate them, and then as a class project I put the questions up on the screen in an editable document. Together we group the questions into categories, discussing which ones can be answered by later events or close watching of the film and which need additional thought or research.

The point of watching the film together is not to get them to ask philosophers' standard questions of what the film is *saying* or *arguing*. In fact, I choose *Coherence* in part because it refuses to answer philosophical questions like "What is the explanation for these events?" and "Is this metaphysically possible?" and "Does this character make the ethically correct choice?" Rather, I encourage students to ask as many different questions as they can. Typically, most of their questions regard plotting ("What will happen next?") or request clarification ("What's the relationship between these two characters?"). Some questions open up further discussion: why did the filmmakers choose a particular aesthetic, how did they achieve that aesthetic, why do certain filmmaking roles show up in opening credits, how are we encouraged to empathize or identify with certain characters, what should we make of viewers' moral objections to characters' behavior, does the film settle questions about multiverses and branching spacetimes, what are we expected to assume about the rules in fictional universes, how does the film's independent production and lack of A-list stars affect the way that we view the film, and so on. Encouraging students to ask their own questions of films and learning from the questions that others ask are two of the best ways I know to help students understand how and why to love films.

My ultimate goal in this course assignment is to show how the tools, methods, and questions of philosophy and related disciplines can help students pose and answer their own questions and the questions they had never thought to ask before. It is important not to set the bounds too early of what is or is not a legitimate question (or a legitimate philosophical question). With questions that matter to them (because they asked them), we then consider how to answer them. What new knowledge do we need? What tools do we need? By not limiting themselves at the outset to only the question of what a film is arguing or claiming, students realize that to learn what they want to learn and to view films in exciting new ways, they will need to read and discuss much more widely than what philosophers or critics have written about a particular film. Unlike the philosophy-through-film approach, which encourages students to focus on a single thematic or narrative element, this approach is both student-started and wide-ranging. Unlike another common philosophy-of-film approach, this assignment requires students to pay close attention to a particular film, rather than discuss structural elements common to groups of films. By posing questions before covering topics, students can be encouraged to see how later class sessions will build off questions they already have while also posing new questions they hadn't thought to ask. Ideally, the course topics can even be amended to focus on the questions that students raised in these opening sessions.

For subsequent class sessions, I assign readings from philosophers, historians, film theorists, journalists, critics, and filmmakers to help students see how people with diverse professional interests can approach questions regarding medium specificity or the sanctity of the theater or auteurism in divergent and overlapping ways. The questions I ask in each class session contain a mixture of standard philosophical questions (such as the role of a filmmaker's intentions in determining a film's meaning and whether narratives can make arguments) and questions that students are familiar with but are unlikely to have posed in a classroom (such as the ethics of spoiling a movie's end and of texting in theaters, what obligations "based on a true story" claims create for the filmmakers and the audience, and what makes a film performance distinct from other types of performance).[30] This models active scholarship that doesn't stop at disciplinary boundaries or even at the classroom door, while broadening students' perspective on what can be thought and done. Some of these questions are comfortably at home in either cinema studies classrooms or philosophy classrooms, but new connections and ideas arise by asking them in a class where students read Cynthia Freeland and Berys Gaut alongside Richard Dyer and Lea Jacobs. We don't allow our students to take classes in only one department, reading and discussing issues from only one discipline; we too can find new questions and new insights by modeling omnivorous attitudes.

Blending methods, viewpoints, and issues from diverse sources is more difficult in an introductory philosophy class. I have experimented with using films in the way described, but I find that only in classes with small numbers and alternative schedules (such as intensive, between-semester courses common at some American schools) is it effective. However, a simpler version can work in a standard semester-long introduction to philosophy course. Rather than use films as illustrations of the theories we discuss (*The Matrix* as skeptical scenario, for instance), we can model cinephiliac virtues through how we present films. To give one example, when discussing what activities or experiences would make for the best sort of life, students inevitably raise the question of whether there are objectively true, interpersonal judgments about what sort of experiences are best. At this point, I might show a favorite Buster Keaton short, such as *The Goat* (1921). Few of my students are familiar with films from the silent (pre–synchronized sound) era, so not only do they have a new experience (which lends itself to talking about whether seeking out new experiences is part of living a good life), but I can ramble on passionately about the genius of Keaton and his stock cast and crew, the value of laughing, learning to appreciate how technology and film style interrelate, and any number of seeming digressions. Students don't just discuss the value of new experiences; they have a new experience (a positive one, I would hope, with Keaton). Curiosity and joy in discovery are key cinephiliac virtues, and creating an environment in which students can experience those is an important part of education. Exhibiting how to harness one's passions for film, or anything else (within limits), into worthwhile pursuits is part of what we can do as educators.

One of my emphases in this final section has been displacing a topic-based approach to a question-encouraging model of teaching with film. Both new and experienced teachers can fall into the trap of teaching so as to cover the material. In our attempts to cover the material, we shift the focus from students learning, exploring, and improving to checking items off a list. There are often sound pedagogical reasons for teaching the material we do (e.g., students need proficiency at a skill or familiarity with a topic to take the next course in a sequence), but there are ways to fight the urge to fill the course with topics to cover (and thus items to check off a list) rather than with student-focused educational goals. I have discussed how a virtue-modeling approach can ground an interdisciplinary, student-focused pedagogy. At the heart of this approach is a call to rediscover our own love for what we teach. By reflecting on our cinephilia (and perhaps by extension bibliophilia and paleophilia and so on), we can encourage our students to love and pursue what interests them. We can draw them alongside us as we each make our best attempts at the good life.

TIMOTHY YENTER is Assistant Professor of Philosophy and Affiliated Faculty in Cinema at the University of Mississippi. In addition to teaching and writing about European philosophy of the seventeenth and eighteenth centuries, he regularly teaches courses at the intersection of philosophy and film.

Notes

1. "Popular Culture and Philosophy Series," *Open Court Publishing Company*, accessed May 30, 2016, http://www.opencourtbooks.com/categories/pcp.htm.

2. "Wiley: The Blackwell Philosophy and Pop Culture Series," accessed May 30, 2016, http://www.wiley.com/WileyCDA/Section/id-324354.html.

3. "Philosophers on Film," *Routledge: Taylor & Francis Group*, accessed May 30, 2016, http://www.routledge.com/books/series/philosophers_on_film_PHILFILM/.

4. Thomas E. Wartenberg, *Thinking on Screen: Film as Philosophy* (London: Routledge, 2007), 32–54.

5. The model I propose need not completely displace the philosophy-through-film approach; it could supplement it. I am not providing a sustained critique of specific arguments for film as philosophy, but merely pointing out their pedagogical shortcomings. For this

reason, I am focusing on the advantages of the richer cinephiliac model rather than arguing that we should never use the film-as-philosophy model.

6. Susan Sontag, "The Decay of Cinema," *New York Times Magazine*, February 25, 1996, http://www.nytimes.com/1996/02/25/magazine/the-decay-of-cinema.html; Andrew O'Hehir, "Is Movie Culture Dead?," *Salon*, http://www.salon.com/2012/09/28/is_movie_culture_dead/.

7. Friedrich Nietzsche, *On the Genealogy of Morality*, ed. Keith Ansell-Pearson, trans. Carol Diethe, Cambridge Texts in the History of Political Thought (New York: Cambridge University Press, 1887).

8. Aristotle defended such a view, as did medieval Aristotelians like Thomas Aquinas and neo-Aristotelians like Alasdair MacIntyre, but the approach is broader than anything Aristotle wrote or directly influenced. For instance, even Nietzsche's historical account of the ways in which moral concepts and attitudes are embedded in cultural practices fits this broad description.

9. I do not address many of the philosophical questions lingering, such as whether some virtues are required for success at any practice or whether some practices are illegitimate. My account is incomplete, perhaps necessarily so, but it is true enough and sufficient for the argument that follows.

10. I'm reminded of a conversation I had with an acquaintance. He described himself as someone who loves "all sorts of movies, except the ones with those little angel wings." (He was referring to the laurel wreaths used in promotional materials to signify film festival awards or selections.) Further questions revealed that he was only interested in recent, Hollywood studio-financed films in a variety of popular genres. He would not qualify as a cinephile by the definition I am using.

11. On the rift between academic scholars and "cinephiliac intellectuals" and the possibility of complementary work, see David Bordwell, "Academics Vs. Critics," *Film Comment*, May/June 2011, http://www.filmcomment.com/article/never-the-twain-shall-meet.

12. Molly Haskell's reflection on changing movie theater experiences is typical in some ways but without a thick residue of nostalgia: Molly Haskell, "It Used to Be So Easy. I Remember When, . . ." *New York Times*, March 14, 2003, http://www.nytimes.com/2003/03/14/movies/it-used-to-be-so-easy-i-remember-when.html.

13. This roughly follows the distinctions within ethics among theories that focus on the virtues (virtue theories), those that focus on conformity of actions to a set of moral rules (deontological theories), and those that focus on the consequences of one's actions (consequentialist theories). Nothing I say turns on defending one of these over another. I talk about developing specific virtues (positive character traits), but most moral theories from each of the three categories accept that it is good to develop these character traits. For instance, a consequentialist would accept that we should be generous or fair or courageous because these lead us to act in ways that produce the best consequences. A deontologist like Immanuel Kant defends virtues as allowing one to do one's duty.

14. Reducing happiness (also called *well-being* or *welfare*) to pleasure and pain is known as *hedonism*. Hedonism does not, as often thought, require seeking peak pleasures. For instance, some hedonists, like Epicurus, focus on minimizing pain. Alternative theories of happiness include *mental statism* (happiness reduces to experiences, but experiences do not reduce to pleasure and pain alone), *desire satisfaction theory* (happiness is having one's desires satisfied), *objective list theories* (happiness is living a life that meets a set of criteria that apply to all people), and *perfectionism* (happiness is fulfilling one's purpose as a human being or fulfilling one's nature). For a summary of arguments for and against these theories, see Shelly Kagan, *Normative Ethics* (Boulder, CO: Westview Press, 1998), 29ff. Nothing in our discussion turns

on one of these being the correct theory, but note that perfectionistic theories typically deny a distinction between a happy life, a meaningful life, and a good life.

15. Susan Wolf, *Meaning in Life and Why It Matters*, University Center for Human Values (Princeton, NJ: Princeton University Press, 2010), 10–11. "According to the conception of meaningfulness I wish to propose, meaning arises from loving objects worthy of love and engaging with them in a positive way." Ibid., 8.

16. Leo Tolstoy, *A Confession* (North Hollywood, CA: Ægypan Press, 1879); Jean-Paul Sartre, *Existentialism Is a Humanism* (New Haven, CT: Yale University Press, 2007); Elizabeth Anscombe, "Modern Moral Philosophy," *Philosophy* 33, no. 124 (1958): 1–16.

17. For some examples, see John Cottingham, *On the Meaning of Life* (London: Routledge, 2003); Julian Baggini, *What's It All About? Philosophy and the Meaning of Life* (Oxford: Oxford University Press, 2005); Terry Eagleton, *The Meaning of Life a Very Short Introduction* (Oxford: Oxford University Press, 2008); and Wolf, *Meaning in Life and Why It Matters*.

18. Jonathan Rosenbaum and Adrian Martin, eds., *Movie Mutations: The Changing Face of World Cinephilia* (London: British Film Institute, 2003), ix.

19. Ibid.

20. That a goal or experience matters to a person elevates its importance, but there are limits to this. For instance, a person who finds pleasure in torturing others and who wants to torture a human being born in every country has a subjectively provided goal but one that seems to be impermissible. While some might say their life goes better because they achieved this goal, I think we ought to conclude that their goal was so misguided that their life actually was worse because they achieved it. Provided that cinephilia does not violate some sort of prohibition like this, then we should think that achieving their goals and sustaining the life they've chosen contributes to their living the good life.

21. Allan Bloom, *The Closing of the American Mind* (New York: Simon and Schuster, 1987), 371.

22. For two examples of books that follow Bloom's lead in arguing that universities have lost sight of their mission to transform teenagers into thoughtful adults, but without the belabored attacks on political correctness and cultural studies, see Alexander W. Astin, Helen S. Astin, and Jennifer A. Lindholm, *Cultivating the Spirit: How College Can Enhance Students' Inner Lives* (San Francisco: Jossey-Bass, 2010); and Harry R. Lewis, *Excellence Without a Soul: How a Great University Forgot Education* (New York: Public Affairs, 2006).

23. Roger Kimball, *Tenured Radicals: How Politics Has Corrupted Our Higher Education* (Chicago: Dee, 2008); Dinesh D'Souza, *Illiberal Education: The Politics of Race and Sex on Campus* (New York: Free Press, 1991); and William F. Buckley, *God and Man at Yale: The Superstitions of "Academic Freedom"* (South Bend, IN: Gateway Editions, 1977).

24. Kimball, *Tenured Radicals*, 1.

25. The books that I have referenced as representative were published in the late 1980s and 1990s. For a recent collection of essays focused on the way that political correctness is claimed to be harming universities, see Robert Maranto et al., *The Politically Correct University: Problems, Scope, and Reforms* (Washington, D.C.: AEI Press, 2009).

26. Scott Soames, *Philosophical Analysis in the Twentieth Century: The Dawn of Analysis*, vol. 1 (Princeton, NJ: Princeton University Press, 2005), xiv.

27. One exception is Ludwig Wittgenstein, who plays an important role in Soames's story (and in most histories of the period) but certainly saw philosophy as intimately tied to living life well, although he did not believe that philosophy's contribution is always positive.

28. If we narrow from "What is the good life?" to "What makes a life meaningful?" there is even less written. Robert Adams similarly claims, "Philosophers, at least in the

English-speaking world, have published relatively little about meaningfulness in life, despite its apparently profound human importance. We have found the concept of it a tough nut to crack and pry open" (quoted in Wolf, *Meaning in Life and Why It Matters*, 75).

29. This is the new "crisis of the humanities," in which students are said to be voting with their feet and fleeing humanities disciplines since the 1970s, or are entering a job market for which they are unprepared, or are attending universities that are financially unsustainable. For a general statement of the concern, see Tamar Lewin, "As Interest Fades in the Humanities, Colleges Worry," *New York Times*, October 30, 2013, http://www.nytimes.com/2013/10/31 /education/as-interest-fades-in-the-humanities-colleges-worry.html; and Jennifer Levitz and Douglas Belkin, "Humanities Fall From Favor," *Wall Street Journal*, June 6, 2013, http://online .wsj.com/news/articles/SB10001424127887324069104578527642373232184. This narrative of crisis is not borne out by the data, however, as shown by David Silbey, "A Crisis in the Humanities?—The Edge of the American West," *Chronicle of Higher Education*, June 10, 2013, http:// chronicle.com/blognetwork/edgeofthewest/2013/06/10/the-humanities-crisis; Michael Bérubé, "The Humanities, Declining? Not According to the Numbers," *Chronicle of Higher Education*, July 1, 2013, http://chronicle.com/article/The-Humanities-Declining-Not/140093/; and Nate Silver, "As More Attend College, Majors Become More Career-Focused," *New York Times*, June 25, 2013, http://fivethirtyeight.blogs.nytimes.com/2013/06/25/as-more-attend-college-ma jors-become-more-career-focused/. Additional important points are made by Gary Gutting, "The Real Humanities Crisis," *New York Times*, November 30, 2013, http://opinionator.blogs .nytimes.com/2013/11/30/the-real-humanities-crisis/.

30. In Philosophy of Film, we spend about 5 percent of our total class time on the philosophy-through-film approach. Through associated readings and a very brief lecture, I introduce key positions and arguments about whether films can make philosophical arguments or claims. Students do one required class presentation on a reading that their classmates have not read, and a couple of the options are philosophy-through-film essays.

Selected Bibliography

Affron, Charles. *Star Acting: Gish, Garbo, Davis.* New York: Dutton, 1977.

Allen, Robert C. "Reimagining the History of the Experience of Cinema in a Post-Moviegoing Age." In *Explorations in New Cinema History: Approaches and Case Studies*, eds. Richard Maltby, Daniel Biltereyst, and Philippe Meers, 41–57. Exeter, UK: University of Exeter Press, 2007.

Álvarez López, Cristina. "Double Lives, Second Chances." *Frames* 1 (2012). http://framescinemajournal.com/article/double-lives-second-chances/.

———. "From Idea to Concept." *[in]Transition* 1, no. 3 (2014). http://mediacommons.futureofthebook.org/intransition/2014/09/14/idea-concept.

Álvarez López, Cristina, and Adrian Martin. "The One and the Many: Making Sense of Montage in the Audiovisual Essay." *The Audiovisual Essay* (2014). http://reframe.sussex.ac.uk/audiovisualessay/frankfurt-papers/cristina-alvarez-lopez-adrian-martin/.

Andrew, Dudley. "The Core and the Flow of Film Studies." *Critical Inquiry* 35 (2009): 879–915.

Aquino, Rowena Santos. "To Live (with) Cinema: Documenting Cinephilia and the Archival Impulse." *LOLA* 4 (2013). http://www.lolajournal.com/4/cinephilia.html.

Arenas, Fernando Ramos. "Writing About a Common Love for Cinema: Discourses of Modern Cinephilia as a Trans-European Phenomenon." *Trespassing Journal: An Online Journal of Trespassing Art, Science, and Philosophy* 1 (2012): 18–33. http://trespassingjournal.com/Issue1/TPJ_I1_Arenas_Article.pdf.

Bachelard, Gaston. *The Poetics of Space*, trans. Maria Jolas. Boston: Beacon Press, 1994.

Balcerzak, Scott, and Jason Sperb, eds. *Cinephilia in the Age of Digital Reproduction: Film, Pleasure and Digital Culture, Vol. 1.* London: Wallflower Press, 2009.

Barthes, Roland. *Camera Lucida*, trans. Richard Howard. New York: Hill and Wang, 1980.

Baumbach, Nico. "All That Heaven Allows: What Is or Was Cinephilia?" *Film Comment* (March/April 2012).

Bellour, Raymond. *The Analysis of Film.* Bloomington: Indiana University Press, 2000.

Benjamin, Walter. "On Some Motifs in Baudelaire." In *Illuminations*, trans. Harry Zohn, 155–200. New York: Schocken Books, 1968.

Bennett, Jane. *Vibrant Matter: A Political Ecology of Things.* Durham, NC: Duke University Press, 2010.

Berlant, Lauren. "On the Case." *Critical Inquiry* 33 (2007): 663–672.

Boyer, Ernest L. *Scholarship Reconsidered: Priorities of the Professoriate.* New York: Carnegie Foundation for the Advancement of Teaching, 1990.

Cavell, Stanley. *In Quest of the Ordinary: Lines of Romanticism and Skepticism.* Chicago: University of Chicago Press, 1988.

———. *Philosophy the Day After Tomorrow.* Cambridge, MA: Harvard University Press, 2005.

———. *The Pursuits of Happiness.* Cambridge, MA: Harvard University Press, 1981.

———. *The World Viewed: Reflections on the Ontology of Film.* Cambridge, MA: Harvard University Press, 1979.

Cherchi Usai, Paolo. *The Death of Cinema: History, Cultural Memory and the Digital Dark Age.* London: British Film Institute, 2001.

Costanzo, William V. *Great Films and How to Teach Them.* Urbana, IL: National Council of Teachers of English, 2004.

de Baecque, Antoine. *La Cinéphilie: Invention d'un Regard, Histoire d'une Culture, 1944–1968.* Paris: Librarie Arthème Fayard, 2003.

Deleuze, Gilles. *Cinema 2: The Time-Image,* trans. Hugh Tomlinson and Robert Galeta. New York: Continuum, 1989.

Deleuze, Gilles, and Felix Guattari. *A Thousand Plateaus: Capitalism and Schizophrenia,* trans. Brian Massumi. Minneapolis: University of Minnesota Press, 1987.

de Valck, Marijke, and Malte Hagener, eds. *Cinephilia: Movies, Love and Memory.* Amsterdam: Amsterdam University Press, 2005.

———. "Cinephilia in Transition." In *Mind the Screen: Media Concepts According to Thomas Elsaesser,* eds. Jaap Kooijman, Patricia Pisters, and Wanda Strauven, 19–31. Amsterdam: Amsterdam University Press, 2008.

Doane, Mary Ann. *The Emergence of Cinematic Time: Modernity, Contingency, the Archive.* Cambridge, MA: Harvard University Press, 2003.

Donald, James, Anne Friedberg, and Laura Marcus, eds. *Close-Up 1927–1933: Cinema and Modernism.* Princeton, NJ: Princeton University Press, 1998.

Duckworth, Eleanor. *The Having of Wonderful Ideas.* New York: Teachers College Press, 2006.

Edmundson, Mark. *Why Teach: In Defense of a Real Education.* New York: Bloomsbury, 2013.

Eisenstein, Sergei. "Teaching Programme for the Theory and Practice of Direction: How to Teach Direction." In *Sergei Eisenstein, Selected Works, Volume III, Writings 1934–47,* trans. William Powell, 74–97. New York: Tauris, 2010.

Elsaesser, Thomas. *The Persistence of Hollywood.* New York: Routledge, 2012.

Epstein, Jean. *Jean Epstein: Critical Essays and New Translations,* eds. Sarah Keller and Jason N. Paul. Amsterdam: Amsterdam University Press, 2012.

———. "Magnification," trans. Stuart Liebman. In *French Film Theory and Criticism: A History/Anthology, Vol. 1: 1907–1929,* ed. Richard Abel, 235–241. Princeton, NJ: Princeton University Press, 1988.

Evans, H. M. "Wonder and the Clinical Encounter." *Theoretical Medicine and Bioethics* 33, no. 2 (2012): 123–136.

Fischer, Lucy, and Patrice Petro, eds. *Teaching Film.* New York: Modern Language Association, 2012.

Freire, Paulo. *Pedagogy of the Oppressed.* Harmondsworth, UK: Penguin, 1970.

———. *Teachers as Cultural Workers: Letters to Those Who Dare to Teach.* Boulder, CO: Westview Press, 1998.

Gaudreault, André, and Philippe Marion. *The End of Cinema? A Medium in Crisis in the Digital Age,* trans. Timothy Barnard. New York: Columbia University Press, 2015.

Giroux, Henry A. *Teachers as Intellectuals: Toward a Critical Pedagogy of Learning.* Westport, CT: Bergin and Garvey, 1988.

Graff, Gerald. "Disliking Books at an Early Age." In *Falling into Theory: Conflicting Views on Reading Literature*, eds. David H. Richter, 36–43. New York: Bedford/St. Martin's, 1999.

Grant, Catherine, and Christian Keathley. "The Use of an Illusion: Childhood Cinephilia, Object Relations, and Videographic Film Studies." *Photogénie* (2014). http://www.photogenie.be/photogenie_blog/article/use-illusion.

Grieveson, Lee, and Haidee Wasson, eds., *Inventing Film Studies*. Durham, NC: Duke University Press, 2008.

hooks, bell. *Teaching to Transgress: Education as the Practice of Freedom*. New York: Routledge, 1994.

Johnson, David T. "The 'Flashing Glimpse' of Cinephilia: What an Unusual Methodology Might Offer Adaptation Studies." *Adaptation* 6 (2013): 25–42.

Keathley, Christian. *Cinephilia and History, or the Wind in the Trees*. Bloomington: Indiana University Press, 2006.

Klevan, Andrew. *Film Performance: From Achievement to Appreciation*. London: Wallflower Press, 2005.

———. "Notes on Stanley Cavell and Philosophical Film Criticism." In *New Takes in Film-Philosophy*, eds. Havi Carel and Greg Tuck, 48–64. New York: Palgrave Macmillan, 2011.

Klinger, Barbara. *Beyond the Multiplex: Cinema, New Technologies and the Home*. Berkeley: University of California Press, 2006.

Kracauer, Siegfried. *Theory of Film: The Redemption of Physical Reality*. Oxford: Oxford University Press, 1960.

Lundin, Roger. "What We Have Loved." *Pedagogy* 4 (2004): 133–140.

Manovich, Lev. *The Language of New Media*. Cambridge, MA: MIT Press, 2001.

Martin, Adrian. "The Inward/Outward Turn." *[in]Transition* 1, no. 3 (2014). http://mediacommons.futureofthebook.org/intransition/2014/09/14/inwardoutward-turn.

McKim, Kristi. *Love in the Time of Cinema*. London: Palgrave Macmillan, 2011.

Metz, Christian. *The Imaginary Signifier: Psychoanalysis and Cinema*. Translated by Celia Britton, Annwyl Williams, Ben Brewster, and Alfred Guzzetti. Bloomington: Indiana University Press, 1982.

Monaco, James. *How to Read a Film*. Oxford: Oxford University Press, 1977.

Mulvey, Laura. *Death 24x a Second: Stillness and the Moving Image*. London: Reaktion Books, 2006.

———. *Fetishism and Curiosity*. Bloomington: Indiana University Press, 1996.

Naremore, James. *Acting in the Cinema*. Berkeley: University of California Press, 1988.

Ng, Jenna. "The Myth of Total Cinephilia." *Cinema Journal* 49, no. 2 (2010): 146–151.

Nizhny, Vladimir. *Lessons with Eisenstein*, trans. and ed. Ivor Montagu and Jay Leyda. New York: Hill and Wang, 1962.

Polan, Dana. *Scenes of Instruction: The Beginnings of the U.S. Study of Film*. Berkeley: University of California Press, 2007.

Pomerance, Murray. *The Eyes Have It: Cinema and the Reality Effect*. New Brunswick, NJ: Rutgers University Press, 2013.

Rancière, Jacques. *The Emancipated Spectator*, trans. Gregory Elliot. London: Verso, 2009.

———. *The Intervals of Cinema*, trans. John Howe. London: Verso, 2014.

Ray, Robert B. *The ABCs of Classic Hollywood*. New York: Oxford University Press, 2008.

Richards, Rashna Wadia. *Cinematic Flashes: Cinephilia and Classical Hollywood*. Bloomington: Indiana University Press, 2013.

Rodowick, D. N. *The Virtual Life of Film*. Cambridge, MA: Harvard University Press, 2007.

Rosenbaum, Jonathan. *Goodbye Cinema, Hello Cinephilia: Film Culture in Transition*. Chicago: University of Chicago Press, 2010.

Rosenbaum, Jonathan, and Adrian Martin, eds. *Movie Mutations: The Changing Face of World Cinephilia*. London: British Film Institute, 2003.

Sarris, Andrew. "Film Criticism in the Seventies." *Film Comment* 14, no. 1 (1978): 9–11.

Schwartz, Beth M., and Aeron Haynie. "Faculty Development Centers and the Role of SoTL." *New Directions for Teaching and Learning* 136 (2013): 101–111.

Shambu, Girish. *The New Cinephilia*. Montreal: Caboose, 2014.

Sobchack, Vivian. *The Address of the Eye: A Phenomenology of Film Experience*. Princeton, NJ: Princeton University Press, 1992.

———. "Vivian Sobchack in Conversation with Scott Bukatman." *Journal of E-Media Studies* 2 (2009). doi: 10.1349/PS1.1938–6060.A.338.

Sontag, Susan. "The Decay of Cinema." *New York Times Magazine*, February 25, 1996. http://www.nytimes.com/1996/02/25/magazine/the-decay-of-cinema.html.

Tashiro, Charles Shiro. "Videophilia: What Happens When You Wait for It on Video." *Film Quarterly* 54, no. 1 (1991): 7–17.

Thompson, John O. "Screen Acting and the Commutation Test." *Screen* 19, no. 2 (1978): 55–70.

Toles, George. "Rescuing Fragments: A New Task for Cinephilia." *Cinema Journal* 49, no. 2 (2010): 159–166.

Vendler, Helen. "What We Have Loved, Others Will Love." In *Falling into Theory: Conflicting Views on Reading Literature*, eds. David H. Richter, 27–36. New York: Bedford/St. Martin's, 1999.

Wartenberg, Thomas E. *Thinking on Screen: Film as Philosophy*. London: Routledge, 2007.

Willemen, Paul. *Looks and Frictions: Essays in Cultural Studies and Film Theory*. Bloomington: Indiana University Press, 1994.

Wittgenstein, Ludwig. *Philosophical Investigations*, trans. G.E.M. Anscombe. Oxford: Blackwell, 2001.

———. *Philosophical Occasions*, eds. James Klagge and Alfred Nordmann. Indianapolis, IN: Hackett, 1993.

Index

Lightning Source UK Ltd.
Milton Keynes UK
UKOW01f0835271017
311703UK00006B/383/P